The Secret

What Would the Anabaptists Tell This Generation?

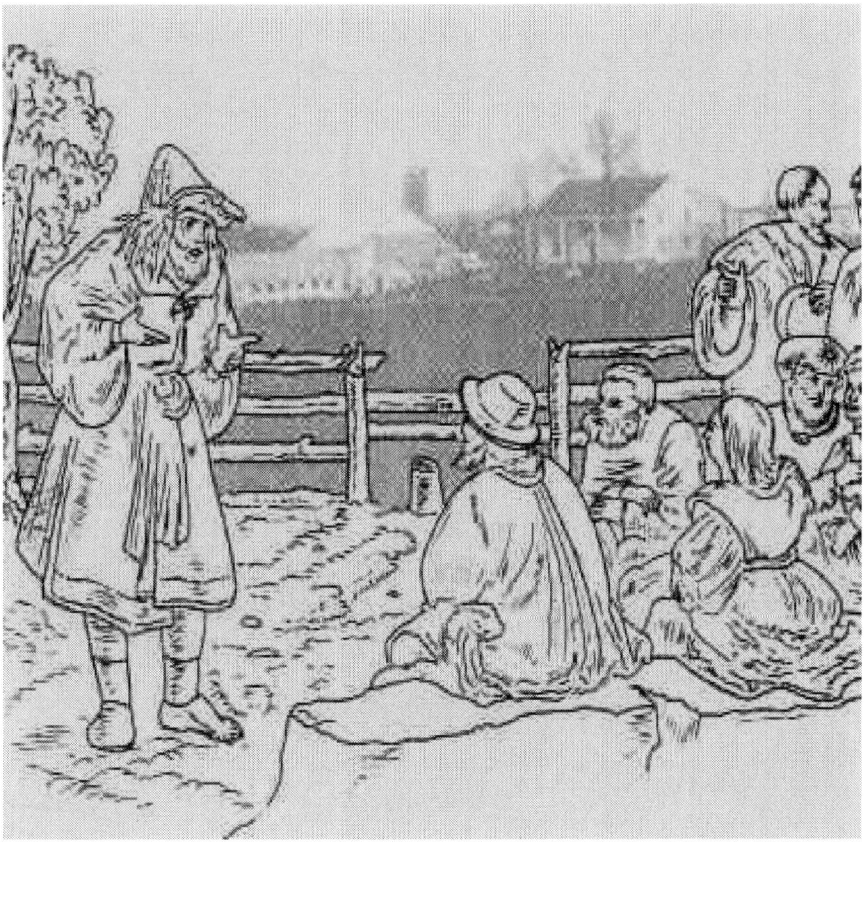

Peter Hoover

FREEDOM FROM COPYRIGHT

The text of this book, in line with the ethics it teaches, is in the public domain. It may be copied, quoted, and reproduced in any way—in its entirety or in part. Only, if portions of it get edited or revised, they should no longer be published under the author's name.

PHOTO CREDITS

All photos are original or in public domain and not copyrighted. In the original text, some photos were copyrighted and used by permission; in this version they have been omitted so as to eliminate any potential copyright issues.

TRANSLATIONS

All translations in this book are original. For readability and to fit them into a book this size, all of them have been abridged. To read the full text in German, follow the references indicated.

PREVIOUS EDITIONS

This book, written in 1991, has been published informally and has appeared online since 1998. Benchmark Press of Shippensburg, PA, first printed it in larger amounts. In 2006 Down to Earth Verlag in Berlin, Germany, published it in German under the title *Feuertaufe*. Spanish and Portuguese translations are also available.

Contents

Introduction

I well remember the first time I faced the stark realization that I was a Mennonite and different. My fourth-grade friend, Gregory, and I were riding home from public school on the bus. We were talking about our future, how we would always be friends and do things together when we grew up. Then he enthusiastically began to describe activities that from my upbringing I knew to be worldly. Desperate to save our lifelong friendship, I turned to Gregory and said, "You will have to leave your church and become a Mennonite when you grow up." Thus, the inevitability of our way of life impressed itself on my eight-year-old mind. A year later I made my decision to follow Christ. Of course, Gregory never joined my church, and I do not even know his whereabouts today.

The theme of separation from the world ran strong in the Cumberland Valley of Pennsylvania where I grew up. But I wrongly assumed that, except for our plainness, we believed the same things that other Christians believed. Then one evening at the Chambersburg Mennonite Church, where I was a member, a visiting speaker jolted me with a graphic picture of my martyr heritage. Even after forty years, I can still see Brother Irvin Martin stepping to the edge of the platform to demonstrate how they shoved the head of Felix Manz beneath the water trying to make him recant. Then the preacher showed us how they stripped his bound hands over his knees, thrust a stick between to hold them, then dumped him into the water to drown while his Anabaptist mother shouted encouragement from the riverbank. From that moment I knew that my destiny lay in the faith expressed by Felix Manz, though I but dimly understood what that meant.

Several years later I visited Zurich, Switzerland and stood beside the Limmat River at the place where it had happened. By then, I knew that it was the Protestant reformers, not the Roman Catholics, who opposed my Anabaptist forefathers in Zurich. I realized that the issues then were freedom of conscience and separation of church and state. Knowing that these were no longer issues in the free land of America, I again wrongly assumed that only our separated lifestyle and nonresistance distinguished us from our neighbors who now actually professed the same fundamentals of faith that we do. This false assumption was driven home by many sermon comments about our "twin distinctive doctrines." It seemed that we were Biblicists just like the fundamentalists around us except for our two distinctives. Unfortunately, my false assumption was a reality in the beliefs and lives of many in my church. But this I did not realize until many years later.

In the meantime, I struggled through a spiritual crisis that obliterated thoughts of history and heritage. Agonizing doubts about my salvation drove me finally in desperation to surrender all of my life unconditionally to Jesus as my Lord. Brimming with new motivation and power of the Holy Spirit, I began my quest for reality. The Scriptures became an absorbing delight, and I made it my purpose to master the Book. Then new movements in the community began to challenge the worldward drift in the church. Earnest preachers called for a return to "what the Bible says." Revival would follow when we had "scriptural beliefs," "scriptural standards," and "scriptural churches." The genius of our Anabaptist heritage, we were told, was our forefathers' insistence on *sola scriptura* (the Bible alone). At first, I agreed. It sounded so right. Certainly, obeying God meant obeying the Bible. But something seemed to be missing.

The secret of my new life was my passion to model my life after Christ, not my preoccupation with the text. For me, the text was not an end in itself, but a means to an end—learning to know the thoughts, feelings, and will of my Lord. But I saw well-meaning people getting stuck in the text. And then the disagreements broke out all around me over what and who were "scriptural." In the confusion that followed, one thing became clear. Much sincere teaching and debate focused on sharpening "scriptural" ideas from the Bible, but not on the example of Jesus Himself.

I saw this discrepancy most clearly in our "scriptural" conclusions about mammon. The "Biblical" discussion was impressive. The exegesis put every verse in its proper place. No one could find fault with the "scriptural" logic. There was only one problem. The conclusion did not match the voluntary poverty of Jesus Himself, nor did it ring true to His many clear teachings on the subject, even though we had "scripturally" explained them all. It was a watershed discovery: Being "scriptural" did not guarantee that we would be Christlike—the whole point of being *Christ*ian.

With new ears I began to scrutinize the teaching around me. The call to follow the Bible was loud and clear, along with the call to obey the Church and separate oneself from the world. But a primary call to focus finally on the example of Christ and follow Him was seldom heard. The rare allusions to modeling the actual life of Christ in everything were usually peripheral to other primary concerns. It was obviously assumed that getting the verses right would make us Christian.

I finally turned again to the Anabaptists. Was Biblicism their secret? To my surprise, I found that the Protestant reformers were the Biblicists, insisting that people turn from the dogmas of the church to the authority of the Bible. Martin Luther gave his people the Bible in German so they could read it for themselves. Zwingli preached through the Gospels verse by verse. Between them, they bitterly debated the meaning of the literal text. It all sounded so familiar. So what then did the Anabaptists do differently?

To be sure, I found that the Anabaptists also turned to the Bible in serious study. But they went "beyond the sacred page" to focus on the Person the Scriptures were intended to reveal. For them, the final appeal was actually *solo Christus*. A credible discipleship was their powerful theme, not a sterile Biblicism that actually misses the life of the Person. They saw the Scriptures as an "outer word" that would lead the genuine seeker to the "inner Word," which was Christ. It was the confirmation I needed for the conviction the Holy Spirit had given to me.

Herein lies the great distinctive of Anabaptism. The "gospel" of the fundamentalist still focuses on the text, manipulating verses into proper theologies.

Somewhere along the way, we unwittingly adopted their emphasis. But we dutifully tacked on our "twin distinctives." It is obvious now that this was not enough to save us, and most of my boyhood friends were finally swept into the camp of the Biblicist reformers. The gap between Reformation theology and Anabaptism is as wide today as it ever was. It is the difference between a misguided Biblicism and the true Word of God.

Our critics will say, "There should be no difference between the Scriptures and the Word." The writer of this book would heartily agree. The glory of this powerful union as well as the tragedy of the unintended separation is shown in his story.

Peter Hoover has not given us a history of the Anabaptists. You can read that history in the many volumes by others. In this book, however, you will meet the Anabaptists in their struggles to live as Jesus would against strong Biblicist opposition. The strength of Brother Peter's presentation lies in the many actual quotes that allow the Anabaptists to speak for themselves. Obviously, these quotes have been selected and no doubt reflect the writer's bias (as all books do). But the reader is heartily invited to judge the truth for himself. Have we really followed Christ as our forefathers so passionately followed Him? Or has His pristine example been obscured by many "scriptural" inventions that they would have rejected outright? Does all our emphasis on the church lead us to experience the unique Anabaptist vision for community? Was "the secret of the strength" what we commonly assume today?

This book will likely provoke much fresh and vigorous discussion. It will challenge many long-held assumptions about what it means to be an Anabaptist. Some will see this as threatening and dangerous. Others will be encouraged to focus with new passion on the Person and example of Jesus Christ. With a fervent prayer to this end, we invite you to consider the story you hold in your hands.

John D. Martin
Chambersburg, Pennsylvania
November 8, 1997

Acknowledgments

For my Friend about whom they asked, "Isn't this the Carpenter?" who wrote no books but about whom and for whom we are still writing, for Susan *and the brothers and sisters of our fellowship in 1997*: Lynn and Wilma Martin, Marvin and Virginia Wadel, John and Patricia Martin, Edsel and Jennifer Burdge, Kore and Elizabeth Byler, Ronald and Edith Martin, David and Starla Goodwin, Eldon and Sherilyn Martin, Conrad and Katrina Hege, Kevin and Jalee Brechbill, Jason and Jill Landis, Dallas and Joy Martin, Gordon and Janelle Ogburn, Conrad and Sharon Sollenberger, Wendell and Marla Martin, Harvey and Arlene Reiff, Kirk and Barbara Anderson, Jonas and Vonda Landis, Mike and Sarah Hostetler, Dan and Esther Mae Wadel, Sheldon and Marge Martin, Piper Burdge, Luke, Elisha and John Byler, Mario Aguilar, Edna Horst, Levi, Malinda and Rhoda Hostetler, Wade and Katrina Anderson, Andrea, Erica, Rantz, Lana, Trent, Anne, Heather, Candace, Craig, Bradlyn and Sharleen Martin, Barry Willis, Marc, Kathy, Byron, Darian and Christa Wadel, *without whom this book would not have become a reality, and* for Christopher, Grace, Justin, Stanley and Stephanie Hoover, Chantel Brechbill, Daniel, Ian, Adam and Andrew Burdge, Salome Byler, Conrad, Felix, Julitta and Anysia Goodwin, Karla, Marjorie, Audrey, Lynette, Leonard and Delbert vi Hege, Bertha Hostetler, Rylan, Rochelle, Jenna, Elyse and Lorielle Landis, Radford, Natalie, Abigail, Winston, Meghan, Alex, Roxanne, Geoffrey, Spencer, Caroline, Lauren, Amy, Rachel, Brady, Dylan, Shana, Kylie, Lance and Colin Martin, Ian, Ariana and Avery Ogburn, Joshua, Jonathan and Joellen Reiff, Travis, Jessica, Heidi and Benjamin Sollenberger, Brendan, Kirby, Maria, Kayla, Micah, Daven, Justin, Joanna, Lindon and Kara Wadel *who, it is hoped, will capture the message of this book and share it with the world.*

Apart from the Christian community that produced it—the men, women, young people and children who have come to share what they have, spiritually and materially, so that none are left with too much and none are found wanting—this book would have nothing to say. It is our challenge. Let us live it. We will need the "secret of the strength" when our trial comes.

My birthplace, the city of Kitchener, Ontario, had much to do with the writing of this book. Founded by Mennonite bishop Benjamin Eby in the early 1800s, the city, with its doors always open to immigrants, provided me with my first contacts with the wider Anabaptist community: the Russian Mennonites, the *Nazarener*, the Hutterites, and others. Special recognition must be given to J. Winfield Fretz and Frank Epp, then of Conrad Grebel College, for spending time with me in my most impressionable years. The same and more must be said for Reinhold Konrath, then of Victoria Street, with his rare collection of Anabaptist books and documents, and for Reg Good, a friend.

My parents, Anson and Sarah Hoover, and great-uncle Menno Sauder of the Old Order Mennonite community north of the city greatly stimulated my desire to know about our past. So did my grandparents, Menno and Leah Hoover and our neighbourhood harness-maker, Matthias Martin, whom I visited innumerable times on foot, cutting across the back fields to his place along the creek.

I would thank Cornelius Krahn of North Newton, Kansas (who gave us a box full of Anabaptist books as a *Poltergeschenk* when we stopped at his place on our wedding trip) and bishop Elmer D. Grove for their inspiration in historical research. I thank the following persons: Amos B. Hoover (in whose library I paged through original Anabaptist writings for the first time), David Bercot, Philip Yoder, John David Hoover, Elmo Stoll, Wayne Chesley, Keiner Barrantes and the rest who played a part in bringing this book to completion.

Claudia Schmiedel Pichardo, writing from Mexico City, München, or Graz added a special dimension to this project, and I am grateful to John D. Martin and Edsel Burdge for their work as editors, Elizabeth Myers Byler and Starla Goodwin for correcting the text, Conrad Sollenberger for its design, and to my wife Susan and our children for putting up with me during long hours of writing and review.

Peter Hoover

A Man Hanging by His Thumb

The sun shines on Klundert, green lowland plains lying flat as far as eye can see. Tourists visit Klundert. They take pictures: fields of flowers and vegetables. Thunderheads rise, making rows of poplars alongside canals of Noord Brabant look small. Long canals, they cut straight through the shimmering plains until they lose themselves in the haze where land and sky meet sea. "We like the peace of Noord Brabant," say the tourists, "It does the heart good."

But there is much the tourists do not know.

Klundert, tidy Dutch village in Noord Brabant, stands on blood. The blood of Anabaptists was shed here.

Anabaptists gathered at Klundert throughout the mid-sixteenth century. They came, sneaking out of nearby cities, to meet in secret on the fields. Sometimes they gathered in the homes of Elsken Deeken or Jan Peetersz, a servant of the Word. On August 5, 1571, about a hundred Anabaptists met at the Peetersz home in Klundert. Some came from Haarlem, some from Leyden, and many from towns not far away. During the meeting a young couple was going to get married, but they did not get that far.

The town magistrate and his assistant were sitting at Gerrit Vorster's house, drinking. Someone told him about the Anabaptist gathering. He said: "We will root up that nest and get rid of them at once!" Twice he sent one of his men to listen at the Peetersz house. "Straight Peter" a tailor lived in the front part of the house. Jan Peetersz lived in the back where the people met. After nine o'clock the spies found the meeting in session. They heard someone preaching and saw the light of many candles in the room. Then the magistrate and his men, well armed with guns, halberds, swords, and other weapons broke in through all doors at once. They grabbed left and right. But most of the Anabaptists, ready for such an emergency, escaped up the stairs, through a hole in the roof, or back through a hall and out of openings in the wall.

When the raid was over, the magistrate's men held six men and several women: Peter the tailor, Geleyn Cornelis of Middelharnis near Somerdijk, Arent Block of Zevenbergen, Cornelis de Gyselaar, and a sixteen- or seventeen-year-old boy who worked for Straight Peter the tailor. The captives were led to Gerrit Vorster's house where the women escaped. They handcuffed the men and kept them under guard. The next morning Michael Gerrits, an uncle of Cornelis de Gyselaar, came to see him. Also an Anabaptist, Michael came to encourage Cornelis to stand for Christ, no matter what might take place. The magistrate seized Michael too.

They confiscated the property of the prisoners, so their wives fled from Klundert with nothing. Then they called on the school teacher to dispute with the prisoners. He wrote up a report in which he said: "They do not baptise infants. They cannot believe that Christ had his flesh and blood from Mary, and they regard themselves as the little flock and the elect of God. But their lives are better than the lives of many others. They bring up their children in better discipline and fear of God than many other people. Their children in school are better students and learn more readily than the rest."

The magistrate kept the prisoners in Gerrit Vorster's house until noon of August 7, 1571. Then he took them to Breda to be tortured. Straight Peter, the tailor, gave up the faith, so they only beheaded him. The rest, including his teenage worker, remained steadfast. One had his hands tied behind his back to be suspended by them and whipped. Another was pulled to the utmost on the rack. While in this helpless condition they held his mouth open to urinate into it and over his body. But Geleyn Cornelis was treated worst of all. They stripped off his clothes and hung him up by his right thumb with a weight hanging from his left foot. Then they singed off his body hair, burning him in tender places with candles, and beat him. Finally the men, tired of torturing the prisoners, took to playing cards. They played for over an hour while Geleyn hung, by now unconscious, until the commissioner of the Duke of Alba said: "Seize him again. He must tell us something! A drowned calf is a small risk."

Jan Luyken, Dutch artist, poet and bar-room entertainer (married to a barmaid) found Christ as a 24-year-old in 1668. Radically transformed, he became a member of an Anabaptist community and spent the rest of his life buy- ing back and destroying what he had painted or composed for the devil. On 104 copper plates Jan engraved scenes, such as this one of Geleyn Cornelis, for the *Martyrs Mirror*, published in 1685.

At first they thought Geleyn was dead. They shook him until he revived, but he did not recant.

They burned Geleyn Cornelis, Jan Peetersz, and the young boy first. The wind came the wrong way and blew the fire away from Geleyn's stake, so the executioner had to push and hold his body into the flames with a fork.

When they led Cornelis de Gyselaar and Arent Block to the stakes, Arent dropped a letter hoping that some Anabaptist in the crowd would notice it and snatch it up. But the Duke's men saw it first and took the two men back to prison for another torturing session. They did not recant and they refused to betray any of their brothers in the faith. Shortly afterward, they burned Cornelis, his uncle Michael Gerrits, and Arent Block.

Since 1571 there have been no more Anabaptists at Klundert. Tourists come—with Bermuda shorts, sunglasses, paper cups of Coke, and with camera strings flapping in the fresh spring breeze. They like Noord Brabant. But there is much the tourists do not know.

Anabaptist home in Noord Brabant where, nearly five centuries after the burnings at Klundert, new conversions and baptisms have again taken place—this time at the hands of Hutterite believers from America. The cost of following Jesus in the Netherlands has not grown less, and today's believers face spiritual opposition of an intensity never seen before. Pray for them.

What Was the Secret of the Strength?

For as long as I can remember, people have told me Anabaptist stories. In fact, I distinctly remember the first time they told me about Geleyn Cornelis, who hung from his thumb. I was not yet going to school. It was on a Sunday evening in southern Ontario, and we had many visitors. (My father was an Orthodox Mennonite minister.) All of us sat around our long kitchen table on which a kerosene lamp stood to light a circle of solemn faces: women in dark dresses with large white head coverings, and men with suspenders and their hair cut round. I was sitting on someone's lap while one of the visitors told the story of Geleyn Cornelis. I never forgot it, and I live to this day deeply aware of the challenge put to me by my Anabaptist ancestors.

I am challenged by the strength of their convictions, by the strength of their endurance in persecution—and above all, by the sheer strength of the early Anabaptist movement itself.

Within thirty years of the first baptisms in Switzerland, in a secret meeting of a few people, the movement drew incredible thousands—perhaps more than a hundred thousand converts to Christ, and this in the face of the bitterest persecution.

Congregations of Anabaptists sprang up almost overnight. On Palm Sunday, 1525, only two months after his own baptism Conrad Grebel baptised several hundred in the Sitter river at Sankt Gallen in Switzerland. Ten years later, the movement had reached the far corners of the German world. All of ancient Swabia: Switzerland, the Tyrol, Salzburg, Württemberg, Bavaria, Ansbach, and the Kurpfalz, as well as central Germany: Hesse, Thuringia and Saxony had been affected. Entire regions of southern Germany, whole towns, were reported to have "gone Anabaptist." In Moravia, Anabaptist communities eventually numbered 60,000 members. In the Netherlands, Belgium, the Lower Rhine region in Germany, Holstein, and along the Baltic Sea to East Prussia, the movement raced like a fire.

Due to favourable winds?

Hardly. Within those same ten years innumerable Anabaptists were imprisoned, exiled, and put to death by Roman Catholic and Protestant authorities. Anabaptists had white-hot rods pushed down their legs, their tongues screwed onto their gums, and their fingers chopped off. Some had gun powder tied to their bodies or crammed into their mouths to be set on fire. Some were beheaded. Some were drowned. Some were buried alive and many more burned at the stake.

The Anabaptist movement was a city movement in the beginning. Born in Zürich, it branched out quickly into the largest cities of central Europe: Strasbourg, Augsburg, Regensburg, Salzburg and Worms. Soon afterward, it reached Aachen, Gent, Utrecht, Amsterdam, Emden, Hamburg, Lübeck, Danzig, and even Königsberg (now Kaliningrad) in East Prussia. On back streets by lantern light, in town squares during public executions, everywhere, Anabaptists preached and lives were changed. Christian communities took shape and in the bond of love that united them the Kingdom of Heaven came to earth.

What was "the secret of their great strength"?

A woman called Delilah once asked that question.

And the more I think about it, the more parallels I see between the Anabaptist movement and Delilah's husband.

The Anabaptists began with spectacular accomplishments—but they met spectacular defeats.

The Anabaptists began as the only peace church, the only nonviolent movement in a violent age—but it did not take long until many divisions weakened them and obscured their witness to the world.

The Anabaptists began in great light from heaven, in true faith and personal conviction—but many of them became bound by tradition, blindly and pitifully treading the mill of meaningless custom.

In the beginning the Anabaptists were free, even in bonds. Now many of them are bound, even in freedom. Truly, their weaknesses and failures, like Samson's, have become apparent to all. But what, in the beginning, was the secret of their great strength?

That is the question I began to ask myself while growing up with horses and buggies, bare houses, and serious-minded German people in southern Ontario.

Was the secret of the Anabaptists' strength their return to the Scriptures? No. Most of the early Anabaptists could not read, and few owned Bibles. Christians today know the Scriptures as well, or better than they—but without the strength.

Was their secret a sound church structure and submission to men in God-given authority? No. The Anabaptist movement spread all over central and northern Europe before it had any structure at all. Its early leaders were self-appointed and unofficial, many of them in their late teens or in their twenties. Many of them got killed.

Was their secret a connection to an evangelical tradition that had gotten passed on from generation to generation in the mountains of Europe? No. The Anabaptists inherited no sacred "body of tradition" from anyone. They were all new converts—not tradition keepers, but tradition breakers. There is no evidence of a single contact between them and the Waldenses, Albigenses, or other movements before them.

So what, finally, was their secret? Was it a return to perfectly correct doctrine and applications? No. All of the first Anabaptist leaders taught some things that were incorrect: an impossible view of the incarnation, mistaken eschatology, misunderstood Latin terms about separation from the backslidden, and the like. And in their applications of Bible principles, the early Anabaptists varied greatly. But for more than a century the Spirit of God moved among them in a truly miraculous way.

What a great secret! What a mystery! In spite of appalling weaknesses and a lack of education, of seasoned leadership, of church structure, of unified practice, of experience, of established tradition ... even in spite of errors in their teaching, the Anabaptist movement shook Europe so that like the first Christians, they were accused of turning the world upside down.

"Anabaptist Compound" says this sign on a Slovakian street corner, in translation. The first Anabaptists, particularly those that lived in community of goods, liked to rent ghetto-like courtyards, surrounded by multi-storied housing and shops in cities that tolerated them. This allowed everyone to work and live as members of one family in Christ.

Four centuries later, I grew up inwardly aware, always conscious of our glorious "Anabaptist heritage" . . . and wondering, already as a child, how they could accomplish so much and we so little. We heard our parents tell about the Anabaptists on long winter evenings. We learned about them in school, and we heard about them in the unpainted, wooden interior of our meetinghouse where we met to sing and pray. But already as a child I began to suspect the Anabaptists, like Samson, knew something—some secret—that we did not.

Now I am beginning to sense there is yet more to the Samson comparison: After Samson lost his strength and spent a long time blind, shackled, and treading the mill in prison, his secret came back to him. Little by little his great strength came back.

He could feel it in his bones! Then, on the day of the feast in the idol's temple, poor old blind Samson came back. Thousands came to see him. Some smiled and giggled, pointing at his blindness and chains: "There he is! There is the man who sent the foxes through our fields! There is the man who struck down a thousand with a donkey's jawbone and walked off with our city gates. But just look at him now! He's blind. He doesn't know who's leading him around. Just look at the funny old man!"

While the words were still in their mouths, the Philistines began to stare. What was Samson doing! What was going on! He was pushing. Great muscles rippled along his biceps. Mighty legs braced themselves, and the pillars began to move, the roof began to sway . . . and nobody remembered the crash, for the screams and curses of thousands who slid and thousands who saw them fall were silent, after the idol's temple came down.

In the end, Samson's great strength came back to accomplish more in death than in life—and his name went down with the faithful in Hebrews eleven.

Any parallels?

I am fascinated with the possibility of an ongoing parallel between Samson's life and the Anabaptist movement.

The Anabaptists, like Samson, were once the terror of the populace. Governments spent all they had to get rid of them. Their writings were outlawed on pain of death.

But the Anabaptist movement, like Samson, grew old and feeble. No one is afraid of it anymore. Thousands come to look at the Mennonites, the Amish, and the Hutterites (the Anabaptists' descendants). Some smile and giggle, pointing at their quaint clothes and customs: "There they are! There are the people who dared defy the pope (and Luther, Zwingli, and Calvin besides)! There are the people who sang on their way to be burned at the stake, who had their fingers chopped off or their tongues cut out rather than give up what they believed. But just look at them now! They're blind. They don't know who's leading them around. Just look at the funny people!"

What they don't know is that the Anabaptist movement, like Samson, may yet have some life in it.

Something may be happening. New faces, new family names, new tradition-breakers (home-schoolers, seekers, hungry and thirsty Bible readers) are popping up out of nowhere, right out of our modern Dark Ages, to stir up the old Mennonite, Amish, and Hutterite communities. What would happen if some of those seekers, and some of those "plain people" should start remembering together—if they would rediscover the secret of the strength, the muscles would start rippling, the shackles would fall, and the pillars of the idol's temple would start to move?

Just what would happen?

In this book I want to allow the first Anabaptists to answer that question.

The Woman Who Had a Baby in Jail

In 1637 they caught the minister, Hans Meyli, of the Horgerberg, in the foothills of the Alps south of Lake Zürich in Switzerland. They tried him and threw him into the Oetenbach tower dungeon, but after forty-three weeks he escaped. The Protestant authorities (of Zwingli's Reformed Church) were furious. They did continual house searches and harrassed the believers. Thirty *Täuferjäger* (Anabaptist hunters) found out where the Meylis lived and with bare swords and firearms stormed the house, hacking through doors and throwing things around to find the escaped minister. They cursed and swore and blasphemed God. When they realised that he was not there, they took his two sons, Hans Jr. and Martin Meyli captive. Martin was already married. They grabbed his young wife and tied her up tightly. Her name was Anna. She had a fourteen-week-old baby, which they took from her and gave to people from the state church to keep. They took the captives to Zürich, tried them and locked them up in the Oetenbach tower.

They took off the men's clothes and chained them to the stone floor for twenty weeks, torturing them with spiders and caterpillars. They gave them just enough food and water to stay alive. But the prisoners would not recant. After one year the two men escaped "with undamaged consciences" and after two years, on Good Friday, 1641, Anna escaped as well. They fled from place to place, but the people betrayed them. Anna fell into the hands of the *Täuferjäger* again and was imprisoned, first at the Oetenbach, then in the Spital jail. This time she was expecting a baby. They left her shackled until the pains of labour came upon her. Then they loosened her to have the baby, and "with the help and grace of God" she escaped. After her husband found her they fled across the mountains and through the Black Forest to Germany.

That woman, Anna (Baer) Meyli, was my ancestor, eleven generations removed.

When I repented and chose to follow Christ at the age of fifteen, I wanted nothing more than to follow her on the narrow way to eternal life. But I did not know for sure which way that was.

We lived among twenty-five kinds of Mennonites and Amish in one densely populated county in southern Ontario. From the most acculturated to the most traditional, every type of Anabaptism was represented there. Every group claimed to be a legitimate heir of the "Anabaptist heritage" we all had in common, and they all claimed to be travelling on the narrow way. But their claims became jumbled in my mind.

During the 1950s, my parent's group (which had left another one in 1917) suffered a deep inner crisis. My parents then took part in establishing the group in which I was born and spent my childhood. When I was 13 we entered another time of turmoil, and my father became the lead minister of a new brotherhood. Then, two years later, we practically disintegrated, and now, by the time I was a young teenager, we were not attending meetings at all.

Today's Anabaptists, of the more conservative groups, tend to live in orderly, quiet seclusion, as on this Old Order Mennonite farm in Ontario, Canada. To be "the quiet in the land" and to keep themselves from the corruption of the world has become their ideal.

That a true remnant of the true church still existed somewhere—surely somewhere —among the Anabaptists' descendants, we felt certain. My father spoke of making a trip through the eastern United States and visiting all groups that looked like possibilities for a safe church home. But we had little hope that the trip would do any good. All our lives we had lived in a constant struggle over lifestyle issues—what to allow, or what to reject as "worldly" and of the devil. My parents never wavered in their dedication to Anabaptist beliefs. They kept on looking for something suitable among the groups. One of my sisters had contact with the Amish. But I turned, on long Sundays at home, to the Anabaptist writings. . . .

Late on a cold afternoon in 1975 a Städtler (a man from the city) stepped from the Canadian winter into the dim light of our horse stable where I was working. His car had slid off the road and he had gotten stuck. I pulled him out with the heavy team and he gave me fifteen dollars. Another man gave me ten for the same reason, and I began to look forward to fresh snowfalls. With my money I bought the *Complete Writings of Menno Simons*, the *Aelteste Chronik der Hutterischen Brüder*, the *Ausbund*, the *Artikel und Ordnungen der Christlichen Gemeinde* and all other Anabaptist-Mennonite books I could afford. A friend of our family, J. Winfield Fretz of Conrad Grebel College, took a special interest in my studies. He gave me valuable books and directed me to Mennonite college archives in the United States and Canada. Another Mennonite professor, Frank H. Epp, became a personal friend and inspiration to me. He let me "work" on his unpublished manuscripts and introduced me to Anabaptist social concerns.

Then I met a World War II refugee from Yugoslavia. This man, living in the city of Kitchener, Ontario, knew history and owned a wealth of rare and untranslated Anabaptist writings. He was not primarily a historian, nor a scholar, but he spent hours with me, a fifteen-year-old, intensely, earnestly, calling me beyond what I knew of the Anabaptists into strange and exciting territory.

It was in my contacts with this man, and while reading the literature he gave me from the Anabaptists in southern Germany and Moravia, that I began to sense, for the first time, a clue to their secret. I began to sense an incredible power behind the things they wrote, the power of a *new world coming, a time when men are free . . . and we shall be his people and He shall reign in peace!*

Beyond the darkness and gloom of four centuries, beyond the tunnels of the traditional, the historical, and the academic, I began to see a strange new light in the accounts of those who went out "with shining eyes" to die. Dimly at first, but slowly and surely it dawned on me as a young teenager, that this light from heaven would surely break forth again, and that *someday a strong wind would blow and the raindrops and clouds would be gone . . . and the darkness would leave me, and the sunshine would see me, as I walk . . . as I walk . . . a new road.*

That new road has been longer and rougher and narrower than I expected, and it is definitely taking me to where I did not plan to go. It is taking me from the shelter of a long-established "background" into the raw uncertainty of going out, not knowing where to or with whom. It is taking me from the riches of my "goodly heritage" into dreadful loneliness—the forsaken loneliness of the cross, where all men are equally poor. Out of the familiar traditions of my childhood into a frightening, totally unknown world, where "backgrounds" do not count, where terrible consequences must be taken in stride, where glances into the dark night ahead make the blood run cold . . . with visions of hatred and rejection, of high-sounding religious denunciations, of fierce opposition from family and friends, a world of coercion, of fire-arms and murder, of castle dungeons and bloody torture, of treachery and terror and death.

This new road, I have discovered, is the road of the woman who had her baby in jail.

Do you want to be on it?

If not, you should forget about finding the secret of the strength and stop reading this book.

From Where Did the Anabaptists Come?

They came from "no where." Right out of the Dark Ages, out of incredibly corrupt state churches, the Anabaptists (Ludwig Keller and E. H. Broadbent notwithstanding) stepped as a totally new and different movement.

Were they somehow connected to the first Christians?

No, they were not. The early Christians were Jewish, Greek, or Latin people in flowing robes. The Anabaptists were north Europeans in black hats and broadfall trousers.

The Anabaptists, although they respected the early Christians, made no attempt to "reproduce" them exactly. A thousand miles and a thousand years apart, they had little in common except the New Testament *and the secret of the great strength.*

Once this became clear to me I started seeing things in history:

Jewish Christians

After Pentecost, Jews from Parthia, Media, Elam, Babylon, Cappadocia, and other places joined the Jews of Judaea who believed in Christ. Jewish Christians, all of whom could trace their ancestry back to Abraham, were circumcised and wore beards. They ate Kosher foods and kept the Sabbath holy. But they followed Christ, and Christianity soon broke out of the bounds of Judaism.

Greek Christians

After Paul's conversion and Peter's visit to Cornelius, hundreds and eventually thousands of Greeks from all over Alexander's former realm—Greek merchants and lawyers, Greek doctors, educated Greeks, Greeks given to profound thought, athletic Greeks, Greeks used to idolatry and total abandon to immorality, Greek masters and slaves—repented, believed, and got baptised. They followed Christ, and it wasn't long until Christianity was predominantly Greek, centred in Hellenistic Syria, Egypt, and Asia Minor. Paul wrote his letters in Greek and the rest of the New Testament, if not originally conceived in that language, was soon known only in Greek texts.

Greek, the "world language" and "world culture" of the times, gave the Christians a place on the cutting edge of current events. But Christianity soon broke out of the bounds a Greek world.

Latin Christians

With the decline of Greek influence in the western part of the empire, Latin Rome came into its own. Jews from Rome witnessed the birth of Christianity in Jerusalem. Perhaps it was they, or other early missionaries who carried it to Latin

Italy and northern Africa. Whatever the case, it wasn't long until thousands of clear-thinking Latins, Europeans at heart and, like the Greeks, uncircumcised, had joined the Jews and the Greeks in following Christ. From these Latin Christians, centred at Carthage and Rome, came such inspired thinkers as the bishop Clement of Rome, Mark Felix, and Tertullian. Latin Christians carried the Gospel throughout the far reaches of the Roman empire: to the Celts in Britain and Ireland, to Iberia (Spain and Portugal), to the Gauls in what later became France, and to Celtic tribes living in the Alps and down the Danube valley. But Christianity soon broke out of the bounds of the Roman Empire.

German Christians

As early as 1800 B.C. (about the time Jacob fled to Padan- Aram) small bands of families had found their way from Mesopotamia and the Indus valley north through Persia and the Ukraine, through central Europe to the shores of the North Sea. There they called themselves *Teutsch* (German).

The Germans lived a wild life, planting few crops and hunting to make up the slack. The "Indians of Europe," they thrived in cold forests and wetlands along the sea. They grew rapidly in number, pushing ever southward until they inhabited the Black Forest and the mountains of Swabia. They pushed north (the Vikings) to occupy Scandinavia, west into England, east into Russia, and eventually south into Italy and Asia Minor.

These German raiders had no taste for Latin or Greek culture. They smashed temples, slaughtered ruthlessly, and took children along with their spoil. Through this practice they unwittingly brought home something that changed their ways forever.

On a raid to the south, around the time of Constantine the Great, German tribesmen kidnapped a Cappadocian boy named Ulfilas. He believed in Christ.

Unlike most captives before him, Ulfilas did not lose himself in barbarian ways. Carried north through the Balkan mountains, he crossed the Danube river with his captors and found himself outside the Roman Empire—out in the wilds with a wild people, but he did not lose heart. He learned German and began to tell his captors about Christ. Long blond hair falling around their fur-clad shoulders, rough men with beards and hefty women sitting around campfires listened to him, fascinated. Their hearts responded to the story of Christ. One by one they believed, repented of their sins, and began to follow Christ themselves.

Ulfilas baptised them in water. Before long, a nucleus of Christians developed among the wild people north of the Danube. Ulfilas, using the Greek and Latin he knew, invented for them a German alphabet. He taught them how to read and translated first the Gospels, then the letters of Paul, and finally most of the Old Testament into German.

In 341 A.D. Ulfilas travelled south to his homeland in "civilised" Asia. In Nicomedia, the city where an old bishop, Eusebius, lived, he told of the Germans who had turned to following Christ. Eusebius ordained Ulfilas to be an apostle to the Germans.

The Germans Become Catholic

Ulfilas's Christian movement did not survive. Already during his lifetime the Latin and Greek Christians of the south had became powerful. What they believed became almost like a national religion under Constantine the Great. Constantine tried to unite all Christians under one great church organization that would cooperate with the Roman government. He called councils to draw up rules and define catholic (universally accepted as genuine) doctrine. In the process of these councils Ulfilas and the German Christians became classed officially as heretics.

Ulfilas taught that Christ was the Son of God, but not exactly like God the Father in every respect. He taught that the Holy Spirit was subordinate to God. In short, Ulfilas preached aChristianity as he knew it before the councils of Constantine. But now it was no longer considered "catholic."

The new "catholic" Christianity first reached the Germans by way of a man called Remigius. Remigius was a Latin youth who loved to study and spoke well. At the age of twenty-two he became bishop of the catholic congregation at Reims in what is now France.

During Remigius's time many Germans followed a ruthless chief called Clovis who had a Christian wife. Clovis came to know Remigius and his little church at Reims but he did not care for Christianity. He ignored Remigius's frequent attempts to "convert" him until two things happened to change his mind: His son got sick and was healed, and he won a great victory over his rivals at Zülpich, after praying (as a last resort) to the Christians' God. Then Clovis wanted to get baptised.

Clovis hurried to Reims and had Remigius baptise him, his warrior chiefs, and more than three thousand of his soldiers at once. "Catholic" churches then sprang up all over Clovis's domain. Tribe after tribe of the remaining Germans fell before his "Christian" sword, and thousands were baptised en masse. Missionaries followed (and in some places preceded) the army in its task of conversion. Gall of Down, an Irish Catholic missionary, reached Switzerland in 612. He built a mission at Sankt Gallen. Boniface (Wynfrith of Wessex) followed him in 716, baptizing thousands more—both pagans and those who had belonged to what was left of Ulfilas's "uncatholic" congregations. By doing this Boniface cleaned up what he called a "haphazard Christianity" propagated by "heretical and free living clerics."

Boniface anointed a German chief, Pepin the Short, to rule over all his German converts. Then, to be sure that Pepin's rule would be "catholic," Boniface led him to be crowned by bishop Stephen of Rome.

The Church of the Dark Ages

Pepin the Short had one outstanding son named Karl, later known as *Karl der*

Große — Charlemagne. Karl grew up speaking old High German, a language similar to the Pennsylvania Dutch of today's Amish. He was baptised in the "catholic" Christian church and loved to fight. When he became king he resolved to convert and civilise all the remaining "Indians of Europe": the German tribes east of the Rhine river.

Karl fought and baptised valiantly. He meant business. But his converts never understood him like they had understood Ulfilas. They could not read the Latin New Testament with which he forcefully replaced Ulfilas's German translations. The converts said the Lord's prayer in Latin (law demanded it), but they did not know what it meant. They accepted the sprinkling of baptism, but it looked to them like a magical rite. They ate the sacred bread, but they did not get the mumblings of the priests who consecrated it with words that sounded like "hocus pocus." In Saxony, where some Germans had second thoughts about accepting these "catholic" traditions, Karl had four thousand, five hundred, massacred in one day. He made his point.

Then, in November, 800 A.D., Karl, the German chieftain, visited his friend Leo, the bishop of Rome. At this time the bishop of Rome was still under the oversight of the Greek church at Byzantium, but he was unhappy. Leo and Karl got to discussing things and came up with a great idea.

On Christmas day, both Karl and Leo entered St. Peter's church in the middle of town. Thousands of people had come for the Christmas service. The festive atmosphere was exactly right for Leo to anoint and crown Karl as a new Roman Emperor— Charlemagne—and for Karl to take Leo as his religious head of state.

A Christian empire! A *holy, Roman,* empire! Bishop and warrior, church and state became one on Christmas day 800 A.D., and a split between the old *Greek* catholic church and the new *Roman* catholic church became inevitable. Karl felt good with his new role as Roman Emperor—even though he modestly confessed that if he would have known what Leo was going to do, he never would have set foot in St. Peter's church. Leo, at the same time, exulted in his liberation from Byzantium and forged a document to prove that Constantine had always wanted the bishop of Rome to be the head of Christendom.

The wedding of the Holy Roman Empire to the Roman Catholic Church, on Christmas day, 800 A.D. drew the curtain of the Dark Ages securely down on Europe.

The Christian movement among the Jews had been glorious. Among the Greeks yet more so. Latin Christians had carried the Gospel west and north. Many Germans had gotten converted. But now, this Christianity of the Dark Ages swallowed everything up and was worse than no Christianity at all. It was the wolf of north European barbarianism decked in the sheep's clothing of Christ's Gospel. What a potent disguise! The church of the Dark Ages might well have been the end of Christianity—had it not been for its preservation of the New Testament.

Anabaptist Christians

Fortunately, not all German converts to Roman Catholicism were totally given to hunting wild pigs and drinking beer. The church, corrupt as it may have been, succeeded in drawing young Germans into the religious life (monasteries and convents). There they learned to read Latin, and there a few of them came across the New Testament in the early 1500's.

Johannes Gutenberg, working in the German cities of Strasbourg and Mainz, contributed greatly to the spread of published materials, through his invention of movable type, and printing the entire Bible (in Latin) in 1455. Within a century of his time all of Europe was flooded with printed literature—Bibles and spiritual writings (including thousands of Anabaptist writings) among them, but not all of them for the good.

Here a German monk (Martin Luther of Wittenberg), there a German priest (Menno Simons of Witmarsum), here and there and everywhere, with the invention of the printing press, educated Germans began to read with alarm the words of Christ and the Apostles. Suddenly they realised that they had been short-changed by the missionaries who had "converted" them. Suddenly it became clear to them that they had been Christians for a thousand years without ever knowing Christianity at all! Martin Luther, Huldrych Zwingli, Balthasar Hubmaier, Hans Denck, Michael Sattler, and Pilgram Marpeck—German after German rose to the challenge of the outrage. Powerful tracts, Latin tracts at first, but soon German tracts and German translations of the New Testament swept the entire German populace, from Switzerland to the North Sea and from Scandinavia to East Prussia, into flame. The church of the Dark Ages had totally underestimated the effect that the New Testament could have on an ignorant population.

No longer could the Germans be controlled. No more could they be hoodwinked into believing fantastic stories about the virgin, the saints, baptism, and the mass. Once the Bible was printed and the Germans had it in their hands, the dark days of the apostate "catholic" church in northern Europe were over.

Luther did not go all the way. Neither did Zwingli. But just a few years after the New Testament hit the German world, more than a hundred thousand Germans pressed all the way through to Christ and broke out of the Dark Ages. Because they followed Christ's example and baptised adults, people called them *Anabaptists* (rebaptisers). In this book you may meet them and consider what they wrote.

Literarily . . . An Explosion!

Conrad Grebel, a young Anabaptist, wrote on September 3, 1524:

> I am full of words and the spirit of my belly constrains me. Behold my belly is as new wine without a vent, which bursts the wineskins. I shall speak and I shall breathe a little more freely: I shall open my lips and make answer. [1]

Hans Denck, a widely-travelled Anabaptist messenger from southern Germany, wrote:

> I open my mouth against my will. I speak reluctantly about God, but he compels me to speak so I cannot be silent.... Some brothers think they have utterly explored the gospel, and whoever does not agree with everything they say must be a heretic. Should one wish to give an account of one's faith to those who desire it, then they say that one causes discord and tumult among the people. If one ignores the wrong things they say, they insist that one shrinks from the light. Very well, let God draw me out of my corner then, and I will say what is on my mind. Whether it will do any good, only God knows. For there are many who ask for the truth, but few who like to hear it.[2]

Fortunately, Conrad Grebel, Hans Denck, and other Anabaptists, did not stay silent. And they did more than just speak. They wrote. From the beginning of the movement their writings shook the populace. Roman Catholics burned them. Luther cursed them. Zwingli and Bullinger wrote scathing replies. Practically all European governments made the publication, the distribution and the ownership of Anabaptist writings a capital offence. But they survive to speak today.

The Anabaptist Writings

Unlike the writings of the first Christians, which survive only in rare manuscripts and in limited quantity, the writings of the Anabaptists survive in amazing abundance, and more are coming to light all the time. When Roman Catholic authorities ransacked the Anabaptist communities of Moravia and drove the brothers away, they hauled off wagonloads of handwritten books. Many of them survive, even after World War II, and are being discovered in the libraries and church archives of Europe.

The difficulty in preparing this book was not in finding material to use, but in deciding what *not* to use. Without constant effort and many deletions, this book could have grown to the size of the *Martyrs Mirror* and the *Aelteste Chronik* combined! But it was deliberately kept brief. This regrettably required the use of fragments and abbreviated passages. Those who can do so are urged to read these writings in their original languages and in their context if possible.

---

1 Job 32:18-20, quoted in a letter of September 3, 1524, to Joachim von Watt (Vadian).

2 From *Was geredt sey* . . . published at Augsburg in 1526.

Spontaneous Literature

"How did they do it?" I have asked myself time after time. Out of money, driven from their homes, when paper was scarce, ink expensive, and the publishing of their books was a mortal risk, the Anabaptists produced thousands upon thousands of books for free distribution!

The only thing I can see is that God helped them.

The first Anabaptists had no central organization. For the most part (outside of Moravia) they had no publishing houses or editorial committees. Their earliest writings were nothing but the spontaneous efforts of individuals here and there, many of them in jail. Their originality shows in poetry that doesn't quite rhyme, Scriptures quoted by memory, words and names written in a vast variety of German dialectic spellings and misspellings, a lack of punctuation, and in many cases a lack of style or form. But God spoke through their literature and it moved Europe.

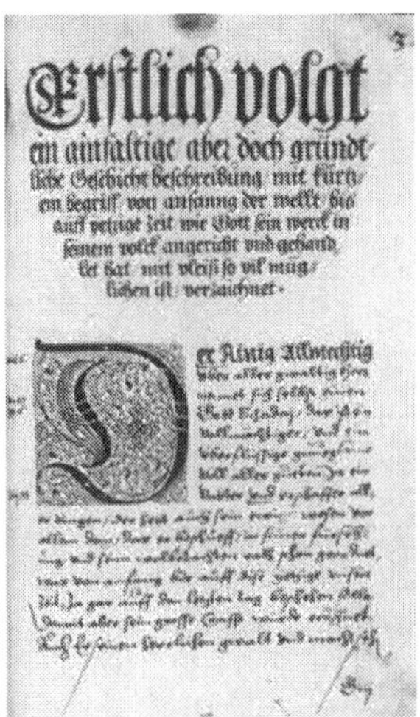

Erstlich volgt

Anabaptist writers and publishers used printing presses where possible. But printing, in the sixteenth century, continued to be a costly, time- consuming affair. Copying writings by hand was much simpler, even though it did not allow for as wide a distribution of the finished product.

This page from the Hutterite *Gross-Geschichtbuch*, first written on vellum during the 1500s and recopied many times, is an example of what came from the *Schreibstuben* (scriptoriums, writing rooms) of the believers in Moravia. Young men and women, working under gifted teachers like Hauprecht Zapf, reproduced thousands of writings, some of them surviving in European libraries and in Anabaptist communities today.

In this book you will often read what "the Anabaptists said" or "the Anabaptists believed." Such statements, in light of the spontaneity of my sources cannot be taken as all-inclusive absolutes. The Anabaptists shared the secret of the strength of their movement, but many of them did not share the beliefs of the majority in every area.

A Word of Caution

You will, in fact, almost certainly disagree with some things the Anabaptists said and believed. If you are a descendant of the Anabaptists themselves, you may feel disappointed and unsettled (I did). You may be sorely tempted to doubt my sources, to write off the men I quote as "unsound"or "marginal" characters, or simply to dismiss this book by saying: "Well, the Anabaptists were off on some things too.

They probably were. But I encourage you not to react like my friend from Pennsylvania did. Several years ago I wrote a paper on threefold baptism as taught by the Anabaptists. The night after I gave him the paper I was startled to suddenly have him knocking on my door. Because he lived a good distance away, my first thought was that something terrible must have happened. He looked dishevelled and excited. "Peter!" he exclaimed as he burst through the door. "I read your paper and just had to come to talk things over. What is going on?"

"Did you read the whole paper?" I asked him.

"No," he confessed. "I didn't get past the first paragraph where you spoke of being buried in baptism. I thought it sounded like you were going off track and teaching immersion. . . ."

I understood my friend's concern. I grew up like he did. But our Anabaptist forefathers could not have understood it at all, and this book, which consists largely of what they wrote, reflects their insensitivity to our doctrinal touchiness.

My prayer is that such "details" in this book will not divert your attention from its theme. My prayer is that you will find your way through the superficial, the transient, and that which you did not expect, to get your hands on the truth behind the Anabaptist movement of the sixteenth century. If that can happen, and if a light comes on in your heart as a result, I shall feel amply rewarded for having prepared this book in the English language.

A Word on Anabaptist Research

Knowing what the Anabaptists taught is not enough. Thousands, now-a-days, both know what they taught and are able to expound on it at length, but their lifestyle remains unchanged.

This book is written with a general distrust of Anabaptist scholars who do not live in an "Anabaptist" (radically nonconformed) way. It is written with little sympathy or appreciation for the conclusions of most modern-day Anabaptists. What can those who have gone the way of the world in education, in economics, in dress, and in entertainment contribute to the understanding of what was believed by their forefathers in the sixteenth century?

Can a man describe the inner feelings of a woman?

How can those who have isolated themselves in culturally elite, rural communities in North America, or those who have become wealthy property owners and businessmen, identify with the Anabaptists who were often at the bottom of the working class, landless, and city dwellers?

This book is written with the premise that only those who choose the life which the Anabaptists chose will in the end discover what they thought and believed.

Anabaptist Quotations in This Book

Most twentieth-century Christians do not know Anabaptist writings because they cannot read them. The Anabaptists wrote in a variety of German dialects. ("Standard High German" had not yet become a standard in their day.) Some of their important writings have never been translated into English. Those that have been translated are in some cases hard to read because of the cumbersome English used to portray German thoughts. (How, for instance, do you best translate such graphic terms as *untergeworfen*, *angestrengt*, or *einverleibt*?)

In this book I have tried to make the Anabaptists as readable as possible without altering the sense of their statements. I have used some English translations (such as Leonard Verduin's excellent one of Menno Simons' writings), but even in them I have changed some terms back to correspond more exactly with their German originals (such as "teachings" instead of "doctrine" for the German word *Lehre*, and "nighttime meal" instead of "communion" for *Nachtmal*). I have tried to express original German ideas as accurately as possible. Because of this I favoured the use of standard German above English translations, the gap between standard and dialectic German (or Dutch) being much smaller than the gap between those dialects and English.

Those acquainted with Anabaptist writings will notice that I have in some cases broken up or abbreviated quotations for the sake of readability and brevity. In all such cases I refer readers to the original works or their competent translations for the full text.

References are given to original Anabaptist works, which were my sources, whenever possible, for the quotations used in this book. Of these you may find many translations, both fragmentary and complete, in standard High German and English. A good way to locate them is by searching in scholarly Anabaptist bibliographies in Mennonite college libraries.

This book itself is not a scholarly work. It is not a reference book. Its translations are rough and fragmentary. Its references are incomplete. But I pray that the Spirit who moved the Anabaptist writers will move those who read this book and lead them . ..

On to Jesus

In 1527, two years after the birth of the Anabaptist movement in Switzerland, people already wondered about its secret. Their wondering (with minds just coming out of the Dark Ages) led them to suspect magic. Somewhere in the deep valley of the River Inn, between the snow-capped mountains of Austria, a strange story began to circulate. People said the Anabaptists had a magic container, a little vial, filled with a liquid about which the devil himself had no clue. They said the Anabaptists forced their converts to drink from the vial. One little sip of its contents was enough to bring anyone completely under their power. Just one sip and a person became serious-minded, no longer able to do what he used to do, and no amount of money, nothing that life had to offer could bring him back to what he used to be. Once a person tasted from the vial he would die before giving up his strange beliefs.

Leonhard Schiemer, in prison before his beheading at Rattenberg on the Inn, took the time to answer this foolish story in 1527:

> Well you godless crowd, let me tell you how it is. Let us say you are right. Let us say it is true that we must all drink from a little vial. And like you say, it certainly is true that the devil does not know what is in it. If you do not know it either, you are also devils . . . but if you want to know, I will reveal the liquid's secret proportions to you!
>
> Like Caiaphas, you speak the truth without knowing it. You say that whoever takes a sip from the vial is permanently changed. How true! For the liquid in the vial is made from nothing else than a struck down, ground up, rubbed apart, and sorrowful heart pulverised in the mortar and pestle of the cross . . . and it is the liquid which our dear brother and friend, Christ Jesus, drank— mixed with vinegar and gall.
>
> The vial is the one he offered to the sons of Zebedee. It is the one he drank from in the garden. It is the one that caused him to sweat until he sweated drops of blood, and until he trembled and fell into a faint so that angels had to lift him up. Truly the liquid in it is such an awful liquid that no one can drink it without his neighbours taking note that he is totally changed!
>
> Whoever takes a sip from the vial indeed becomes willing to forsake everything he has . . . because the Spirit of Christ teaches him and reveals to him things that no man can express and which cannot be written onto paper. Nobody knows what those things are, save those to whom they have been revealed...[1]

A broken heart and fellowship with Jesus—Leonhard Schiemer answered the foolish story in a truly Anabaptist way.

The first Anabaptists followed Jesus.

It was so simple that people could not understand it. It was so easy to explain it seemed mysterious.

---

[1] From Leonhard Schiemer's writing *Vom Fläschlen, gantz clärlich endteckt, was es bedeytet, allen Frommen Tröstlich zu leesen,* written on the Thursday after Saint Andrew's day, 1527.

Jesus Calling—Me?

When the New Testament fell into their hands in the sixteenth century, many German people naively took it at face value. When they heard Jesus' call to the disciples, "Follow me," they thought it meant them. When they read Jesus' commands, "Turn the other cheek," "Give to him who asks of you," or "Sell everything you have," that is what they did. They thought Jesus was God in human flesh, showing them how to live, and that God expected them to live just like that. They thought that being a disciple of Jesus meant studying his teachings, putting them to practice, and living with the consequences (the cross) of following him.

It never occurred to them that following Jesus (while carrying a cross) would lead anywhere else but to death.

Michael Schneider, before he died under torture at Passau in Bavaria, wrote from the castle dungeon:

> Listen to me, all peoples of the earth. Listen to me, young and old, great and small. If you want to be saved, you need to leave sin, follow Christ the Lord, and live according to his will. Christ Jesus came to the earth to teach men the right way to go, to teach them to turn from sin and to follow him. He said: "I am the way the truth and the life, no-one comes to the father except through me."
>
> He who longs for *Gemeinschaft* (one-ness, community) with Jesus and who wants to take part in his kingdom, needs to do what Jesus did while he was on the earth. He who wants to reign with Jesus must first be willing to suffer for his name. The man who dies with Jesus in this life will enter with him into the Father's kingdom, in eternal joy. But the man who does not follow him is not redeemed by his blood and his sins will never be forgiven.
>
> Those whose sins have been forgiven should live no longer in sin. This is what Jesus Christ, our Lord, teaches us. Those who fall back into sin break their covenant with God. Even greater pain and suffering will be theirs—and their loss will be forever.
>
> Not all who say "Lord, Lord" will enter the kingdom. Only those who keep his covenant will be accepted by him. He who confesses Christ before the world and who stands for the truth to the end will be saved.
>
> Help us to that, God, our Lord, that we may stay with Jesus—that we may always walk according to his teachings, that we may commit no more sins, and that we may be an honour to his name, now and forever . . . into eternity! Amen.[2]

Jesus' Community

Following Jesus, for the Anabaptists was much more than obeying his commandments. It was much more than confessing him publicly or being willing to die for him. It was knowing Jesus, and living like the first disciples in full *Gemeinschaft* with him.

The words of Paul in Philippians 3:10 stated distinctly the goal of the

[2] *Ausbund*, 82

Anabaptists: "I want to know Christ, and the power of his resurrection, and the *fellowship* of sharing in his sufferings, becoming like him in his death, and so, somehow, to attain to the resurrection from the dead."

The Greek word *koinonia*, translated "fellowship" in this verse, was always translated into the German word *Gemeinschaft*. To the Anabaptists, this beautiful word meant both spiritual communion and community of goods. It was the word used in Acts 2:44 and 4:32 for "all things common" (*alle Dinge gemein, es war ihnen alles gemein*). It was the word they found in 1 John 1:7: "If we walk in the light as he is in the light, we have *Gemeinschaft* one with another and the blood of Jesus, his Son, purifies us from all sin." It was the word they used instead of "church."[3]

About this statement, Peter Rideman wrote in chains from his dungeon of the castle at Wolkersdorf, in Hesse, in 1540:

> When we listen carefully to the Gospel and conform to it, we come to take part in the community of Christ, as may be seen in the words of John: "What we have seen and heard we declare unto you, that you may have Gemeinschaft with us, and our Gemeinschaft is with God the Father and with his son, Jesus Christ our Lord, who has given us all things that he heard and received from his father" (1 John 1:3).
>
> Gemeinschaft is nothing else than to have all things in common (*gemein*) with those to whom we are inwardly bound. It is to keep nothing for ourselves, but to share all that we have with others— like the Father keeps nothing for himself but shares all that he has with the Son, and like the Son keeps nothing for himself, but shares all that he was with the Father and with those in Gemeinschaft with him.
>
> Those in Gemeinschaft with Christ follow his example and keep nothing for themselves. They hold all things in common with their Teacher, and with all those who belong to his community, so that they may be one in the Son, as the Son is one with the Father (John 16:13-15).
>
> This is called the "Gemeinschaft of the holy ones" (in the Apostles Creed) because we hold in common holy things: the things through which we were made holy in the Father and in the Son. The Son makes us holy through what he gives us. In this way everything serves to the advantage and building up of one another, and to the praise and glory of God.[4]

Gemeinschaft with Jesus, like earthly Gemeinschaft among men, comes about only at incredible cost and continual struggle. But it is a gift from God. It must be fought for again and again. But it is the only way to peace.

To the Anabaptists, Gemeinschaft with Jesus was worth having at the expense of husband, wife, children, or parents. It was worth the terror of flight and

---

[3] The Anabaptists nearly always spoke of the church as the Lord's *Gemein* (commune), and left the high-sounding term *church* (Kirche) for the Roman Catholics and the Protestants to use. It was also the word they found in the Apostles' Creed in "the communion of the saints" (*die Gemeinschaft der Heiligen*).

[4] From Peter Rideman's *Rechenschafft unserer Religion, Leer und Glaubens,* first published in Moravia in 1545.

torture. The glory of community with Jesus, the "Gemeinschaft of sharing in his sufferings" lit up the deepest dungeon. It shone with an other-worldly radiance above the flames of the *Scheiterhaufen* (the woodpile where the condemned were burned at the stake). It was the light they saw that opened the heavens and allowed them to see right there, almost within reach, the unspeakable joy of eternal fellowship in new heavens and a new earth where righteousness dwells.

Gemeinschaft with Jesus, for the Anabaptists, was the promise of the Kingdom of Heaven. A south German Anabaptist wrote in the mid-1500s:

> Oh God Father, on heaven's throne, you have prepared for us a crown if we stay in your Son, if we suffer with him the cross and the pain, if we surrender ourselves to him in this life and if we struggle continually to enter into his Gemeinschaft. You tell us what we need to know, through your Son, if we have inner Gemeinschaft with him . . .
>
> You gave your beloved Son to us to be our head. He has marked out for us the road we should take, so that we would not lose our way and find ourselves outside of his community . . . Therefore, Christians, oh little flock, let us all look together at how he walked before us here on the earth. Let us become like him in love and in suffering. Let us keep our covenant with him and not stay away from eating his flesh and his blood.
>
> His flesh and his blood, the food he gave us, must be understood like this: In eating his flesh and blood, the Spirit brings us into community with him. . .. God redeems us together with Jesus. He serves us through his Son. His Son is the rock and the cornerstone of his church community—his wife, his companion and his love, through whom he works on the earth. . ..
>
> Therefore come! Come all you newborn Christians! Come in sincerity to Christ the Passover lamb, whose kingdom and communion shall never end![5]

Jesus, the Focus of Their Prayers

The Anabaptists, far removed in Spirit from the wooden christs, the crosses, and the worship of Mary and the saints in the Dark Ages, prayed freely to Jesus. Far removed from the doctrinal "correctness" of the Protestant Reformers (who offered formal praises to "God Almighty, the Lord Sebaoth"), they simply prayed to God the Father or to Jesus their brother, or to both at the same time, knowing that in the Spirit their prayers were heard.

Without this direct communication with Jesus, the Anabaptists could not have followed him. Under torture or on the way to the *Scheiterhaufen*, the Anabaptists, like Stephen, cried to Jesus in their distress. They lived in total confidence of Jesus' words: "Come unto *me* . . . Whoever comes to *me* I will never drive away . . . No one comes to the Father except through *me*."

"Oh Christ, help your people!" cried Michael Sattler before they cut out his tongue and burned him at the stake in 1527.

"Oh Lord Christ from heaven, I praise you for turning away my sorrow

---

[5] *Ausbund*, 55

and sadness!" cried Felix Manz before they threw him into the Limmat River at Zürich, in 1526.

"Fly to the mountain of refuge: Christ Jesus!" wrote Menno Simons. "Commend your affairs to him who has chosen you to be his precious bride, his children and the members of his body."[6]

The Lord Jesus Christ was no dim theological figure, no "marginal character," to the first Anabaptists. He was their friend, their brother, the hero and the focus of their highest admiration. An unnamed Anabaptist wrote in the early 1500s:

> Look at Jesus the friendly knight! Look at the captain! The battle, when you come to this place, is fierce. The enemies—the world, the flesh, sin, the devil, and death—close in around you. But leap to your captain's side! He will kill the enemies! He will help you out of all distress.
>
> Stay with your flag! Do not let them drive you back from your captain, Jesus Christ! If you want the crown and the glory, and if you want to triumph with him, you must suffer and die with him too. They caught Christ our captain and beat him. In like manner they mistreat us, his followers. The hour of distress has come upon all the earth. They hunt us out. In almost every country they try to catch us because we stand for Christ. They try to keep him from coming to help us, barricading all the roads until they have us. Then the strangling and the stabbing, the gruesome violence begins. But wait, our captain, he will avenge it! He will break the power of the enemy, and he will stand with his little flock!
>
> All you beloved knights of God, be strong! Be manly in the fight! This dreadful storm will not be long. Stand fast! Stand true to death! Do not allow them to drive you back. Men and women, trust in God![7]

A Picture of Jesus

Little by little, out of their "community with Jesus" (Phil. 3:10), a picture of Jesus began to take shape in the Anabaptist movement.

Wolfgang Brandhuber, a servant of the Word among the Anabaptists in southern Germany and Austria, wrote in the late 1520s:

> The one who fears God sees the true light and evaluates in it all his thoughts, his words, and his works. That true light is Christ, whose life is the will of God. In actual humanity Christ Jesus showed us what we should do, so that no one may have an excuse on the last day. Our thoughts on the inside and our deeds on the outside—all our life is to become a picture of Christ who said: "I and the Father are one."[8]

Shortly after writing this letter, Wolfgang Brandhuber died with seventy others who

---

6 From *Dat Fundament des Christelycken leers*. . . first published in 1539.

7 *Ausbund*, 78

8 From *Ein sendbrief an die gmain Gottes zu Rottenburg am In*, 1529

were sentenced to death by "fire, water and sword" at Linz, in Austria, in 1529.

The Teacher and the Example

True disciples of Jesus follow his example in everything. Doing this is the way to "learn Christ" (Ephesians 4:20).

Before they beheaded him in 1528, Leonhard Schiemer wrote:

> The educated people of this world start at the wrong end. They hitch the horse to the back of the wagon. They would love to receive the truth of Christ in high institutions of learning, but that is like me going to the goldsmith and telling him to teach me his trade without bothering to take me into the workshop, or like a man learning out of a book how to make shoes.[9]

Learning by doing is the way to learn Christ. It sounds easy: "Do what Jesus would do." But it is not easy. It is "living by faith" instead of sight.

Hans Schlaffer was a Roman Catholic priest in the mountains of upper Austria. But he followed Jesus and became an Anabaptist servant of the Word. On a cold evening, December 5, 1527, while on a trip up the Inn River to his mountain home for the winter, he attended an Anabaptist meeting in the valley, at Schwatz. The police caught him and locked him up in the nearby Frundsberg castle. There, on the night before they beheaded him, he wrote a long letter addressed to God. In the letter (which contained teachings for his survivors) he wrote:

> Oh God, illuminated by your kindness, we understand the word *faith* in the context of *deeds*. He who has faith in Jesus gives himself to you and to your will. He denies himself, takes up his cross and follows Jesus, his teacher, his Lord and his head . . . even into death. He says with Paul, "I live, but not I. It is Christ who lives in me," and "everyone who has not the Spirit of Christ is none of his."
>
> Oh Father in heaven, whoever lives in Christ your Son and suffers and dies with him will rise with him in glory to be in his Kingdom forever. This is how we have understood the holy Gospel. This is how we understand Christ and his teachings, and this is how we now understand the word *faith* which we never understood like this before.[10]

Christ the Head of the Body

Paul's picture of Jesus and the church as a body could for the Anabaptists have only one meaning: The body must follow the head. Because Jesus, the head, suffered, the body must suffer with him.

---

[9] From *Vom Fläschlen. . .* 1527.

[10] From *Ein einfältig Gebet durch ein Gefangner armen Bruder im Herren, zuSchwatz gebetet und betrübt bis in den Tod*, written Monday after Candlemass, 1528.

Looking across the Inn Valley from a window in the Frundsberg castle at Schwatz, in which Hans Schlaffer lay imprisoned in 1527. Michael Gaismair, who led the peasants' revolt in South Tyrol, lived and worked in this mining town as a young man. A large number of his co-workers, sharing his disgust with the greed and hypocrisy around them, found the Lord and got baptised in the 1520s.

Ambrutz Spittelmayr, tortured in the castle at Ansbach before they beheaded him in southern Germany wrote in 1527:

> All who are one with Christ through his divine Word are members of his body: that is, they are his hands, his feet, and his eyes. . . . Jesus Christ is a real man in the flesh. He is the head of the body, and it is through him that the members are governed.[11]

Ambrutz went on to speak of the body's "community of suffering" with the head, but I will quote again the ex-priest, Hans Schlaffer, who wrote the night before his execution:

> Oh my God, how shall it go with me in the hour of my great need? I lay my worries, my terror, and distress on you. You have always been my powerful help. Surely you will not withdraw yourself from me in the hour of my greatest weakness. . .. Surely you will grant me, in the hour of my body's death, eternal life!
>
> You have decreed that the entire Christ, the head with all the members of the body, must suffer . . . the members of his body, of his flesh and of his bones, who have become as one flesh with him. This is a great mystery in Christ, and in his church community.
>
> Now, since Christ the head lived in human flesh (but without sin) he needed to suffer and die, and we who have become the members of his body cannot do anything but go along with our head.[12]

Detachment

Following Jesus, the Anabaptists, especially those of south central Europe, spoke of *Gelassenheit* (a state of detachment, letting everything go) for Jesus. Hans Haffner from the community at Auspitz in Moravia wrote a tract while in the dungeon of the castle in Passau, Bavaria, in the 1530s. Its title was "About

---

[11] From the statement Ambrutz addressed to the court at Cadolzburg in Franconia, on October 25, 1527.

[12] *Ein einfältig Gebet*. . . 1528

the True Soldier of Jesus Christ." In it he spoke of detachment:

> Now let us hear what true detachment is: It is to let go of all things for God's sake . . . and to turn to God so that he may lead us. Jesus Christ called it hatred: "He who does not hate his father and mother and renounce everything he has is not worthy of me." True detachment is to put to death the flesh and to be born another time. The whole world wants to have Christ, but they pass him by. They do not find him because they want to have him only as a gift, only as a giver of grace and a mediator which he certainly is, but they do not want to have him in a suffering way.
>
> The same Christ who says, "All who are heavy laden, come to me and I will refresh you," also says, "Whosoever will not forsake father and mother cannot be my disciple." Whoever loves truth must accept the one as well as the other. Whoever wants to have Christ must have him also in the way of suffering. It is foolish to say: "We believe that Christ has redeemed us, but we do not want to live like he lived."
>
> True detachment involves two things: enduring persecution and overcoming ourselves. When they hit us one cheek we are to turn to them the other. . . . In the second place we must be weaned from the ways of our human nature as a child must be weaned from his mother's breast. We must be willing to forsake wife and children, father and mother, lands and property, our lives and even what God has given to us . . . for Christ.[13]

Madmen or Fools?

Four centuries after Hans Haffner wrote this tract, I spoke about Christian economics at a mission church in Latin America. I read what Jesus said on the subject and implied that we should obey him. No sooner did the meeting end than the missionary (a North American) came to me and wondered what I meant. I said I didn't mean anything but what Jesus said. He replied: "Well, I haven't studied into it much, but I am sure there must be other Scriptures that would give this more of a balance."

Balancing out Jesus—what a difficult assignment! Especially for a missionary who hasn't "studied into it much"!

Leonhard Schiemer, Wolfgang Brandhuber, or Hans Schlaffer—it would never have occurred to them that Jesus needed"balancing out." The first Anabaptists did not ask what Jesus meant. They simply followed him, and people called them fanatics.

The young Anabaptist messenger, Klaus Felbinger, wrote in chains from the castle dungeon at Landshut in Bavaria shortly before they beheaded him on July 19, 1560:

> The world has become a wilderness, sunken in sin, and knows little or nothing of God. And now the very teaching of the Gospel has become a new and heretical teaching, a deception in the eyes of the world. As soon as God raises up a messenger of salvation . . . one who proclaims to them the true Word of God and shows them the right way to go, they refuse

---

13 From *Von einem Wahrhaften Ritter Christi, und womit er gewappnet muss sein, damit er überwinden möge die Welt, das Fleisch und den Teufel*, written ca. 1533.

> to believe him and think he is a madman or a fool. Anyone filled with the Spirit is considered stupid or insane.[14]

It was the Protestants, not the Anabaptists, who studied the New Testament in the sixteenth century to find out "what Jesus meant." It was the Protestants, not the Anabaptists, who arrived at a "place of rest" and at "balanced" and "reasonable" positions on scriptural issues. It was the Protestants, not the Anabaptists, who knew their theology, their soteriology, and their ecclesiology. And certainly, the Protestants had inspired and capable leaders too.

A Monk in Armour

As a sixteen-year-old boy wrestling with a colt to get it untangled from its tie strap, I broke my foot. For several weeks I was laid up and an elderly neighbour brought me books to read from his church library. One of them, a book about Martin Luther called *A Monk in Armour,* moved me deeply.

The story of Martin Luther's conversion struck me to the heart. His conviction and his zeal for the truth inspired me, as few things have, in my Christian life. This is part of the story in his own words:

> No matter how irreproachably I lived as a monk, I felt myself to be a sinner in the presence of God. My conscience bothered me very much. I could not believe that I pleased God with the things I was doing to gain his favour. I did not love God and his justice. In fact, I hated him—if not in open blasphemy, at least with huge murmurings in my heart. I was indignant with him, thinking that on top of condemning us miserable sinners to eternal destruction through original sin and oppressing us with all kinds of calamities through the law and the ten commandments, he had added sorrow onto sorrow by giving us the gospel (impossible to obey) through which his wrath would finally fall on us.
>
> In this way I struggled fiercely and desperately with my conscience, while I continued to knock away at the epistles of Paul, consumed with a burning desire to know what he meant. . ..
>
> Then, at last, I began to understand the justice of God. I began to see that the just man lives by the gift of God that is by faith. I began to understand that the justice of God revealed in the Gospels is to be taken in a passive way, and that God justifies
>
> men not by works but by faith, as it is written: "The just shall live by faith." When I comprehended this, I felt myself to have been born again, and to have entered through open gates into paradise itself.[15]

Martin Luther found rest for his conscience—not in Jesus but in Paul, not in the Gospels but in "sound doctrine." When I was ten years old his great hymn, *From the high heavens I come to you. I bring you salvation and the doctrine of grace.*

---

[14] From *Ein Sendbrief Klaus Felbingers geschrieben aus seiner Gefenknus an die Gemein Gottes in Mähren im 1560. Jahr.*

[15] From the preface to Luther's complete works, which he prepared for publication in 1545.

Sound doctrine I bring you in great amounts, and of that I will tell you singing[16] made a deep impression (through a special occurrence) on me.

Throughout my childhood it was my favourite hymn. But in the years following, little by little, I began to see where Martin Luther and the Anabaptists parted ways.

Martin Luther found the Scriptures. The first Anabaptists found Jesus. Their discoveries led them in totally different directions.

A Balanced Position

At the Diet of Augsburg on June 25, 1530, the rulers and church leaders of Protestant Germany met to draw up the Augsburg Confession of Faith (the "only authoritative and in every way the most significant" confession of the Lutheran church)[17]. Among its "balanced" and "reasonable" positions, based on the Scriptures, the confession states:

> It is taught among us that all government in the world and all established rule and laws were instituted and ordained by God for the sake of good order, and that Christians may without sin occupy civil offices or serve as princes and judges, render decisions and pass sentence according to imperial and other existing laws, punish evildoers with the sword, engage in just wars, serve as soldiers, buy and sell, take required oaths, possess property, be married, etc.

Condemned here are the Anabaptists, who teach that none of the things indicated above is Christian. Also condemned are those who teach that Christian perfection requires the forsaking of house and home, wife and child, and the renunciation of such activities as are mentioned above. Actually, true perfection consists alone of proper fear of God and real faith in God, for the Gospel does not teach an outward and temporal but an inward and eternal mode of existence and righteousness of the heart.

After five other ringing condemnations of the "Anabaptists, Donatists and Novatians," the Augsburg Confession (translated and adapted for use in the Anglican and Methodist churches of today) was signed by John, duke of Saxony; George, margrave of Brandenburg; Ernest, duke of Lüneburg; Philip, landgrave of Hesse; John Frederick, duke of Saxony; Francis, duke of Lüneburg; Wolfgang, prince of Anhalt; the mayor and council of Nuremberg and the mayor and council of Reutlingen.

But the Anabaptists paid no attention to it. They followed Jesus. Further south, in Protestant Switzerland, Huldrych Zwingli and John Calvin also wondered how to handle the "Anabaptist pestilence." In a letter to Vadian (Conrad Grebel's brother-in- law), Zwingli said: "My struggle with the old church (Catholicism) was

---

[16] *Vom Himmel hoch da komm ich her, ih bring euch Heil und Gnadenlehr. Der guten Lehr bring ich so viel, davon ich singend sagen will . . .* (Some German versions have Gnadenmär instead of Gnadenlehr.)

[17] From an English translation of the Augsburg Confession, published by theMuhlenberg Press in 1959.

child's play compared to my struggle with the Anabaptists." John Calvin in his *Brief Instruction to Arm Those of Good Faith Against the Errors of the Anabaptists* wrote:

> These miserable fanatics have no other goal than to put everything into disorder. . . . They reveal themselves to be the enemies of God and of the human race. . .. If it is not right for a Christian man to go to law with anyone to settle quarrels regarding possessions, inheritance, and other matters, then I ask these good teachers what will become of the world![18]

The Anabaptists did not answer John Calvin in writing. They answered him with their lives.

Kappel, in Switzerland, where Huldrych Zwingli met his death in a bloody battle against Catholic opponents from the south, in 1531. The hero of the day, Adam Neff (who rescued the flag of Zürich) had Anabaptist children and grandchildren, whose descendants still live in Mennonite communities

The Way, The Truth, The Life

To the Protestants, the Bible was their manifesto, an end in itself. Once they reached an agreement on how to "properly" interpret it, they revered it and treated it with gallant devotion. They preached and persecuted and fought mighty wars in defence of the Bible and its doctrines.

To the first Anabaptists, the Bible was simply the book that took them to Jesus.

The Protestants found the "key" to Bible interpretation in the epistles of Paul. But the Anabaptists found it in Jesus and his Sermon on the Mount.

The Protestants saw in Paul a great theologian, the expositor of the doctrines of faith and grace. The Anabaptists saw in Paul a man who forsook everything to become a "fool for Christ's sake." They found community with him in his martyr's death.

---

[18] *Brieve Instruction pour armer tous bons fideles contre les Erreurs de la secte des Anabaptistes* (Geneva, 1544)

The Protestants lived to obey their authorities. They spoke much about "God-ordained authority" and held their princes and church leaders in highest esteem. The Anabaptists lived to obey Jesus.

The Protestants worked en masse and waited until "everyone was ready" to make changes in religious practice.

The Anabaptists did, on first opportunity, what they thought Jesus wanted them to do. If no one else joined them, they did it alone.

The Protestants followed a logical course. Theologians, princes and educators planned what to do in a way that made sense.

The first Anabaptists followed Jesus without making plans. That did not make sense. But it was the secret of their great strength. And it led them....

On to Conviction

Nestled into the northern shoulders of the Swabian Alps, lies the old German city of Schwäbisch-Gmünd. The Romans knew this place. Its Johanneskirche (St. John's Church) dates from 1230, and its cathedral of the Holy Cross was already old in 1528 when a strange man came to town.

The young man, Martin Zehentmayer, came from Bavaria and was an artist. At least he had been an artist learning to paint in the city of Augsburg in Bavaria. There, they said, he had joined a fanatical sect and had gotten expelled. Now he was in Schwäbisch-Gmünd.

None of the respectable people in town would have anything to do with him. But Martin made his presence known. A poet who wrote songs, he went from house to house calling on people to follow Jesus. The young people fell for him. His sincerity deeply impressed them and what he said cut right through the stuffy formality of Schwäbisch-Gmünd's society to the innermost longing of their hearts: a longing for peace with God in brotherly community. Before the townspeople caught on to what was happening, Martin had baptised over one hundred people and was secretly celebrating the Eucharist in their homes.

They caught him on a winter night in February, 1529, in a secret meeting—right in the act of "deceiving" the young, the simple, and the poor people of town. Along with Martin they grabbed forty others, including nineteen girls and women.

Many of them they soon let go for their "innocence," but Martin and the most outspoken among them they kept on bread and water in the tower prison on the city wall until the end of the year.

The people in the city who had come to the meetings did all they could to stay in contact with the prisoners. Some women and children climbed the city wall at night to reach the tower and talk to them. They read to the prisoners and sang together. But this stopped when the guards discovered them and prohibited further contact.

They tortured Martin on the rack, accusing him of sexual impropriety. But he had little to confess other than his desire to live like Jesus and his conviction (ridiculous from the authorities' point of view) to hold with the believers all his possessions in common.

On December 4, 1528, they finally brought the seven "obstinate ones" out of their cells and tried them publicly for the benefit of the town. Among the seven stood a woman and the young son of the miller.

The seven prisoners continued in their "stubbornness," so the town council convicted them of heresy and sentenced them to death. Then, three days later they led them in chains from the tower prison to a bare frozen field outside the walls of the city. A contingent of the Swabian League (under the provost,

Berthold Aichele) surrounded them. Noblemen, lords, and judges followed on horseback, and the townspeople, a great crowd, came along behind. The beating of drums made it hard to speak or to be heard.

On the field, the soldiers formed a large circle, with the convicts, the guards, and two executioners in the centre. Then, what was that! The youngest of the seven, the miller's son, was shouting something.

His voice above the sound of the drums was clear, and many could understand what he said: "Stand off from your sins! Turn to God! There is no other way to heaven than through the Lord Jesus Christ who died on the cross to redeem us!"

Some women in the crowd shouted back: "Keep up your courage, young man! Be strong!"

But it was too much for one of the mounted noblemen. He could not bear to see the young man killed. Demanding permission, he rode into the ring to speak with the boy. "My son," he said, "stand off yourself from the error you are in, and make things right! Do not lose your young life! What do you think you will have for it? I will take you home and keep you with me. I will give you a permanent inheritance as my own son and see to your needs for life. You will have many good things. Now come! Come with me and be my son!"

But the young man answered him distinctly: "God does not want me to do that. Should I choose a worldly life and forsake God? I would do evil by making such a choice, and I will not do it. Your wealth can help neither you nor me. I choose greater riches by persevering to the end. I will surrender my Spirit to God and commend myself to Jesus so that his bitter suffering on the cross will not have been in vain for me."

They beheaded the seven on the bare frozen field. It was December 7, 1528, and great fear came upon the people. Someone said he saw lights above the fountain in the town square that night and heard the singing of angels. The city council, just to be sure, kept on round-the-clock duty the soldiers of the Swabian League.

Convicted

Who was convicted at Schwäbisch-Gmünd?

The city court convicted the seven prisoners and sentenced them to die. But did they die for that conviction?

No. They died because their hearts had been touched with an infinitely higher conviction—the conviction that they were doing right by following Jesus no matter what it cost.

Inwardly sure that following Jesus was the right thing to do, nothing could make the Anabaptists feel guilty. They followed Jesus into baptism, into the breaking of bread, into turning the other cheek, into a new and totally different economy, into every area of his life and teachings, even into suffering and death, without it ever occurring to them that they could be wrong. The people who killed them sensed this, and it frightened them. They sensed that against such conviction— conviction that chooses capital punishment over a nobleman's inheritance—no tradition, nor law, nor family, nor emperor, nor sword, nor pope, nor church could stand, because it produces martyrs.

The First Martyr

For the Anabaptists, the first martyr was not Stephen, but Jesus,[1] and it was easy for them to see their lives as parallels— imperfect human parallels—of his.

Jesus Christ refused an easy life, earthly glory, and all the kingdoms of the world. He withstood his family, the religious leaders of his day, and the government of the Roman Empire. He walked without hesitating to a gruesome death (even when twelve legions of angels could have saved him) because he felt in his heart the calm assurance that he was doing what was right.

The first Anabaptists, following him, were touched with that same assurance. And from there it was a small step to calling their own religious leaders the "crowd of Caiaphas" and their own government officials "Pilate's children."[2] And it was also a small step to drawing the final parallel between them and Jesus in a martyr's death.

The Anabaptists saw Jesus as one who did what was right even when every soul on the earth abandoned him. And in that "loneliness of Christ" where every man must take up his cross to follow him, they found inner communion with him. In it they came to "know Christ and the Gemeinschaft of his sufferings, becoming like him in his death," and in it they hoped to attain, with him, "to the resurrection from the dead" (Phil. 3:10).

Following the martyr Christ, the Anabaptists, at the close of the Dark Ages, chose with him the way of the cross that leads to eternal life and light.

What Made the Dark Ages Dark?

The early Christians, up to the time of Ulfilas, followed Jesus. But the light went out when they became afraid to do what was right (like Ulfilas among the barbarians) alone.

---

[1] The *Martyrs Mirror*, first published by the Anabaptists of the Netherlands in 1660, begins with the account of "Jesus Christ the Son of God, crucified in Jerusalem". The third song of the *Ausbund* begins even further back, with the Old Testament prophets and John the Baptist.

[2] The *Aelteste Chronik* especially, uses these terms, but they also appear in the *Ausbund*, the *Martyrs Mirror* and elsewhere.

Afraid to do right if "the whole group" was not behind them, the early Christians stopped being a movement of convicted believers and became an organised religious body. They stopped being "rebels," "fanatics," and "those who turn the world upside down" to became a respected element of society. The world stopped fearing them. With that, it stopped hating them, and the age of persecution faded away.

Within the church conviction died as "submission" took its place, and "God-ordained authorities" found it necessary to tell everyone what to do and what to believe. The voice of the church took its place above the voice of a Christ-directed conscience, and "Christian Europe" lay for a thousand years in ignorance, bondage, and fear.

Ideas from the "Infidels"

The church of the Dark Ages tried to control everything the people of Europe did. Even worse, it tried to control what they thought. The church had long convinced the people that it was more important to submit than to think. The people no longer dared to think. In fact, after a thousand years, almost everyone had forgotten how, until strange things began to happen.

The pope, to keep the church of the Dark Ages together, called, in the name of the Lord Jesus, for "Christian crusades." No longer united by love nor by principle, the church sought unity in common hatred of the Muslims who had taken over the Middle East and northern Africa, and were pushing from all sides into Europe itself. The "infidels" had overrun "Christian" Spain and now threatened to take even the Spanish town where the apostle James's bones were said to lie.[3]

In the 1400's the pope and the Roman Catholic rulers of Spain finally drove the Muslims back. But in that conquest, the "Christian" armies of Europe (unwittingly, like the Germans a thousand years earlier) brought back with their plunder their own undoing. This time it was not a Cappadocian boy, but a collection of old Muslim and Jewish books. The books were translations from Greek, and after the invention of printing in the 1450s they released a flood of new ideas upon Europe. These exciting ideas gave birth to a new faith in man and a new hope for his future—the movement called *humanism*.

The humanists, after a thousand years of darkness, once more dared to "think for themselves". They even dared to question the traditions of the church, and in so doing they set parts of Germany, the Netherlands and Switzerland on a course to the Protestant Reformation.

This led to greater discoveries . . .

---

[3] Compostela, in the northwestern corner of Spain (Galicia), a major pilgrimage site in mediaeval Europe.

Beyond Humanism

Like the popes and bishops of the Dark Ages, the Protestant Reformers knew nothing but to build churches on the principle of submission to God-given authority. But they did so with a much more impressive authority than the Roman Catholics. The Roman Catholics' only claim to authority was their continuity—their "apostolic succession." The Reformers had something far better. Their claim to authority was sound doctrine (sola fide) and the Bible itself (sola scriptura). Against such a church, a "Biblical church," who would dare to rebel?

Johannes Denck dared.

A university student at Ingolstadt in Bavaria, Johannes Denck did not look like a rebel. He was "tall, very friendly, and of modest conduct."[4] He was also intelligent. One professor described him as "surpassing his age and seeming older than what he was."[5] Enrolling in the university when he was seventeen years old he graduated two years later with a bachelor's degree, fluent in Latin, Greek, and Hebrew. In his first job, he undertook the editing of a three-volume Greek dictionary.

At 23 years of age, Johannes Denck (*Hans* as everyone called him) accepted an appointment to the position of rector at the Sankt Sebald school of Nürnberg in Bavaria. He married a young woman of the city and they had a baby.

But all was not well.

Deep down in his heart, Hans (who had learned to "think for himself" in the university) knew his thinking was getting him nowhere. Like his "enlightened" Protestant friends, he had no victory over sin in his private life. He felt guilty and disappointed. "Surely there must be more to life than this!" he told himself. "But what?"

Hans was not the only one to ask this question. All around him people were grumbling about the "Reformation farce." Some were actually going back to the Roman Catholics. Then Hans found the answer in the call of Jesus: "Follow me!"

It changed his life.

Hans took as his motto, "No one truly knows Christ unless he follows him daily in life," and began at once to follow him to the best of his ability. That made trouble. The faculty and board of Sankt Sebald's school roused themselves. His parents-in-law told him to be careful. But Hans did what he believed was right—even when they summoned him to court.

---

4 From Johannes Kessler's *Sabbata* a cultural and church history written at Sankt Gallen, in Switzerland, in the mid-1500's.

5 Joachim von Watt (Vadian), the reformed scholar of Sankt Gallen.

The city court of Nürnberg demanded an explanation for his "odd behaviour." Hans replied in writing:

> I confess that I am a poor soul, subject to every weakness of body and spirit. For some time I thought I had faith, but I have come to see that it was a false faith. It was a faith that could not overcome my spiritual poverty, my inclinations to sin, my weaknesses and my sickness. Instead of that, the more I polished and adorned myself on the outside (with my supposed faith) the worse became my spiritual sickness on the inside. . . . Now I see clearly that I cannot keep on in this unbelief before God, so I say: Yes Lord! In the name of the Almighty God whom I fear from the bottom of my heart, I want to believe. Help me to believe.[6]

The court decided, in spite of his humble testimony, that Hans could not stay in Nürnberg. On January 21, 1525, in the dead of winter, they expelled him from the city with orders not to come closer than ten miles to it, on pain of death, for the rest of his life. They confiscated his property to support his wife and child who had to stay behind, and he found himself on the road, among the mountains and snow-laden forests of southern Germany, with nothing but the clothes on his back—and the inner conviction that he was doing what was right.

Joy in Surrender

By the time he left Nürnberg, Hans Denck had rejected his humanistic education that had taught him to "think for himself." Inner peace, he now knew, is not discovered in thinking for oneself, but in thinking like Jesus and in following him, no matter if one has to do it alone.

Once he comprehended this, Hans entered, with the Anabaptist movement, into actual Gemeinschaft with the martyr Christ. And in this he discovered, with them, the joy of submitting to Christ within us, the hope of glory (Col. 1:27).

In prison, before they beheaded him at Rattenberg on the Inn, Leonhard Schiemer wrote in 1527:

> There are three gifts of God. The first gift is the Word given to us by the Father. It is the law, the light of God within us. This light of God within us shows us what sin is, and what it is not. All men have this light, but not all of them make use of it.
>
> The second gift is Christ, the righteousness of God. The first light (the light within us) is our guide to this second light which is Christ. But there is only one way to get to the second light. It is through the melt-oven of true surrender (Gelassenheit). . . .
>
> The third gift is the gift of joy. It is the promise of the Holy Spirit and of the glory of God. The life of the world begins in happiness but ends in sadness. The life of the one who fears God has a sorrowful beginning; then the Holy Spirit comes to anoint him with unspeakable joy.[7]

With Hans Denck and Leonhard Schiemer the first Anabaptists found

---

6 From Hans Denck's confession of faith, written on January 14, 1525.

7 From the article *Was die Gnad sey . . .* 1527

Christ, the "true light which lights every man that comes into the world" (John 1:9), and the great joy that comes in total surrender to him.

Like a Willing Bride

God, the Anabaptists taught, gives to all of us the freedom to think and to believe what we want. But God, they also taught, convicts all of us when we sin and gives us a longing to do what is right. This gift from God, this knowledge of the truth—our *Gemüth* (intuition)—is a light within us to guide us in the choices we make. We all have the freedom to choose to follow it and to find joy in Gemeinschaft with Jesus, but many of us do not "make use of it."

The Anabaptists respected the conscience (*Gewissen*) highly. Menno Simons spoke of guarding what we learn "in the little chest of the conscience." But they saw the *Gemüth*, our inborn knowledge of the truth, as a yet higher authority than the conscience.

The conscience can be wrong. The Anabaptists, when they left Catholicism, struggled with their consciences about leaving the "holy, mother church." But another voice within them, the voice of truth working through their *Gemüth*, compelled them to override their consciences and do what was right no matter what they felt like doing. It was this obedience to the truth that disentangled the Anabaptists from the Dark Ages and set them free—free to think, free to believe, and free to stand for what was right.

The first Anabaptists used their freedom to think, but not to "think for themselves." They thought like Jesus.

The first Anabaptists used their freedom to believe, but not to promote their own beliefs. They believed like Jesus.

The first Anabaptists used their freedom to stand, but not to stand for "personal convictions." They stood for Jesus, and Jesus within them became the conviction that carried them through prison, through torture, through violence and death—to eternal life.

Free to choose, free to live like they pleased, the first Anabaptists knew that they were totally free. But they chose to give their freedom to Jesus and follow him. Hans Denck taught that the highest thing we can choose with our freedom of choice is to choose to give our freedom of choice back to God, and that there is "no other way to blessedness than to lose one's self-will completely." This, for the Anabaptists was the way to *wahre Gelassenheit* (a true "letting loose" or surrender), and it led them to community with Jesus and his body, even in material things. Hans Denck wrote that "the church surrenders her freedom of choice to Christ like a willing bride surrenders herself to the groom."[8]

---

[8] *Was geredt sey . . .* 1526

Menno Simons wrote:

> We have but one Lord and master of our conscience, Jesus Christ, whose word, will, commandment and ordinance we obey, as willing disciples, even as the bride is ready to obey her bridegroom's voice.

Michael Sattler wrote:

> They threatened us with bonds, then with fire and the sword. But in all this I surrendered myself completely into the will of the Lord, together with all my brothers and with my wife, and prepared myself to die for his testimony.[10]

Shortly after Michael Sattler and his companions died in public executions, Heinrich Hug, the Roman Catholic chronicler of Villingen wrote, "It was a miserable affair. They died for their conviction."

A young Anabaptist, Hans van Overdam, wrote before they burned him at Gent in Belgium, on July 9, 1551:

> We would rather suffer our bodies to be burned, drowned, racked or tortured, whatever you may wish to do with them, and we would rather be whipped, banished, or driven away, or robbed of our goods, than show any obedience contrary to the Word of God.[11]

This true surrender (a true "letting loose") became within the Anabaptists the conviction to follow Jesus no matter what it cost—and it led them to decisions like that of the miller's son.

What happened at Augsburg

After eight months of wandering through the mountains of Switzerland and southern Germany, Hans Denck reached the old city of Augsburg in Bavaria, by September, 1525. He was tired and ready to stay at one place for the winter, but he found the city sharply divided and in a turmoil. Some followed Luther. Some followed Zwingli. Some had remained Roman Catholic, but very few, only two or three people in the city, seemed to show interest at all in following Jesus.

Everyone fought about doctrine—"correct", "Biblical" doctrine. Everyone fought to have the most members and for the control of the city. But the "light of God" within them, Hans observed, they totally ignored. "What would it help you if you should reject all ceremonies?" he wrote in frustration to one Protestant leader. "Or what would it help you if you should keep all of them? What you need is to teach one another to know God. . . . I see not only the people of this city, but also

---

10 *Ein Sendbrief an die Gemeine Gottes in Horb,* 1527

11 *Ein Brief von Hans von Oberdam, der er an die Herren des Gerichts zu Gent und an die Ratsherren den Tag vor seiner Gefangenschaft gesandt hat,*1551

the pastors going astray."[12]

Hans felt great disappointment in the "Christians" of Augsburg, but he knew that no matter what they did, he needed to follow Jesus. He found a job teaching Latin and Greek to a nobleman's children and met from time to time with a few seekers who wondered where they should go.

Joining the Roman Catholics was not an option for any of them. The Lutherans had some impressive arguments. The Zwinglians seemed more sincere. But finally, with Hans' encouragement, they decided to take as their criteria nothing but the life and teachings of Jesus. They decided to ask this question about everything: "Is it like Jesus?" Then, whatever doctrine, whatever practice, whatever church, whatever tradition, whatever law, whatever decision was not like Jesus, they would simply ignore . . . to follow him.

This led them to meet on Easter Sunday, 1527, in a house near the gate of the Holy Cross at Augsburg where Balthasar Hubmaier baptised five people on confession of faith. Hans Denck was one of them. A year and a half later the congregation numbered over a thousand souls.

Go Ahead!

Suddenly, not just in Augsburg, but in Nikolsburg, Strasbourg, Wassenberg, Amsterdam, Antwerp . . . everywhere throughout the German lands of Europe, seekers felt that *now* was the time. The time to get up and follow Jesus was *now*—no matter who was with it or who was not, who gave permission or who did not.

In Zürich it had already happened two years before on the evening of January 21, 1525. Conrad Grebel, Georg Blaurock (an ex-priest from Chur) and a number of others had found their way through the back streets to the house where Felix Manz lived.

Then, according to the *Aelteste Chronik* this took place:

> And it came to pass that they were together until fear rose up within them and came upon the gathering. They were constrained in their hearts. Then they got down on their knees before the highest God in heaven. They cried to him because he knew their hearts. They prayed that he would help them to do his will and show his mercy to them, because flesh and blood or human instigation had not brought them to this place. They well knew that their patience would be tried and that they would have to suffer for this.
>
> After the prayer, Georg of the house of Jakob got up. He had asked God to show him his will. Now he asked Conrad Grebel to baptise him with the correct Christian baptism upon his faith and testimony. When he knelt down with this desire, Conrad baptised him because at that time no servant had been ordained to handle such a work. After this the others

[12] *Wer die Wahrheit wahrlich lieb hat* . . . 1526

> asked Georg to baptize them, which he did upon their request. In this way they gave themselves together to the name of the Lord in high fear of God. They commended one another to the service of the Gospel. They began to teach and hold the faith, to separate themselves from the world, and to break themselves off from evil works.[13]

Only a few months earlier, Conrad Grebel had written to Thomas Müntzer, urging him to go ahead and do what was right:

> Go ahead with the Word and establish a church community with the help of Christ and his teachings, as we find in Matthew 18 and lived out in the epistles. Use determination and common prayer, and make decisions about faith and life without commanding or forcing the people into anything; then God will help you and your little flock to real sincerity.[14]

Then, in 1525, Conrad encouraged the Reformed pastor of Hinwil in Switzerland:

> Do not have respect of persons! Do not worry about the authorities. Just do what God has told you to do.[15]

When Melchior Hofman presented his beliefs to Christian, Duke of Denmark, and four hundred representatives of the nobility and clergy in the chapel of the Barefoot Friars at Flensburg in Holstein, they threatened to punish him severely. But he said: "All the scholars in Christendom cannot hurt me. Even if God would permit that you should treat me violently, you cannot take from me more than this robe of flesh which Christ will replace with a new one on the day of judgement."

The Duke was surprised. "Is this the way you talk to me?" he asked.

Melchior replied: "If all the emperors, kings, princes, popes, bishops, and cardinals should be together in one place, nevertheless the truth shall and must be known to the glory of God."

"Who stands with you?" asked the Duke of Denmark.

"No one that I know of," answered Melchior Hofman. "I stand alone on the Word of God, and let all men do likewise!"

Once the conviction to follow Jesus had taken control of their hearts, there was nothing the Anabaptists could do but *go ahead* at the price of their lives.

Disobey the Church?

To oppose the world to follow Jesus was one thing. But to oppose the

---

[13] From the entry for 1525 under the heading: *Geörg vom Hauß Jacob oder Blabrock sampt etlichen gleerten ersprachten sich aus Gottes wort vom rechten Tauff unnd begert e einer vom andern getaufft zu werden weil sie kein verordneten Diener dises wercks darzu nit heten.*

[14] *Ein Brief an Thomas Müntzer,* September 5, 1524.

[15] From a statement made to Hans Brennwald, August 9, 1525.

church was another—and the Anabaptists, after a thousand years of authoritarian teaching, had to overcome a deeply rooted feeling of guilt before they could do so.

The first Anabaptists were not leaving the old corrupt church of the Dark Ages. They were leaving the new "Biblical" and "evangelical" church of Huldrych Zwingli in Switzerland. But in following Jesus, they got to where it made no difference. They could walk only with a church that followed Jesus, and wherever it did not, they felt "constrained in their hearts" to disobey it. For Menno Simons, the courage to do so became the turning point of his life.

For two years Menno Simons had lived with a problem. He was a Catholic priest, but he doubted whether the wafer and the wine in his hands really turned into Jesus' body and blood. "Such doubts," he told himself, "must come from the devil." But he could not get rid of them. They did not go away, until in desperation he turned to the New Testament.

Menno Simons did not question the authority of the church. He hoped the New Testament would confirm it and help him to be a better Catholic. But to his dismay it did the opposite. The more he read, the hungrier he got for the truth, and the more he realised how far from Jesus his church's teaching was. Eventually his inner conflict reached a climax. He had to decide which authority was to rule his life: the church or the Word of Christ.

Really, Menno would have liked to obey them both. He had always "known" that disbelief in church doctrine meant eternal death. Then he found a book Martin Luther had written as a young man. In it Luther taught that one is not damned if he disobeys the church to obey the Bible. Slowly that truth soaked in. And slowly it led to a yet greater truth—that one is not damned even if he disobeys a "Biblical" church to follow the example of Jesus. Once he placed the Word and example of Jesus above all human authority, Menno felt free to leave both the Roman Catholics and the Protestants behind, to be baptised, like Jesus, on confession of faith. "Then I surrendered myself, body and soul to God," he wrote. "I committed myself to his grace and began to teach and baptise according to the contents of his holy Word. I began to till the vineyard of the Lord with my little talent. I began to build up his holy city and temple and to repair the tumble-down walls."[16]

Disobey the Government?

Huldrych Zwingli said, in a public debate at Zürich,Switzerland, in 1523: "The authorities dare not call for anything but that which the holy and unchangeable writings teach. If they fail to do so and adopt some other course, which I do not expect, I would preach against them, severely, with the Word of God."

But Zwingli, when he came to the test, did not keep his word. His government, in cool defiance of his words went ahead and called for exactly that—infant baptism and the continuing of the mass—and Zwingli backed down. He did

---

16 *Een Klare beantwoordinge, over een Schrift Gellii Fabri . . .* 1554

not want to make trouble (or lose his position) by being more "Biblical" than what his government would allow. Two months after he made the above statement there was another debate in Zürich. Zwingli proposed to leave the matter of whether to celebrate mass in the hands of the city council. Then Simon Stumpf, a supporter of Conrad Grebel, got up and said: "Master Huldrych, you do not have the right to place the decision on this matter into the hands of the government, for the decision has already been made. The Spirit of God has already decided. . . . If the government adopts a course that would be against the decision of God, I will ask for his Spirit and I will preach and act against it."

The first Anabaptists felt free to disobey the government whenever they needed to do so to follow Jesus. And patriotism, for them, was a thing of the world.

Eccentrics and Individualists?

Some time ago, after I spoke about the Anabaptists following the voice of inner conviction, a Christian woman asked me: "But how would that work? How could we maintain our unity if we just let everyone go out and follow their convictions?"

Another question that must be asked is, "How does it work if we don't?" The first Anabaptists believed that unity is not the result of group consensus. It is the result of many individual commitments to Jesus. It is not the work of men, but a gift from God. They believed that true unity can be nothing but "the unity of the Spirit" that comes from Gemeinschaft with Jesus (Eph. 4:3). Such unity, they believed, cannot be forced nor regulated, for the Spirit of God is like the wind that "blows wherever it pleases. You hear its sound, but you cannot tell where it comes from or where it is going" (John 3:7-8).

By 1527, the Anabaptists had already published two books about man's freedom of choice and his duty to obey the voice of Jesus within him. In Augsburg, Hans Denck wrote:

> Everyone should know that in matters of faith we should all proceed in a free, voluntary and uncompelled way.[17]

Kilian Auerbacher, from Moravia, wrote:

> Christ's people are a free, unforced and uncompelled people, who receive Christ with desire and a willing heart. What people believe is not to be forced, but is to be accepted as a gift of God.[18]

---

17 *Was geredt sey. . .* 1526

18 *Ein Brief an Martin Butzer,* 1534

Menno Simons wrote:

> Christ alone is the ruler of the conscience, and besides him there is no other. Let him be your emperor, and his holy Word your law. You must obey God before the emperor and hold what God says above what the emperor says.[19][19]

That this teaching rocked the foundations of every establishment in Europe—church, state, and family—can well be understood.

If what people believed was not the "God-ordained authorities'"business to decide, whatever would become of society? If people were free to believe what they wanted to believe, free to obey what they felt led to obey, and free to follow the voice of conviction within them whenever and however they wanted to follow it . . . what would become of public order? Of the church? And of the laws of the land?

The Protestant Reformers woke up with their eyes round. They roused themselves with a roar. Joining forces with the Catholics and the church of the Dark Ages, they responded to this "heresy" with a tidal wave of persecution, hatred, and "holy" rage, the likes of which has not been seen before or since.

This was sedition! This was high treason! "Unauthorised men preaching on the street corners" wrote Martin Luther "are a sure sign of the devil."[20]

John, duke of Saxony, made a law at once to stop secret baptisms and communions. Imagine! Baptising or celebrating communion without the church's consent! Without properly authorised men in charge! In secret! Not in church buildings but in private homes! This, wrote Luther, is blasphemy, blasphemy, blasphemy . . . and after his book *Of the Sneaky Ones and the Corner Preachers* came book after book and sermon after sermon loaded with his bitterest invectives against the Anabaptists who "dared to take the Scriptures into their own hands and overthrow the authority of the church."

The "Sitzrecht"

Martin Luther and the Protestant Reformers did not have a problem with the Anabaptists because they called for changes in the church. Everyone was calling for changes. Luther himself was a leader in making them, and he, with the other Reformers, was only too willing to sit down (at the beginning) and "lay everything out on the table" to discuss it. But when Luther and the Reformers discovered that

the Anabaptists were committed to making changes with or without the church's consent, their "friendliness" turned to alarm.

There is only one way to make changes in church practice, the Reformers

---

[19] *Dat Fundament des Christelycken leers* . . . 1539

[20] From *Von den Schleichern und Winkelpredigern*, 1532

believed. That is by presenting "new ideas" to the God-ordained leaders of the church. Working with the church and its leaders, changes could be made "in a God-fearing, honest, and orderly way."[21]

The Reformers did not require (like the church of the Dark Ages) total agreement with its practices. They were actually quite lenient in offering the Anabaptists the freedom to believe what they wanted, as long as they obeyed the church and practiced what its leaders saw fit to allow.

The Reformers appreciated the way the Anabaptists lived, and frequently said so. They asked the Anabaptists to help them toward greater holiness and fear of God in the state churches. Luther, on several occasions acknowledged the Anabaptists' steadfastness, and the other Reformers wrote about their holiness, sobriety, and excellent reputation among the people.

But what the Reformers could not tolerate—what made them fearful, and eventually furious, with the Anabaptists—was the Anabaptists' high regard for inner conviction and low regard for the voice of the church. "This heretical persistence in following an inner word," thundered Martin Luther, "brings to nothing the written Word of God!"

In a sense he was right.

The first Anabaptists did not follow the Scriptures (and their "correct interpretation") like Martin Luther wanted them to be followed. They followed a man. And in following him (instead of Luther's church, or Luther's Bible) they got their hands onto the thread that pulls the fabric of civilization apart. This, the Reformers correctly discerned, and it made them desperate enough to pass the death penalty upon them.

Huldrych Zwingli began and Martin Luther kept on violently denouncing the "stirring-up spirit" (*aufrührerischer Geist*) of the Anabaptist movement, which they found, above all, in their "silly teaching" of the *Sitzrecht* (the "sitter's right").

The first Anabaptists took literally the words of Paul in 1 Corinthians 14: 30-31: "And if a revelation comes to someone who is sitting down, the first speaker should stop. For you can all prophesy in turn so that everyone may be instructed and encouraged." They called this the "sitter's right" and calmly implied that they, when moved by inner conviction, had as great a right to speak and to act as any pastor, any priest, any Reformer or bishop or pope. This audacity, this "Sitzrecht from the pit of hell," Martin Luther and his friends believed, could be dealt with only by fire,

---

[21] An idea expressed, for example, in Justus Menius, *Der Wiedertäufer Lehre und Geheimnis*, of 1530, Urbanus Rhegius' *Widerlegung des Bekenntnisses der Münsterischen neuen Valentinianer und Donatisten und zur Neuen Zeitung von den Wiedertäufern zu Münster*, of 1535, in Luther's instructions to the pastors of Saxony, and in his other writings and published sermons against the Anabaptists.

water, and the sword.

"Even though it is terrible to view," Martin Luther admitted, he gave his blessing to the death sentence upon the Anabaptists, issued by the elector, princes, and landgraves of Protestant Germany on March 31, 1527. The sentence was based on the following four points:

1. The Anabaptists bring to nothing the office of preaching the Word.
2. The Anabaptists have no definite doctrine.
3. The Anabaptists bring to nothing and suppress true doctrine.
4. The Anabaptists want to destroy the kingdom of this world.

"For the preservation of public order" both Martin Luther and Huldrych Zwingli promoted the total elimination of the Anabaptists (through capital punishment) as a matter of utmost urgency. They accused the Anabaptists of a crime against the public, "not because they taught a different faith, but for disturbing public order by undermining respect for authority."

Philipp Melanchthon, Luther's close friend and adviser wrote: "The Anabaptists' disregard for the outer Word and the Scriptures is blasphemy. Therefore, the temporal arm of government shall watch here too and not tolerate this blasphemy, but earnestly resist and punish it."

Urbanus Rhegius, the Reformer of Augsburg, wrote: "The Anabaptists cannot and will not endure Scripture." And within twenty years, no less than 116 laws were passed in the German lands of Europe, which made the "Anabaptist heresy" a capital offence.

On to Strasbourg and Worms

Called to court by Urbanus Rhegius, in the fall of 1526, Hans Denck decided to flee. He found his way through the Swabian Alps and up the Rhein to Strasbourg. Here where the Protestant rulers of the city had a reputation for tolerance, he hoped to find a place to stay. But they gave him none.

Instead, they called him to court. Alarmed by his insistence on following Jesus, they told him to leave, once more in the dead of winter. It was December, 1526. The day after his departure, Wolfgang Capito, the Reformer of Strasbourg wrote to Huldrych Zwingli:

> Hans Denck has disturbed our church very much. His apparent sacrificial life, his brilliance, and his decent habits have wonderfully captivated the people. . . . He left yesterday. His going left some disturbance behind, but the remaining problems can easily be settled with diligence and caution.
>
> From Strasbourg, Hans Denck travelled through Bergzabern (where he visited the Ghetto and publicly invited the Jews to follow Jesus), and from there to Landau and Worms.

The venerable city of Worms, seat of Catholic bishops on the Rhine River since 600. A.D., had turned Protestant just the year before. One of its new Protestant pastors was a young man, Hans Denck's age, by the name of Jakob Kautz.

Hans and Jakob soon became friends, even though their activities were not the same. Hans stayed in seclusion in an old house of the city, translating the Hebrew prophets into German. Jakob preached every Sunday to great throngs of people in the Protestant churches of the city, until the call of Jesus—"Follow me!"—made it impossible for him to continue his career.

They called Jakob to court in March, 1527, to warn him. But he could not change his preaching. He followed Jesus, and the situation with the church grew steadily worse. By June 1527, Jakob was ready to let everyone know where he stood. He tacked a sheet of paper with seven statements to the door of the cathedral and invited all who cared to discuss them with him in a public meeting:

1. The word which we speak with our mouths, hear with our ears, write with our hands and print onto paper is not the living, true, eternal Word of God. It is only a witness, pointing to the inner Word.

2. Nothing external, neither Word, sign, sacrament or promise, has the power to assure the inner man, comfort him, or make him sure that he is doing what is right.

3. The baptism of infants is not of God. It is against God and his teaching given to us through Christ Jesus, his beloved Son.

4. In the sacrament of the Lord's nighttime meal the literal body and blood of Christ are not present. Our tradition here in Worms is wrong. We have not been celebrating the sacrament in a proper way.

5. Everything that died with the first Adam, comes back to life in a better way with the second Adam, that is with Christ who walks on ahead of us. Everything unfolds and opens up in Christ. Everything becomes alive in Christ.

6. Jesus from Nazareth did not suffer for us in any way, he did nothing to satisfy God for us, as long as we do not follow him in the way he went before us—unless we follow the commands of the father, like Christ follows them—every man according to his ability.

7. Like Adam's outward biting into the forbidden fruit would not have hurt him nor his descendants if his inner being would not have been involved in the disobedience, so the outer suffering of Christ is no redemption nor work of grace for us if there is no inner obedience and desire within us to obey the will of God.[22]

On the day appointed, June 13, 1527, Jakob Kautz appeared with Hans Denck and Ludwig Haetzer at six o'clock in the morning on the town square to tell everyone what he believed. It was market day, and a great crowd gathered to hear him.

Jakob explained to the people what he had written in the seven statements. He told them that their struggling to find the "right church" and to be good Christians was in vain, as long as they were not moved by the Spirit of God within them. Many turned to Jesus and sealed their covenant with him in baptism at Worms. But it made trouble. . . .

---

[22] *Sieben Artikel zu Worms von Jakob Kautzen angeschlagen und gepredigt. Verworfen und widerlegt mit Schriften und Ursachen auf zwen weg, Anno MDXXVII.*

Two Protestant pastors of the city tacked seven other statements to the door of the church. They contradicted Jakob Kautz and Hans Denck, calling the people back from "following their own ideas" to following the voice of God-ordained church authority. Two weeks later, on July 1, 1527, they expelled the "troublemakers" (including Jakob Kautz and Hans Denck) from the city, and a day later a book appeared: *A Faithful Warning from the Preachers of the Gospel at Strasbourg, against the Statements of Jakob Kautz.* Even Huldrych Zwingli took the time to refute the "troublemakers" in writing, and of the believers at Worms who followed Jesus into baptism, more than one hundred were soon put to death.

Jakob Kautz baptized twenty believers in the nearby town of Alzey. From here others went out to teach and baptize. The Kurfürst Ludwig V set a bounty on their heads. His men caught fourteen Anabaptists, beheading the men at Alzey and drowning the women. When a kindhearted bystander tried to comfort the victims in their distress, Ludwig's men caught her too and burned her alive. Three hundred and fifty believers died in a short time but more than one thousand two hundred escaped to find refuge in Moravia. A great number of them joined the community at Auspitz led by Philip Plener.

Only a Movement

Neither the Roman Catholics nor the Protestant Reformers could see a *church* in the Anabaptist movement. All they saw was an assortment of "perverted sects" whose leaders were eccentric individuals, "unbelievably stubborn" and "wildly obstinate" heretics "who have forsaken much, but can never forsake themselves."[23]

About Menno Simons, John Calvin said: "Nothing could be prouder, nothing more impudent than this donkey." Perhaps, if we would have been in his shoes we would have seen it that way too.

The Reformers came from a comfortable background of "group conviction", where everyone submitted to the leaders and believed like everyone else in the group. The first Anabaptists rejected "group conviction." They believed that just as everyone needed to repent and believe on his own, so the "light of God" (inner conviction) was a personal matter.

The Reformers believed that faith got handed down, like tradition, from generation to generation, and that it was imparted from parents to children in baptism. The first Anabaptists rejected this "historic" and "handed-down" faith. They believed that faith was of the Spirit, and that the Spirit's movings could no more be preserved nor handed down than the wind can be preserved in a box, or the current of a river in a jar.

The Reformers, influenced by humanism, believed that along with "group convictions" it was alright to have some "personal convictions," providing one did not make an issue out of them and kept on cooperating with the

[23] The Reformer, Martin Bucer's description of Pilgram Marpeck.

church. But the first Anabaptists rejected "personal convictions" when they "let loose" and truly surrendered their personal ideas, personal views, and personal rights to Jesus.

All they had left was the inner conviction that it was right to follow Jesus. This conviction alone gave them direction on what to obey and what not to obey, what to believe and what not to believe, what to do and what not to do, and how to understand the Scriptures. This conviction alone led them to submit themselves one to another in the freedom of allowing all men to follow Jesus "in an uncompelled way."

How could they build church like that?

They couldn't. Nobody can . . . except God. And God does not "build churches" the way people do. He moves. He is a Spirit. God is the Spirit that moves in Jesus and in those that live in Gemeinschaft with him. The church is a movement, moving from age to age, from place to place, and from people to people, wherever God finds broken hearts, truly surrendered, in which to dwell.

The Jews looked for an earthly kingdom with an earthly Messiah. The Christians, after a few centuries went the way of the Jews. "But the kingdom of God," Jesus said, "does not come with your careful observation, nor will people say, `Here it is', or `There it is', because the kingdom of God is within you!" (Luke 17:20-21)

.

For some time, right after the Dark Ages, this "inner kingdom," the Kingdom of Heaven, came down to touch the Anabaptist movement. It touched it with the clear light of conviction that shone from the face of the miller's son, sixteen years old, who could say at the price of his life: "God does not want me to do that." And it led the first Anabaptists . . .

On to the Teachings of Christ

In the Gospels the Anabaptists found the teachings of Christ, to which the following passages are the open door:

> As Jesus was walking beside the Sea of Galilee he saw two brothers, Simon called Peter and his brother Andrew. They were casting a net into the lake, for they were fishermen. "Come, follow me," Jesus said, "and I will make you fishers of men." At once they left their nets and followed him.
>
> Going from there, he saw two other brothers, James son of Zebedee and his brother John. They were in a boat with their father Zebedee, preparing their nets. Jesus called them, and immediately they left the boat and their father and followed him (Matthew 4: 18-22).
>
> Another disciple said to him, "Lord, first let me go and bury my father."
>
> But Jesus told him, "Follow me and let the dead bury their own dead" (Matthew 8: 21-22).
>
> As Jesus went on from there, he saw a man named Matthew sitting at the tax collector's booth. "Follow me," he told him, and Matthew got up and followed him (Matthew 9: 9).
>
> Then Jesus said to his disciples, "If anyone would come after me, he must deny himself and take up his cross and follow me. For whoever wants to save his life will lose it, but whoever loses his life for me will find it" (Matthew 16: 24-25).
>
> Large crowds were travelling with Jesus, and turning to them he said: "If anyone comes to me and does not hate his father and mother, his wife and children, his brothers and sisters—yes, even his own life—he cannot be my disciple. And anyone who does not carry his cross and follow me cannot be my disciple" (Luke 14: 25-27).
>
> "In the same way, any of you who does not give up everything he has cannot be my disciple" (Luke 14: 33).

Teachings of Salvation

Jesus' words as recorded in the Gospels, especially in the Sermon on the Mount, were for the first Anabaptists the *seligmachende Lehre* (teachings of salvation) to which the Old Testament was an introduction, and to which the New Testament epistles gave testimony. The first Anabaptists did not regard any of the Scriptures lightly (they used and quoted from apocryphal books without apology), but the Gospels were for them the doorway to them all. Every understanding of the Scriptures was a mistaken understanding, they believed, if it did not match Jesus' example and his teaching in the Gospels.

With the Christ of the Gospels as their guide, no doctrine, to the first Anabaptists, looked complicated or "profound." They may have known the German word for doctrine (*Doktrin*), but both the term and its connotation were foreign to Anabaptist thought, and they did not ordinarily use it. They simply spoke (English translations notwithstanding) of the *Lehren* (teachings) of Jesus.

Menno Simons, in his book, *A Foundation and Clear Direction to the Teachings of Our Lord Jesus Christ Which Are Able to Save You* wrote:

> We do not have a new teaching, as people would like to make you believe. We teach what was taught and practiced in the church 1,500 years ago. It is the teaching which brought the church into being, through which the church is, and through which it will be to the end of time.[1]

In another tract Menno wrote:

> I speak with sure conviction. I speak not because I had a vision or some special revelation from heaven, but I speak by the sure Word of our Lord. From my innermost being I am convinced that this teaching is not our teaching. It is the teaching of the one who sent us: Jesus Christ. . . . Those who love darkness rather than light curse the truth we find in the Gospels. They call it heresy and handle it like treason. But the Word of God shall remain unbroken to the last day.[2]

Steps to Understanding the Teachings

After a thousand years of darkness, the first Anabaptists rediscovered the first step to understanding Jesus' teachings. That step is to get up and follow him. We need to submit to him (*throw ourselves under him* as the Anabaptists wrote) in true detachment from this world's things. As long as we have not done this the study of the Scriptures is useless—or even harmful. Leonhard Schiemer wrote before they beheaded him in 1528:

> He who has not learned what he knows from God, but from men, has a faith that cannot stand. . . . If I should try to teach someone who has not thrown himself under Christ, I would be running ahead of Christ, and I would be a thief and a murderer. For such a man's heart and mind are in the dark. Paul says that man is a stranger to the life that is from God. Trying to teach such a person about spiritual things is like lighting candles for a blind man. He still cannot see.[3]

The second step to understanding Jesus' teachings is to let his Spirit teach us. Only after the Spirit of God "shines in our hearts to give us the light of knowledge" (2 Cor. 4:6) can we hope to understand the Gospels. "The understanding of the truth does not come from human study," testified an Anabaptist before the court at Regensburg in Bavaria. "It comes only to those to whom it is given by grace through the light of his Spirit."

Before they beheaded him at Konstanz in 1529, Ludwig Haetzer wrote:

> He who goes only by the Scriptures receives knowledge. But it is a useless knowledge that does not change anyone for the better. No man, no matter how learned he may be, can understand the Scriptures until he comes to know them and learns them in the most inward part of his soul. If he speaks about the them before this takes place, he speaks like a blind man about colour.[4]

---

[1] *Een Fondament ende clare aenwijsinghe van de salichmakende Leere Jesu Christi* . . . 1558

[2] From *Die oorsake waerom dat ick M. S. niet of en late de leeren, ende te schrijuen* . . . first published at Antwerp ca. 1542.

[3] Vom Fläschlen . . . 1527

[4] Quoted in Karl Hagen's second volume of Deutschland's literarische und religiöse Verhältnisse im

Strasbourg, at the convergence of the Ill River with the Rhein, where Germany meets France, has been a gathering place for centuries. Open to nonconformist ideas, the city sheltered many Anabaptists, including Pilgram Marpeck, who assisted in the engineering of its drainage canals.

The third step in understanding Jesus and his teachings is to love him. Before his death in the massacre at Linz, Wolfgang Brandhuber wrote:

> Oh brothers, if true love is missing, what does it help to know much, to speak or to teach? Oh brothers, let every man act according to the truth in his heart, before the face of God. . . May the Father of all Grace give to those that hunger the true Bread and the ability to discern the Scriptures and the way they are tied together, because the Spirit of God does not want to be bound.[5]

Teachings in the Heart

Obeying the teachings of their consciences and obeying the teachings of Jesus in the Scriptures was for the first Anabaptists the same thing. They made no difference between the Word in their hearts and the Word of the Gospels, but looked to the complete Word of Christ as their highest authority.

The "outer Word" (the Scriptures written with paper and ink) the Anabaptists taught, is nothing but the lamp from which the light of the true Word shines. Ulrich Stadler, servant of the Word at Austerlitz in Moravia, wrote:

> The outer Word is only a sign of the inner Word, like the sign on an inn telling of the wine in the barrels inside. The sign is not the wine. It satisfies no-one's thirst. But we know when we see it that the wine is there.[6]

Hans Denck who found the "wine of the inner Word" when he decided to follow Jesus at any cost wrote in 1525:

Reformationszeitalter (Erlangen, 1841-44).

5 From *Ein sendbrief von Wolfgang Brandhueber an die gmain Gottes zu Rottenburg am In*, 1529

6 Vom lebendigen Wort und geschriebenen, ein kurzer Unterschied und Bericht, ca. 1530

> When Christ the sun of righteousness arises in our hearts, then the darkness of unbelief is overcome for the first time. . . . The man who does not listen to the voice of God speaking within him, but who tries to explain the Scriptures for himself (which only the Spirit of God is able to do) makes a total abomination out of the secrets of God which the writings contain.[7]

Concealed within the written word, the first Anabaptists found a great treasure—the dwelling place of Christ. Balthasar Hubmaier, before they burned him at the stake, wrote:

> The Scriptures are the friend of God. Christ Jesus lives in the Scriptures, and in them he makes his home and rests.[8]

Putting the Teachings to Practice

The first Anabaptists did what children might do with the Scriptures. They read them to see what Jesus said and did so they could imitate him. They believed that by putting his teachings to practice they could please him and live with him forever.

Menno Simons wrote:

> The bright light of the Gospel shines again in these last and dreadful times. God's only begotten Son, Jesus Christ, is gloriously revealed. His gracious will and holy Word concerning faith, the new birth, repentance, baptism, the nighttime meal, and all of his saving teachings and example has again come to light. It has come through seeking and prayer, through action, through reading, through teaching and writing. . . . Now let us go on and build his church community in the apostle's way.[9]

"The words I have spoken to you," said Jesus, "are spirit and they are life" (John 6:63). The Anabaptists, by putting his words to practice, discovered that this was true. Menno Simons wrote in 1552:

> The brightness of the sun has not shone for many years. Heaven and earth have been as copper and iron. Brooks and springs have not run nor dew descended from heaven. Beautiful trees and verdant fields have been dry and wilted—in a spiritual sense. But in these last days God in his love has opened the windows of heaven again. The dew of his Word has fallen upon us so that the earth produces green branches of righteousness bearing fruit for God. The holy Word and the sacraments of our Lord have been rescued from the ashes.[10]

---

[7] From the written testimony of Hans Denck, presented to the court at Nürnberg, in January, 1525.

[8] Preislied des göttlichen Wortes, ca. 1526

[9] *Onderwijs . . . van de excommunicatie,* 1558

[10] *Een grondelicke en klare bekentenisse* . . . 1552

What is Heresy?

When the first Anabaptists put Jesus' teachings to practice, people called them heretics. That was because they had forgotten, after a thousand years, what Jesus had said and done. This led Menno Simons to ask:

> Who are the real heretics and deceivers? Who are they that teach contrary to the teachings of the holy church? According to the venerable Bede, the word *heretic* means one who picks out, one who chooses or gleans. . . . Men cry against us saying: Heretics! Heretics! Drown them, kill them, and burn them! And this for no other reason than that we teach a new life, baptism on confession of faith, and bread and wine for all members in a blameless church community.[11]

While identifying the real heretics (and who they were not), Menno Simons wrote:

> I have taught no other baptism, no other supper, no other ordinance than that which was implied by the unerring mouth of our Lord Jesus Christ and the example of his apostles. . . Put your trust in Christ alone and in his Word. Put your trust in the sure instruction and practice of his holy apostles. Then by the grace of God you will be safe from every false teaching and the power of the devil. You will walk with a free mind before God.[12]

The Rediscovery of Jesus' Teachings

The story of King Josiah finding the book of the law while cleaning out the temple in Jerusalem, moved the first Anabaptists and became Menno Simons' theme when he wrote:

> Behold, the book of the law, the saving Gospel of Christ which was hid for so many centuries by the abominations of the Antichrist, has been found! The book of Christ, by the grace of God has been found again! The pure unadulterated truth has come to light . . . at the expense of much of the property and blood of the saints.[13]

And as in Josiah's day, the discovery of the book had far- reaching effects. Menno Simons described them in *The Cross of the Holy Ones*:

> God has again, in these last days of unbelief and abomination . . . opened the book of eternal truth which had been closed for so many centuries. He has raised the dead from their graves. Those who all their lives lay in wickedness he has called to a new and blameless life. Yes, God is calling the distressed, starving sheep out of the jaws of ravening wolves. He is leadingthem out of the desert of human teachings to the green pastures of the mountain of

---

11 From *Verclaringhe des christelycken doopsels in den water duer menno Simons wt dwoort gods*, first published at Antwerp, ca. 1542.

12 From *Christelycke leringhen op den 25. Psalm*, ca. 1528.

13 *Van dat rechte christen ghelooue ende zijn cracht*, ca. 1542

> Israel—to the care and custody of the eternal shepherd, Jesus Christ, who bought them with his blood.[14]

Guided by Jesus' gentle teachings, the Anabaptists found their way . . .

---

[14] *Eyne troestliche vermaninge van dat lijden, cruyze, vnde veruolginge der heyligen, vmme dat woort Godes*, 1558

On to the Word

"I saw heaven standing open and there before me was a white horse, whose rider is called Faithful and True. With justice he judges and makes war. His eyes are like blazing fire, and on his head are many crowns. He has a name written on him that no one knows but he himself. He is dressed in a garment dipped in blood, and his name is the Word of God" (Rev. 19:11-13).

The Word of God, for the first Anabaptists, was a man. A man whose voice we hear in our hearts and in the Scriptures.

Some years ago I heard a minister explain how the first Anabaptists used the Bible. He said their slogan was *sola scriptura* (only the Scriptures) and that they were known as "the people of the book." At the time it sounded right, but since then I have made other discoveries.

The slogan *sola scriptura* was invented and used by Huldrych Zwingli (the Anabaptists' mortal enemy) and the "people of the book" are the Jews or the Muslims.

The first Anabaptists aimed for something infinitely higher than *sola scriptura.* Their aim was full community with Jesus. And they were not "people of the book." They were "people of the man." The first Anabaptists did not read in the Gospels that the Word was made paper and ink. They read that "the Word became flesh and dwelt among us, and we beheld his glory, the glory as of the only begotten of the Father, full of grace and truth" (John 1:14).

In agreement with Jakob Kautz who taught that the written word is "only a witness, pointing to the inner Word," Hans Denck wrote:

> I value the Scriptures above all of human treasure, but not as highly as the Word of God which is alive, strong (Heb. 4:12), eternal, and free. The Word of God is free from the elements of the world. It is God himself. It is Spirit and not letter, written without pen or paper so that it can never be erased.
>
> As a result of this, salvation is not bound to scripture, even though the Scriptures may help one on to salvation (2 Tim. 3:16). We need to understand, the Scriptures cannot possibly change an evil heart, even though they may educate it well. A godly heart, on the other hand, in which the little light of God shines, can learn from all things. We see then, how the Scriptures help those who believe toward salvation and holy living. But to those who believe not, they serve only for condemnation. . . .
>
> If salvation depended only on reading the Scriptures or hearing them preached, many illiterate people, and many towns to whom no preacher has come, would be lost.[1]

[1] *Widerruf*. . . 1528

Before they burned him at the stake in 1528, Balthasar Hubmaier wrote:

> The Word of God is water to all those who thirst for salvation and is made alive in us through the Spirit of God, without whose work it is only a dead letter.[2]

One Anabaptist testified before the court at Regensburg in Bavaria:

> The Scriptures and the outer word are merely the witness of the inner Word of God. A man can well be saved without the preaching or the reading of the Scriptures. (Otherwise, what should happen with those who are deaf or cannot read?) We understand God our Redeemer, not through the lifeless letter, but through the indwelling of Christ.[3]

The Word of God is One

Because the first Anabaptists spoke of an inner and an outer Word, their enemies accused them of making two Words of God. "But the outer, preached or written word," wrote Pilgram Marpeck, "and the inner Word are One."[4]

Truly surrendered to Jesus, the Anabaptists found perfect unity between the voice of Jesus in their hearts and the Scriptures in their hands. Ulrich Stadler, Anabaptist servant of the Word at Austerlitz in Moravia, wrote in his book *Of the Living and Written Word, or of the Outer and Inner Word, and how they work in the Heart*:

> The inner Word is not written, neither on paper nor on tables of stone. It is not spoken nor preached, but man is assured by it through God in the depths of his soul, and it becomes engraved in a heart of flesh through the Spirit by the finger of God.

Hans Denck wrote about the inner and the outer Word in three of his books. He taught that the inner Word (the voice of the Spirit) comes before the outer word (the Scriptures) and makes it possible for the latter to be received. Without the Word inside, the written word is unintelligible because "the man without the Spirit does not accept the things that come from the Spirit of God." They are foolishness to him, "and he cannot understand them, because they are spiritually discerned" (1 Cor. 2:14).

Hans Langenmantel wrote before they beheaded him at Weißenhorn in Bavaria in 1528:

> Luther says he preaches the Gospel of Christ and with his physical voice he brings Christ into the hearts of his hearers. But I say that there must first be something within us that can receive the physical voice.[5]

---

[2] From *Eine Christliche Lehrtafel, die ein jeder Mensch, bevor er im Wasser*

[3] Quoted in Hermann Nestler's *Die Wiedertäuferbewegung in Regensburg*, 1926.

[4] From a letter to Helena von Streicher, ca. 1544.

[5] From *Ain kurzer Anzayg, wie doctor M. Luther ain zayt hör hatt etliche schrifften lassen ausgeen vom Sacrament, die doch straks wider einander*, 1527.

Leupold Scharnschlager, Anabaptist servant of the Word in Austria and Switzerland, wrote:

> If the Scriptures are not opened in the heart by the Spirit of God, then not only they are dead, but Christ himself with his teachings, his life, his sufferings, and his death, yes, even his resurrection, is dead. To know all about these things without the Spirit of God within is useless, even though one may read about them and study them as long as he likes. Without the Spirit, one becomes learned, but he does not learn.[6]

Beyond Literalism

In Gemeinschaft with the inner Word, the first Anabaptists caught the spirit of the Scriptures. This kept them from the bondage of a systematic theology. It kept them from focusing on the details at the expense of the theme. And it kept them from an empty literalism in their interpretation.

When they burned Georg Blaurock and Hans Langegger at the stake, near Klausen in Austria[7] in 1529, an eight-year-old boy stood wide-eyed among the spectators. His name was Peter. He could not forget. As a young man he began to follow Jesus, and at twenty-one years of age the he was a servant of the Word. In his early twenties, Peter Walpot wrote one of the confessions of faith most widely used among the Anabaptists of Austria and Moravia. On taking the Scriptures literally, he wrote:

> Because Jesus said, "I am the true vine," he was not physically a grapevine. He is called a lamb, but he is not physically a lamb. He called Simon Peter a rock, but Peter did not turn into stone.
>
> He remained human. Paul says of Sarah and Hagar that they were the two testaments. Should that make them literal documents?
>
> No, they only stood for the documents.
>
> Jesus said, "I am the door into the fold, and I am the way." He said that whoever believes on him will have rivers of living water flowing from within him. But he does not mean a literal river. Jesus spoke of a man having a beam in his eye, but this does not mean a literal log or the tongue of a wagon. He said to Mary on the cross: "Woman, behold your son," and to John he said: "Son, behold your mother." According to these plain words, John would have been the natural brother of Jesus, but he was not. His mother was someone else. Jesus said the seed is the Word of God and the field is the world. The seven fat cows and the seven lean cows were seven years—the Scriptures speak many times in words like these. If we should take everything literally many foolish things would happen. In the same way, when Jesus said the bread was his body and the wine was his blood, it was not physically the case, but it stood for those things.[8]

---

[6] Quoted in the *Zeitschrift des Vereins für die Geschichte Mährens und Schlesiens*, 1928

[7] After World War I, the city of Klausen, and the surrounding territory became a part of Italy. In Italian, it is known as Chiusa.

[8] From *Fünf Artikel des grössten Streites zwischen uns und der Welt*, 1547.

Beyond "Biblicism"

"The Anabaptists," some take for granted, "were avowed Biblicists. They gave the Bible first place in their lives and died in its defense. . . ."

But were they?

That the first Anabaptists followed Jesus and all his teachings in the Bible is apparent. But that they felt about the Bible like modern day Biblicists or Fundamentalists is not so clear.

The first Anabaptists must have known the German word for Bible (*Bibel*). But they never used it. They spoke of the writings (the Scriptures)--or the holy writings (not in capital letters, in spite of modern German rules on the capitalisation of nouns).

The first Anabaptists stated no opinions on the correct "version" or "translation" of the Bible. German translations were just beginning to appear. Not all of them were accurate, and the principal one came from Martin Luther, their arch enemy. Beyond this, only a few Anabaptists such as Menno Simons, Conrad Grebel, and Hans Denck, could read the Latin Vulgate (the Roman Catholic Bible).

The first Anabaptists had no clear position on the "canon of Scripture." They accepted, and freely quoted from all the books of the Apocrypha, including the third and fourth books of Ezra and the third book of the Maccabees. They seem to have been influenced by the books of Pseudo-Dionisius, the Gospel of Nicodemus, the Testament of the Twelve Patriarchs, and literature on the saints. The Ausbund commemorates in song the deaths of Saint Laurence, Saint Agathe, Saint Margaret, Saint Catherine, and others. The *Martyrs Mirror* includes more of the same.

For more than 150 years after the beginning of the Anabaptist movement they wrote very little on what they believed about the Scriptures. That belief, while they followed the Word of God riding on a white horse and dressed in a garment dipped in blood, needed no explanation.

Beyond Mysticism and Pietism

"What were they then," a sister asked me, after I spoke about the first Anabaptists following the Word that lived in their hearts. "Were they some kind of mystics or Pietists?"

No.

Without a doubt, the first Anabaptists felt the influence of mediaeval mysticism, but they left the mystics behind when they got up to follow Jesus.

The mystics, and later on the Pietists, found their delight in secret communion with Jesus alone. They managed to "follow Jesus" in such a way that most of them could keep on living in peace in the state churches. For the Anabaptists, this was unthinkable.

Both the mystics and the Pietists found their delight in experiences of the soul and in revelations that threatened to eclipse the example of Jesus in the Gospels. But the Anabaptists found their delight in the Word of Christ. Menno Simons wrote in 1539:

> I have received no vision or angelic inspirations. Neither do I desire such, lest I be deceived. The Word of Christ alone is sufficient for me. If I do not follow the Word, then all I do is in vain. Even if I had special visions and inspirations they would have to agree with the Word and the Spirit of Christ, or else they would be mere imaginations, deceit, and Satanic temptation.[9]

The Word, Above All Human Authority

Dirk Philips, after he left a Franciscan monastery and joined the Anabaptists at Leeuwarden in Friesland, wrote:

> The Gospel of Jesus is the real truth, and the only foundation on which everything must be built (1 Cor. 3:11). Beside this truth and this foundation there is nothing that will stand before God.[10]

Conrad Grebel wrote to a friend in 1524:

> Do your utmost in preaching the Word of God without fear. Set up and defend only the institutions that are of God. Count as precious only that which is good and right, only that which can be found in the pure, clear Scriptures. Then reject, hate, and curse all proposals, all words, all opinion, and all institutions of all men, including your own.[11]

Michael Sattler wrote:

> Let no one tear you from the order that is laid down in the Scriptures, the order sealed by the blood of Jesus and witnessed to by many of his followers.[12]

The Word in Their Hands

Martin Luther condemned the Anabaptists for "taking the Word of God into their own hands." His charge was not without foundation.

The first Anabaptists rejoiced in "that which was from the beginning, which we have heard, which we have seen with our eyes . . . and *our hands have handled*, of the Word of Life" (1John 1:1). They took Peter literally where he said that "no prophecy of the scripture is of any private interpretation." They believed that no church leaders nor denomination held the exclusive right to handle the Word of God. And they believed that the written word was for all to hear, see,

---

9 *Die oorsake waerom dat ick M. S. niet of en late te leeren ende te schrijuen,* 1542

10 From *Enchiridion oft Hantboecxken van de Christelijcke Leere ende Religion, in corte somma begrepen* . . .1564

11 From a letter to Thomas Müntzer, September 5, 1524.

12 *Ein Sendbrief an die Gemeine Gottes in Horb*, 1527

touch, and understand. Conrad Grebel wrote in 1524:

> Just as our forefathers fell away from the true God and the knowledge of Jesus Christ and of the right faith in him . . . so today, too, every man wants to be saved by a superficial faith without fruits. . . . In the same error we too lingered, as long as we heard and read only the evangelical preachers. But after we took the Scriptures into our own hands and consulted them ourselves on many points, we have been instructed.[13]

Grebel criticised Martin Luther for his "irresponsible sparing" of the German populace by not giving them the Scriptures to handle and interpret for themselves. Grebel saw Luther as guilty of "hiding the Word of God, mixing the commands of God with commands of men, and damaging and frustrating all that comes from God."

The Word Prohibits What It Does Not Command

The first Anabaptists believed that churches do not have the right to make rules about things on which the Scriptures are silent. Conrad Grebel, who frequently mentioned the "example and commands" of the Scriptures (*Beispiel und Geboten*), wrote:

> Whatever we have not been taught by clear teaching and example we should take as something completely forbidden, just as if it were written: "Do not do this." If the apostles did not do it, we should not do it either.[14]

Dirk Philips wrote:

> Whatever God has not commanded, that he prohibits us to command. Therefore all worship and practice that is not instituted by a direct command of God is wrong, no matter how many human arguments defend it.[15]

Menno Simons wrote:

> Beware **of** all innovations and teachings that do not come from the Word of Christ and his apostles. . .. Point to Christ and his Word at all times. Let all those who would introduce anything more than what Christ teaches in his Word be anathema. For other foundation can no man lay than that is laid which is Jesus Christ (1 Cor. 3:11).[16]

The Old and the New Testaments

The Protestant Reformers, the first Anabaptists believed, got the old and the new covenants of God confused because they did not approach the Scriptures

---

13 Letter to Thomas Müntzer, 1524.

14 From a letter to Thomas Müntzer, September 5, 1524.

15 *Enchiridion*, 1564

16 *Kindertucht. Een schoon onderwys ende leere, hoe alle vrome olders haer kinderen (nae wtwijsen der schriftueren) schuldich ende gheholden zijn de regieren, te castyden, te onderrichten, ende in een vroom duechdelick ende godsalich leeuen op te voeden. . .* ca. 1557.

through Jesus. They tried to climb in some other way, through the "doctrines" of Paul, through the laws of Moses, or through the Old Testament prophets. This made them "thieves and murderers." It made them take wrong examples from the wrong people, and led them to use the written Word in a way that did more harm than good.

The Protestant Reformers failed, for instance, to follow Jesus' example in loving his enemies because they looked to David's example in war. They did not follow Jesus' example in economics because they looked to Abraham and Job. They did not understand Jesus' kingdom because they looked at the kingdom of Israel.

The Anabaptist servant of the Word, Hans Pfistermeyer, testified before the Swiss authorities at Bern in 1531:

> The New Testament is better than the Old. The Old was fulfilled and interpreted by Jesus. Jesus taught a higher and better way and made with his people a new covenant. I make a great difference between the Old and New Testament and believe that the New Covenant which was made with us is much better than the old that was made with the Jews.[17]

In a public debate at Frankenthal in the Kurpfalz in 1571, the Anabaptists said:

> The Old Testament writings offer strong proof that Jesus is the true God and Saviour of whom all the prophets testified. . . . Moses points us forward to Christ our Saviour. . . . We believe that the New Testament surpasses the Old. The parts of the Old Testament that can be reconciled with the teachings of Christ we accept. . . . If teaching necessary for salvation and a godly life was not taught by Christ and the Apostles, but is found only in the Old Testament, we would like to see it.[18]

Dirk Philips might have expressed the same willingness, but he did not expect to see anything like it. He wrote:

> False prophets disguise their teachings by appealing to the letter of the Old Testament, which consists of figures for things to come. Whatever they cannot defend by the New Testament they try to establish with the Old. This has given rise to many sects and many false religious forms.[19]

Afraid of the Word

In Canada, where I spent my childhood, some believed that people who "read the Bible too much" got strange ideas, lost their minds, or left the church. One

---

[17] From *Ein christenlich gespräch gehallten zu Bernn zwüschen den Predicanten und Hansen Physter Meyer von Arouw den Widertauff, Eyd, Oberkeyt und andere Widertoufferische Artikel betreffende*, 1531.

[18] From *Protocoll, Das ist Alle handlung des gesprechs zu Franckenthal inn der Churfürstlichen Pfaltz, mit denen so man Widertäuffer nennet*, 1571.

[19] *Enchiridion,* 1564.

older man explained it like this, "The Bible is like a stream. As long as you are content to drink from the surface, its water stays clean and pure. But if you get in too deep, you stir it up, and its waters become muddy and unfit to drink."

The first Anabaptists faced similar logic. For a thousand years the church of the Dark Ages had convinced the people the Scriptures were dangerous. The people had come to believe that if an "unlearned" man handles the Bible, he may offend God and bring damnation upon his soul.

Following Jesus, the first Anabaptists lost these fears. They no longer worried about "getting in too deep" or about bringing condemnation upon themselves. Veit Grünberger, Anabaptist messenger arrested at Salzburg in Austria in 1576, mentioned in a letter from prison that he hoped to learn at least one hundred chapters from the New Testament by memory. He regretted that he had not known the Scriptures sooner so that he could have memorised the entire New Testament.

The Anabaptists started with the Gospels, but they did not neglect nor minimise the remainder of the written Word. "Read the epistles with diligence," wrote Wolfgang Brandhuber. "Ask God to help you understand them and he will teach you all things if you attend his school and accept his discipline."[20]

"When we hear or read the Scriptures, it is just as if we heard the Lord Christ or his apostles speaking to us," wrote Leupold Scharnschlager. "Everyone knows that the materials with which they are written are in themselves dead ink and paper, but if we comprehend them right, they are more than that."[21]

The Scriptures helped the first Anabaptists into Gemeinschaft with Jesus. They felt totally at home in the Scriptures. But they feared them too—when people misused them.

Heinz Kraut, Anabaptist messenger from Frankenhausen in Thüringen, fell into the hands of Martin Luther's men on November 20, 1535. Resolving to win him over to their side, the Lutherans imprisoned him at Jena and had their best scholars, Kaspar Kreutzinger and Philipp Melanchthon dispute with him.

The Lutheran scholars quoted scripture after scripture in defense of their positions. Finally Heinz could keep quiet no longer. "You, Master Philip," he said, "have killed more people with your dead Scriptures than have all the hangmen in Germany!"

The Lutherans answered by beheading Heinz Kraut at Jena on January 26, 1536. "The Scriptures are valuable for those who use them right," testified one Anabaptist at the Regensburg trials in Bavaria. "But their misuse is the source of all heresy and unbelief. To the scribes and the Pharisees the Scriptures were

---

[20] *Sendbrief,* 1529

[21] From *Erleütterung durch auszug aus Heiliger Biblischer schrifft. . . zu dienst und fürderung ains Klaren urteils von wegen unterschied Alts und News Testaments. . . genant Testamenterleütterung,* ca. 1544.

not a guide to Christ, but a hindrance and eventually a punishment."[22]

"Man's salvation is not to be bound to the outer word," stated another Anabaptist defendant at Regensburg. "Salvation is a matter of the inner Word alone." And to this Ulrich Stadler added that it is dangerous to bring people to depend on the outer word because it "makes an idol out of the preacher, out of the writings and out of their words. But all these are merely images, signs, or tools."[23]

Bold with the Word

Because they had full confidence in the Word of Christ and in their Spirit-led understanding of it, the first Anabaptists lost their fear of men. Before the court that sentenced him to death, Michael Sattler said:

> We will be convinced through the Scriptures. If we see that we are wrong we will gladly bear our punishment. But if, according to the Scriptures, we are not wrong, then I hope before God that you will all change your minds and allow yourselves to be taught.

At this the judges "stuck their heads together and laughed." Michael's request to use the Scriptures in their original languages as a basis for discussion seemed ridiculous to them. "You shameless and renegade monk," sneered the presiding secretary, "shall we dispute with you? We'll let the hangman do that!"

When the chief judge, Count Joachim von Zollern, asked him if he wanted to receive a just sentence, Michael replied: "Servants of God, I am not called to judge the Word but to be a witness for it. . . . We are ready to suffer for the Word of God whatever punishment you lay upon us. We will stand fast on our faith in Jesus as long as we have breath, that is, until we can be shown from the Scriptures a better way."

"Yes, you will be shown," retorted the secretary. "The hangman will show you. He will dispute with you."

"I appeal to the Scriptures," was Michael's last reply.[24]

The Word and the Cross

After a recent church division, one minister said: "The other group wants to live only by the Word of God. You know, that is a dangerous position for a conservative church to take."

He was right. Living only by the Word of God is dangerous. The day

---

[22] Quoted in Hermann Nestler, *Die Wiedertäuferbewegung in Regensburg*, 1926.

[23] *Vom lebendigen Wort und geschriebenen* . . . ca. 1530

[24] From the eyewitness account of Klaus von Graveneck to live only by the Word of God. You know, that is a dangerous position for a conservative church to take."

Menno Simons decided to do it, he became a hunted man. Dutch authorities set a price on his head. Giving him a bed became a capital offence. He fled by night. He preached much. He suffered much and finally died, an old man with a crutch, banished to the cold windswept moors of Schleswig-Holstein along the Baltic Sea. But Menno was not sorry:

> "Which of the two shall we follow?" he asked. "Shall we follow the truth of Christ Jesus, or shall we follow the lies of the world? If you answer that we should follow Jesus, your judgment is right. But the result for the flesh will be anxiety, the loss of our belongings, arrest, banishment, poverty, water, fire, sword, the wheel, shame, cross, suffering, and bodily death—then eternal life. If you answer that we should follow the world than you judge wrong. Even though the result of such a choice brings us honour and liberty, even though it brings us ease and material advantages, it ends in eternal death."[25]

The cross the Anabaptists carried was heavy. But they carried it for the Word, dressed in a garment dipped in blood, who led them….

---

[25] *Verclaringhe des christelycken doopsels . . .* ca. 1542

On to a New Life

"In Christ Jesus neither the cutting away nor the foreskin is of any value, but a new creature," wrote Menno Simons on the title page of his book *Of the Heavenly Birth and the New Creature* in 1556. He quoted Paul. And with Paul and Menno Simons, the Anabaptists rejected all external means of salvation.

Salvation for the Anabaptists was Jesus. To be saved was to turn to him in the heart and follow him in a new life, like Hans Betz who got converted and baptised at Donauwörth in the FränkischeAlb in 1530.

Hans was a young man with many friends. He learned how to run a loom and earned a good wage in a linen shop. Old enough to know what happens in town at night, he took part in it. He thought he had a good life and that he enjoyed it . . . but he felt guilty.

Then an Anabaptist messenger came to town. Hans heard him speak and felt an inner call. He repented of his sins, got baptised, and gave up all he had to follow Jesus.

After some time, Hans found a place among a community of believers at Auspitz in Moravia. When they needed to flee he fled and was captured with them. His captors threw him into the dungeons of the castle at Passau on the Danube. There he had time to write his testimony:

> In the beginning, God created me to be his child. He created me clean. He gave me his image when I was still in my mother's womb. But when I was born onto the earth I lost my goodness and was robbed of the innocence God had given to me. I grew up in the world, surrounded by all the impurities of sin. I sought only possessions and money, which are against God. Whatever my eyes lusted after, I sought in my heart.
>
> Even though the law of God within me resisted the common sins in which I lived, I did not obey it. I was perverted from the bottom of my heart. My mouth could speak only bad things, and my vices were many. Even though my spirit would have been willing to stay away from sin, I was too weak in the battle and soon found myself lying on my side. The good that I wanted to do I could not accomplish because the power of sin kept forcing me to do wrong. I led an uncontrolled life, driven by the lusts of my heart. I lost God's gift and sinned to the limit. Then the law of God judged me, and even though it was given for life, it condemned me to death.
>
> When I recognised the law of God, I began to see the magnitude of my sins, my vices, and my shame. The law wounded me and condemned me to death and hell. There, surrounded by sin, death and hell I looked for God and he brought me to life again. He moved me with his law to where I found again the grace which I had lost for so long a time. . . .
>
> The law taught me to recognise sin and drove me back to God's gift, given in Christ. I would not have known what sin was if God had not spoken to me. Like sin rules the man who lives in it, God's grace rules the man whom Christ bears again. He is led out of all sin to live in what is right.
>
> When the law wounded my conscience I began to cry for God's grace and

> mercy. I began to cry to him to help me out of my sin and to accept me once more as his child for his mercy's sake.
>
> God in his grace, heard through Christ my cry. He brought me out of death, forgave my sins, took me again as his son, and through him I overcame sin when he made me new. Because I had fallen from God through sin and come under his wrath, he bore me again as his child. He bore me in his Son, the Lord Jesus Christ, who is the man in between, so that I would not be lost.
>
> No one comes to God unless God draws him. Therefore he shows us Christ so that none of us will run away from him when we see through the law the punishment we deserve.[1]

Adam and Jesus

"Jesus Christ, through his obedience, undid the disobedience of Adam and all his descendants," wrote Menno Simons. "And by his painful death he restored life."[2]

"That which Adam lost, we find again in Christ, beautifully adorned and clear,"[3] wrote an Ausbund writer.

What did Adam lose?

The first Anabaptists believed that Adam, when he sinned, lost his innocence. They believed that innocence is a gift of God and that we are all born with it. But when we grow up and lose our innocence, we lose the image of God, which can only be found again in Christ.[4]

Coming to Jesus, the Anabaptists believed, is coming back to the love, the freedom, and the innocence of childhood. Sin, and the laws made to control sin, no longer affect us in Jesus. In Jesus we live above sin and above the law, compelled by nothing but love.

---

1 *Ausbund,* 112

2 *Dat Fundament des Christelycken leers* . . . 1539

3 *Ausbund,* 51:6

4 After Balthasar Hubmaier (who wrote two books on the subject: *Von der Freyhait des Willens* and *Von der Freywilligkeit des Menschens*), Hans Denck was the Anabaptist who wrote most about man's problem with guilt and his freedom to choose. In his book, *Was geredt sey* . . . (1526), Hans taught that God created us to fulfill his desire for voluntary obedience, as opposed to the blind obedience of a log or a stone. He did not believe that God forces us to obey him, but that he permits sin so that we need to use our freedom of choice. Like Balthasar Hubmaier, Hans believed that only our flesh (our natural desires) became corrupted in Adam's fall, and that our spirits became prisoners of our flesh. Sin is a kind of sickness. To recover from it, we must surrender ourselves totally to God. Only then can our spirits dominate our unwilling flesh. Only then can we keep the law of love in obedience to God and live a new life.

Wolfgang Brandhuber, shortly before they killed him at Linz in Austria, wrote:

> If we want to be one with God, we need to be one with his will (Christ Jesus). That happens when we tell him about our great needs and when we tell him that we love him. If we love him we keep his commandments because love—if it is love—comes from the heart. How could true love be anything but from the heart? And love continually seeks love, like the bride in Solomon's song who can sing and speak of nothing else. True Christianity works on nothing but love. It needs no law because it fulfills the commands of God out of pure love and exercises itself in this day and night. It leaves everything earthly behind. It despises everything earthly to the pit, and asks: "Why bother with that?" It seeks because it loves. The more it loves the more it seeks to be loved—engaging itself to the Beloved One and peering out through the lattice work to watch him come from afar.[5]

Hans Betz, before he died under torture in 1537, at Passau in Bavaria, wrote:

> Christ shows us the law of God for man: "Do to others as you would have them do to you." He shows us what is good and what is bad so that we may live in a different way. Christ is the fulfilment of the law that was given in figures to Moses. All the figures of the law end in Christ because Christ is the law. To obey the law, says Christ, is to love God with all the strength of our souls, and to love our neighbour as our self. In these short commands the law is gathered up in Christ.
>
> Faith and love out of a pure heart, says Paul, is the sum of all commands. The one who lives in God's love is a disciple of Christ and knows the truth. Love is is kind and friendly and does no one harm. It bears everything and keeps away from sin. . . . This is how the law and the prophets are fulfilled in Christ our Lord. This is the way he has shown us that leads to the Father and eternal life. . . .[6]

A Turning Around

The first Anabaptists spoke often of being born again. Menno Simons quoted Jesus: "Except a man be born again, he cannot see the kingdom of God. . . . Except a man be born of water and the Spirit, he cannot enter into the kingdom of God." Then he wrote:

> Listen! These are not words invented by men. They were not resolved or decided on in any church council. These are the words of the Son of God! The Word is powerful and clear and means not only Nicodemus but all of Adam's descendants who have come to a mature age. It is too bad that the Word has been hidden by the ugly yeast, the dung of human commandments, human rules, and human interpretations to such an extent that scarcely one or two out of a thousand is left who understands the heavenly birth anymore.[7]

A new birth, a heavenly birth, a baptism of the Spirit—the first Anabaptists used all of these terms, but none more often than the term *Bekehrung* (conversion), which in German means literally "a turning around." They got the word from the German Gospel of Matthew: "Unless you *turn yourselves around* and become like

---

[5] *Sendbrief,* 1529

[6] *Ausbund,* 112

[7] *Een corte vermaninghe van de wedergeboorte* . . . ca. 1537

little children you will not enter the Kingdom of Heaven" (Matthew 18:3).

Hans Betz wrote:

> Listen to how one receives Christ. You need to make a covenant with him. In the depths of your heart you need to turn from sin. Then you will be clean. Christ will come to you and show you his Spirit—and he will bear you again.[8]

Menno Simons wrote:

> If you wish to be saved, your earthly, carnal, ungodly life must first be made new. The Scriptures with their admonitions, their reproof, their accounts of miracles, ceremonies, and sacraments teach us nothing but repentance. If you do not repent there is nothing in heaven or on earth that can help you, for without true repentance we comfort ourselves in vain. . . .
>
> We must be born from above. We must be transformed and made new in our hearts. We must be transplanted from the unrighteous and evil nature of Adam into the true and good nature of Christ, or we can never in all eternity be saved by any means, be they of men or of God. Whoever has not truly repented and found a new life (I speak of those who are of the age of understanding) is lost.
>
> This is unmistakably clear. Everyone who does not wish to be deceived should guard this in the little chest of his conscience.[9]

An Ausbund writer wrote:

> Listen all you Christians who have been born again! God's Son from the Kingdom of Heaven died on the cross and suffered death and shame. Let us follow him! Let us take up our cross! The blood of Jesus washes away the sins of those who leave all to follow him, and who believe on God alone—even though they have sinned much. The Holy Spirit is given to those who believe and are baptised, if they follow Christ. With the Spirit they kill the flesh and find peace with God.Those who are washed and made free from sin with the blood of Christ walk in the Spirit with broken hearts. The Spirit rules them and shows them the way. Therefore, purified children of God— born again—keep yourselves pure! Let no man deceive you! The one who does right is right. The one who sins is a slave to sin.[10]

No Turning Back

The first Anabaptists could not talk about the new life without mentioning Gemeinschaft with Christ, found through suffering with him, and the need of total Gelassenheit (letting go). The material on this subject is vast. It is overwhelming—by far the most popular theme of the Anabaptist writings of southern Germany and Austria. I will quote only Hans Betz who drew a parallel between the Christian's surrender and Lot leaving everything behind when he left Sodom to begin a new life.

---

[8] *Ausbund*, 107:22

[9] *op. cit.*

[10] *Ausbund*, 114

Hans Betz wrote:

> Let us fight valiantly on, pressing toward the prize. The one who turns to one side or the other will perish with Lot's wife who turned to look back, feeling sorry for the possessions she left behind.[11]
>
> Let him who has laid his hand on the plough not look back! Press on to the goal! Press on to Jesus Christ! The one who gains Christ will rise with him from the dead on the youngest day. . . . Remember Lot's wife! When she looked back she was punished by God and became a pillar of salt. Let this be your example, you who have chosen the Way. Do not turn around! Do not look back! Declare yourselves for Christ and go ahead! If you overcome you will live with him in eternal joy![12]

No Cheap Grace

"The proud world wants to be Christian too," wrote an Ausbund writer. "But the world is ashamed of the cross. The world says: `No. That cannot be. Why should we suffer if the sufferings of Christ were enough to redeem us from our sins?' Oh blind world, you will be put to shame! Your faith will not save you! Repent! If you do not want to suffer forever, come out from among the world and sin no more!"[13]

Maeyken Wens, arrested at Antwerp in 1573 wrote beautiful encouraging letters to her husband, her children, and to her friends. Her fifteen-year-old son, Adriaan, watched, but fainted, as they burned her at the stake on the morning of Oct. 6, 1573. Afterward, he dug through the ashes for the tongue-screw with which they had kept her from speaking—as a remembrance of his mother.

Othmar Roth of Sankt Gallen in Switzerland wrote in 1532:

> Man, are you tired of being sad? . . . Leave the world! Leave your possessions! Leave your goods and your money! The one who thinks of death chooses the best and Christ

[11] *Ausbund*, 113:18

[12] *Ausbund*, 111:11-12

[13] *Ausbund,* 79:10

earns grace for him.

It is difficult for the one who loves to talk to get to know himself. If he would think of who he is, he would not have so much to say. Look at yourself! Leave the rest. Do not gossip. Be quiet . . . so that in the end you may not be put to shame.

What you measure out will be measured to you. Christ treats all men fairly. No sin remains unpunished. Therefore fear God and keep his commands. No good deed remains without its reward. Pray for grace, early and late, and pray that we may be spared. If you want to be saved, keep away from sin! To be carnally minded is death. Leave the world! Leave your possessions! Leave your goods and your money! The one who thinks of death chooses the best and Christ earns grace for him.

God will not forsake the one who lives in the truth. God is ready to hear us if we hate sin. Oh Jesus Christ, it is your spirit that comforts us. Do not leave us! Be merciful to us and intercede for us . . . as we near the end of time.[14]

Menno Simons wrote:

With a sincere heart we desire to die to sin, to bury our sins with Christ, and to rise with him to a new life, just as our baptism signifies. We seek to walk humbly and in a holy way with Christ Jesus in this covenant of grace. . . . For even as the death of our Lord would not have profited us, had he not risen from the power of earth. . . . so it will not help us anything to bury our sins in baptism if we do not rise with Christ from the power of sin unto a new life.[15]

Once they discovered a new life in Christ, the Anabaptists moved…

[14] *Ausbund,* 58

[15] *Dat Fundament des Christelycken leers . . .* 1539

On to Baptism

South of Lake Constance, where the land rises to the shimmering peaks, Säntis, Altmann, and Kreuzberg, the city of Sankt Gallen lies in the valley of the Sitter River. For more than a thousand years after 612 A.D. when the missionary, Gall of Down, settled here, monks lived in Sankt Gallen.

Over the centuries their monastery grew. Its library grew to become the most important one in Europe north of the Alps. Its abbots grew in importance until Sankt Gallen became a free city and its abbots princes of the Holy Roman Empire.

In 1525 people knew Sankt Gallen for two things: its ancient monastery and its textiles. For generations, the weavers of Sankt Gallen had made the finest linens of this part of Europe. They had become wealthy and formed an association, a "weavers' guild," and the son of the guild leader was a boy named Wolf.

Wolf Ulimann's father, in spite of his growing wealth and his eye for business, did not overlook the tender conscience of his son. He sent Wolf south to Chur (in the Grisons where the Romans had lived behind the Rhaetian Alps) to become a monk.

While Wolf Ulimann studied in quiet seclusion, another young man of Sankt Gallen, Johannes Kessler, travelled north to the University of Wittenberg in Germany. On his way he stopped one night at Jena in Thüringen at the Black Bear Inn. Some knights came to the inn. At least he thought they were knights, but one was not. That one was Martin Luther, disguised in a knight's armour, on a secret mission out from the Wartburg Castle where he was hiding.

Johannes Kessler, the student, and Martin Luther, the pope- defying monk in knight's armour got acquainted, like travellers get acquainted on cold evenings at hotels, and their talk turned serious.

When Johannes Kessler returned to Sankt Gallen he committed himself to the study of the Scriptures. Holding meetings at his house in the evenings, he read the words of Christ and explained them to the young people who came to learn. Wolf Ulimann, during a time at home, attended a meeting and his heart was moved to stay and become a regular participant. He listened and read and prayed until the Spirit led him to inner repentance and a new life in Christ.

The city council of Sankt Gallen (that by now had turned Protestant) asked Johannes Kessler to stop having the classes. They "caused unrest in the church." But Wolf did not want them to stop. He invited those who sought for the truth to the meeting room of his father's guild and began to lead the Bible studies himself. More people came than ever. The Scriptures Wolf translated from Latin to German came to life in their discussions. All over Sankt Gallen people began to think and to pray, and the Spirit of God moved their hearts. Then Lorenz Hochrütiner came back.

Lorenz, one of the Sankt Gallen linen weavers, had gone to Zürich where he became a zealous, but immature, follower of Christ. One Sunday, after mass in the Zürich suburb of Stadelhofen, Lorenz joined a crowd of people so moved to "do away with dead idols" they ripped out and smashed the church's crucifix. For this he got banished.

Now back in Sankt Gallen, Lorentz attended the meeting in the weavers' hall where Wolf read Romans, chapter six. The study hinged on the meaning of verse four: "We were therefore buried with him through baptism into death, in order that, just as Christ was raised from the dead through the glory of the Father, we too may live a new life."

A burial in baptism and a rising to a new life—Lorenz Hochrütiner stood up and explained what he saw in this verse. Wolf Ulimann became powerfully convicted.

Several months later, Lorenz returned to Zürich and Wolf needed to go on a short trip as well. On the road from Konstanz to Schaffhausen along the Rhein he met Conrad Grebel.

Wolf and Conrad talked. They both felt inwardly moved to follow Christ no matter what it cost.

"Baptise me!" said Wolf. "I must be baptised, not just with water poured from a bowl, but buried in the water like Christ."

Almost before Conrad knew what was happening, Wolf had stripped off his clothes and was heading with him into the frigid waters of the Rhein in February, 1525. There, where the water got deep, Conrad "pressed him under and covered him completely," and Wolf came out—fully surrendered to Christ. [1]

Sankt Gallen, the city that grew up around its famous monastery (the monks' twin-towered chapel illuminated on the right) eagerly embraced Reformation ideas. But to go the whole way, to follow Christ and get baptised as believers, seemed far too radical for most of its people in the sixteenth century.

---

[1] In the words of Johannes Kessler: "Er wollte nicht mit einer Schüssel mit Wasser allein begossen, sondern ganz nackend und bloß, hinaus in den Rhein von dem Grebel untergedrückt und bedeckt werden" (*Sabbata*, ca. 1530).

From this time onward, things happened fast. When Wolf got back to Sankt Gallen, people filled the weavers' hall, standing along the walls on March 18, to hear his testimony in which he said: "The Lord has shown me that I should leave the Church. What the Church teaches is not true. They have never preached the truth in this Church, and they are not doing so now."

On March 25, Conrad Grebel came. Along with him came a man named Eberhard Bolt from the Canton of Schwyz. Eberhard (*Eberli* as everyone called him) had not been baptised. In fact he was against the baptism of adults. But he was a sincere believer, and after talking with Wolf and Conrad, he became convicted, too. Immediately after his baptism the people asked him to preach for them. He was a gifted speaker and had a "God-fearing and compassionate" spirit.[2]

"Almost the entire city of Sankt Gallen" came out to the Berlisberg, where they sat on the sun-warmed grass to hear Conrad and Eberli speak. It was Palm Sunday, April 9, 1525. The rich were struck to the heart. The poor were lifted up in Christ. Many of the women and young people believed, and a great crowd streamed down to the Sitter River at the end of the meeting "as if it would have been a day of parades."[3]

There Conrad, Eberli, and Wolf baptised those who believed— hundreds of converts—in the Sitter River, and a new church community was born.

The people chose Eberli to be their leader, and for a whole week they had services every day. They broke bread in their homes and found the joy of giving up everything for Jesus. One rich man, Anthoni Roggenacher, threw a hundred golden crowns at the feet of the gathered believers. . . . Then they got called to court.

The city court of Sankt Gallen, working on behalf of the Protestant church, was most concerned about baptism. Baptising people without authority, without the blessing of the church, and on top of that baptising by immersion—such things simply were not done in Switzerland in 1525!

Wolf Ulimann spoke before the court. "We know only one baptism," he said. "Baptism is nothing without believing in Christ, dying to sin, and coming to a new life."

The court, under the influence of Johannes Kessler and Dr. Joachim von Watt (Vadian), moved cautiously. They asked Eberli Bolt kindly to leave Sankt Gallen. He obeyed and made a trip to his home at Lachen in the Roman Catholic canton of Schwyz. There he spoke to the priest who became converted. The authorities burned both Eberli and the priest at the stake on May 29, 1525. They walked "gladly into the flames."

---

[2] According to Johannes Kessler.

[3] From the eyewitness account of Fridolin Sicher, the Protestant chronicler of Sankt Gallen.

The city council of Protestant Sankt Gallen admonished Wolf to stop baptising "for the sake of brotherly love" in the Lord's church.

"I cannot do that," Wolf answered. "I follow Christ."

"Then we must expel you from the city," the court decided. But they did not expel him at once. The "evangelical leaders" of the city felt compelled to prove themselves right and Wolf wrong. They arranged two public debates. At the last debate they read from Huldrych Zwingli's book *On Baptism, Rebaptism, and Infant Baptism*. To that Wolf replied in a clear voice before the great crowd of people who had come to listen: "You can have Zwingli's word, but I will have the Word of God!"

By June the Anabaptists of Sankt Gallen were strictly forbidden to assemble. On July 17, 1525, they were banished.

Wolf fled with a group to Moravia. He travelled and spoke and baptised. After a year he was back in Switzerland and they banished him from the city of Basel. Then he led another group from the Sankt Gallen area toward Moravia. But they did not get there. At Waldsee, across the Rhein in Swabia, they got caught. The authorities dispersed the children, drowned the women, and beheaded and burned the men. "In this way," wrote a brother from Moravia named Kaspar Braitmichel, "they witnessed with their bodies, like knights, that their faith and baptism were founded on the truth of God."[4]

Wolf Ulimann would have called it his third baptism—the baptism of blood.

A Threefold Witness

The first Anabaptists looked to Jesus for their example in baptism. Jesus was baptised in the water. The Spirit came upon him, and he spoke of another baptism he had to go through: the baptism of suffering (Luke 12:50). The Anabaptists understood this in the light of 1 John 5:6-8: "This is the one who came by water and blood—Jesus Christ. He did not come by water only, but by water and blood. And it is the Spirit who testifies, because the Spirit is the truth. For there are three that testify: the Spirit, the water, and the blood; and the three are in agreement."[5]

The first Anabaptists believed that Spirit baptism, water baptism, and baptism by blood, were the three witnesses of their souls' salvation. Jörg

---

[4] *Geschichtbuech unnd kurtzer Durchgang von Anfang der Welt wie Gott sein Werck inn seinem Volck auff Erden angericht gehandlet unnd triben hat*, ca. 1570.

[5] Martin Luther's German Bible, read by the Anabaptists, did not include the additions to 1 John 5:7-8, which appeared in Greek texts after the sixteenth century and in the English King James Version. The words appear in some later German editions, but not as part of the main text in Bibles now in use among the Amish, the Old Order Mennonites and the Hutterites.

Rothenfelder, servant of the Word in Bavaria and Switzerland, wrote:

> Baptism is not for the unknowing, as practiced by those who are against Christ, but only for those who believe. The order of Christ must be observed, and the three witnesses, Spirit, water, and blood, must be kept together. It is not enough to have only an "inner baptism" as some perverted spirits teach. Inner faith demands an outer witness.[6]

From 1 John 5 came the teaching of baptism being a "co- testimony" (*Mitzeugnis*), as it was frequently called by the Anabaptists of southern Germany. From John the Baptist came the picture of Jesus' baptism by fire (the fire of suffering) through which all his followers need to go.

Suffering to the Anabaptists was more than being tortured or burned at the stake. They believed it comes on us in three ways: the suffering of persecution (*Verfolgung*), the suffering of temptation (*Anfechtung*), and the suffering of sorrow or anxiety (*Trübsal*). When they asked Ambrutz Spittelmayr—a young,Latin-speaking Anabaptist messenger arrested at Erlangen in Franconia in 1527—what he asked people to do before he baptised them, he said:

> Just like a man submits to the water in baptism, so he must throw himself under God and stay faithful to him in spite of prison, the sword, or whatever trial may come. . . . You understand the words of Christ in John 6 in a wooden, literal way. You think you eat his body and drink his blood in the mass. But to do so is something else. It is to suffer with him. It is to be baptised like him, in blood. Whoever does not want to be baptised with the Spirit, with the water, and with the blood will be baptized in the lake of fire.[7]

Shortly after giving this testimony to the German court, Ambrutz completed his third baptism. They beheaded him at Cadolzburg near Ansbach in Franconia, on February 6, 1528. Ordained as a messenger by Hans Hut, he had spent only seven weeks in freedom as an Anabaptist.

A Mark

On April 16, 1525, shortly after the beginning of the Anabaptist movement in Switzerland, Conrad Grebel visited the mountain town of Oberwinterthur. He stayed in the home of Arbogast Finsterbach, brother-in-law to his friend Marx Bosshard. When Conrad spoke to him about following Jesus, Arbogast asked him: "What must a person do before he can be baptised?"

Conrad answered, "To be baptised a person must stop fornicating, gambling, drinking, and charging interest on his money."

`On another occasion Conrad Grebel answered that question:

---

6 From a letter to Ulrich Agemann, written from Sankt Gallen, in Switzerland, on October 15, 1562.

7 From Ambrutz's written testimony to the court, 1527

> Baptism is for those who want to better themselves, take on a new life, die to immorality, get buried with Christ and rise out of baptism to newness of life. . . . Baptism is the mark of change in the inner man. It is the mark of a new birth, a washing away of sin, and a promise to walk according to Christ.[8]

It took me some time before I understood Conrad Grebel, but his words become clear in the context of what other Anabaptists taught.

An Ausbund writer wrote:

> Come with joy, and dressed in new clothing! Come discerning the evil from the good! . . . Come and draw near to the Passover feast if you have taken his mark: his Spirit, the water and the blood. This is the Christians' possession, and to this they cling. It is the mark of baptism, which they receive of their own free will, and in which their old flesh drowns.[9]

Like Jesus, who responded with commandments (love your neighbour, sell what you have, etc.) when people asked what they must do to be saved, the first Anabaptists responded with commandments. But they taught that commandments (the law) can be obeyed only when we follow Jesus and become born again. They taught that Jesus bears us again in the Spirit, the water, and the blood of baptism.

Water does not save us. "We are not born again when we are baptised," wrote Menno Simons, "but we are baptised when we are born again by faith in God's Word." The new birth, for the first Anabaptists, was not complete without the mark of water baptism. Dirk Pietersz, arrested after holding meetings in his house on the dike at Edam in the Netherlands faced interrogation. The interrogator asked him: "How long is it since you were baptised?"

"Ever since I was born," Dirk replied.

The interrogator did not catch the implication. (Dirk was speaking about his new birth.) But when the matter became clear, they sentenced him to burn at the stake in Amsterdam, on May 24, 1546.

A Seal of Faith

Just as circumcision was the seal of God's old covenant, the first Anabaptists saw water baptism as the seal of God's new covenant. Menno Simons wrote, "Outward baptism with water is a seal or proof of our faith, just as outward circumcision was to the believing and obedient Abraham.[10]"

---

[8] From *Protestation und Schutzschrift*, 1524.

[9] *Ausbund*, 55:10-12

[10] *op. cit*

The Anabaptists quoted Tertullian who in German translation spoke of a *Versieglung* (sealing), and they believed that "the seal of God on men's foreheads" in Rev. 9:4 was water baptism—the counterpart to the mark of the beast. Baptism, they taught, is the stamp of legitimacy on faith that makes it a saving faith. Faith without baptism is like a document without a seal.

Menno Simons wrote:

> Do you suppose, dear friends, that the new birth is just like the world says, just a plunging into the water, or a little speech: "I baptise you in the name of the Father, and of the Son, and of the Holy Ghost" ? No, dear brothers. No! The new birth consists not in water nor in words. The new birth is a heavenly life-giving power, the power of God in our hearts. Power flows from God when the Word is preached. Then when we believe the Word, it quickens, renews, penetrates, and remolds our hearts so that we are changed from unbelief to faith, from sin to righteousness, from evil to good, from carnal to spiritual, from earthly to heavenly, from the nature of Adam to the nature of Christ. . . . Those who go through this change are the truly born again. They are the regenerate ones to whom Christian baptism is a seal of faith by which they receive remission of sins.[11]

No Empty Seal

Catholic and Protestant baptism, the baptism of infants or of anyone else who did not "produce fruit in keeping with repentance," was no baptism at all to the first Anabaptists. They did not feel guilty of *anabaptism* (baptising twice),[12] for the only seal they counted valid was the seal of water on faith.

Menno Simons wrote:

> The word of God must be taught and understood before baptism. To baptise before that which is represented by baptism, namely faith, is found in us, is as logical as to place a cart before the horse, to sow before we plow, to build before we have the lumber on hand, or to seal a letter before it is written.[13]

Leonhard Schiemer wrote:

> To sum it all up, baptism with water is the testimony of the covenant we make with God in our hearts. Baptism may be compared to a man who writes a document and then asks that it be sealed. Nobody will seal it or sign it for him without knowing what the document says. Whoever baptises a child puts his seal on a blank document.[14]

Baptism for Remission of Sins

An Ausbund writer wrote:

---

11 *op. cit*

12 The state churches called them *Wiedertäufer* (rebaptisers). Using a play on words some Anabaptists, in turn, called them *Widerchristen* (Anti-Christians).

13 *Opera Omnia Theologica*, 1681.

14 *Von dreyerley Tauf*. . . 1527

> He who is born out of water and Spirit is no longer a sinner. His flesh rules him no longer. . . . True Christians have buried all their fleshly lusts with Christ.[15]

Concerning Peter's command at Pentecost that repentant believers be baptised for remission of sins, Menno Simons wrote:

> We preach that remission of sins takes place in baptism, not on account of the water of the rite performed (Jesus Christ is the only means of grace) but because men receive the promises of the Lord by faith and obediently follow his Word and will.[16]

Peter, enlightened by the Holy Ghost, commanded us to get baptised like Jesus said, for remission of sins. We must, therefore, receive baptism as it is commanded in the Scriptures. Otherwise we cannot obtain remission of our sins, nor will the Holy Ghost fall upon us. Who has ever received remission of sins contrary to the Word of God? Surely we cannot take the remission of sins and the Holy Ghost from God as by force. If we then desire the remission of sins, we must do and fulfil all that God has taught us through Christ Jesus and through the holy apostles.[17]

The Limmat River in Zürich, Switzerland, where Felix Manz experienced the final dimension of his threefold baptism—that of suffering—on the day Protestant authorities drowned him for what he believed, January 5, 1527. Huldrych Zwingli's church, the Grossmünster, stands tall in the background.

The forgiveness of sins takes place during baptism according to the Scriptures. Baptism is the putting on of Christ. It is an immersion into the community of Christ, not on account of the water or the administered signs (else the kingdom of God would be bound to elements and signs), but on account of the promise that we receive by obedience through faith.[18]

With all this, Menno Simons was careful not to imply that sinners can go through baptism and come out saints. In 1539 he wrote:

---

[15] *Ausbund, 94:20-21*

[16] *Dat Fundament des Christelycken leers* . . . 1539

[17] *Verclaringhe des christelycken doopsels* . . . ca. 1542

[18] *Dat Fundament des Christelycken leers* . . . 1539

> As Christ died and was buried, so we ought to die to our sins and be buried with Christ in baptism. Not that we are to do this for the first time after baptism, but we must have begun all this beforehand.[19]

Not Water Alone

The Anabaptists' enemies thought they could regenerate babies in baptism. They believed that baptism was a channel of grace. This, the Anabaptists steadfastly denied. Hans Betz wrote:

> Baptism alone will not wash you from lust and sin. It only shows that you are clean in Christ. The righteousness of Christ is the garment you are to put on in baptism, when lust, sin, and deceit— your Adam—is washed away.[20]

Thomas von Imbroich wrote:

> The washing of water is joined to the Word. No one is cleansed by the washing of water but by the Word, as the Lord says: "Now you are clean through the word which I have spoken unto you" (John 15:3).[21]

Menno Simons put it plainly:

> As long as men's minds are not renewed and they are not of the same mind with Christ—as long as they are not washed inwardly with clean water from the fountain of God—they may as well say, "What good can water do?" For as long as they are earthly and carnally minded, the entire ocean is not enough to make them clean. . . .
>
> He who seeks remission of sins only through water baptism despises the blood of the Lord and makes water to be his idol. Therefore let everyone be careful lest he ascribe the honour and glory due to Christ to ceremonies performed and to created elements. . . .
>
> Do not imagine that we insist on elements and rites. I tell you the truth. If anyone were to come to me, even the emperor or the king, desiring to be baptised, but walking still in the lusts of the flesh—if the holy, penitent, and regenerate life were not in evidence—I would rather die than baptise such a person. Where there is no regenerating faith that leads to obedience, there can be no baptism. Philip said to the eunuch, "If you *believe* with all your heart it may take place."[22]

Baptism and the Cross

Baptism literally pictured life and death to the first Anabaptists. To get baptised on confession of faith was to sign your own death sentence in the sixteenth century. Luther, Zwingli, and Calvin had mercy on rebaptised people and only beheaded them. But beheading in Roman Catholic countries was considered far too

---

19 *ibid.*

20 *Ausbund,* 108:9

21 *Confessio,* 1558

22 *Dat Fundament des Christelycken leers. . .* 1539

mild a punishment. (It was reserved only for those who recanted.) Baptised adults were usually burned at the stake.

Menno Simons wrote:

> All who hear and believe the Word of God get baptised. With this they declare they will live no longer according to their own will, but according to the will of God. They declare they are prepared to forsake their homes, possessions, lands and lives. They declare they are ready to suffer hunger, affliction, oppression, persecution, cross and death, for Christ. In baptism they express their desire to bury the flesh with its lusts and arise with Christ to eternal life.[23]

Baptised into a life of the cross, the first Anabaptists followed Christ . . .

[23] *ibid.*

On to the Covenant

On a dark, rainy day in November, 1977, I got baptised in the old Lutheran church at Hesson, Ontario. We Mennonites had purchased the building, torn out its baptismal font, turned its Gothic windows into rectangles and were now using it for our meetinghouse. After my baptism and public testimony the bishop gave me a card. On it were the questions I had been asked and the vows I had made. The card's title was *Covenant Reminder*.

Many times since my Mennonite baptism I have been reminded of that covenant I made with Jesus. And the thought of a covenant in baptism, I have discovered, is not new. In the 1520s Balthasar Hubmaier wrote:

> Oh my Lord Jesus Christ, reestablish the two bands with which you have outwardly girded and bound your bride into a covenant. Your bride is the church community. The bands are proper water baptism and the nighttime meal.[1]

Ambrutz Spittelmayr told the court at Ansbach in Franconia: "We make a covenant with God in the Spirit, in water baptism, and in drinking the cup which the Word calls the baptism of blood."[2]

Leonhard Schiemer wrote: "Water baptism is the seal of our faith and of the covenant we make in our hearts to God."[3]

Hans Hut, Anabaptist messenger through southern Germany and Austria, said:

> Baptism follows preaching and believing. Whoever is willing to accept the suffering that God will place on him when he joins himself to Christ, and whoever is willing to stay with Christ and forsake the world, makes a covenant in baptism before his church community.
>
> The community of Christ may open the door of the covenant to those that desire it with all their heart, just like he said: "What you bind on earth will be bound in heaven." The person who makes this covenant (in baptism) may be sure that he has been accepted as a child by God, and as a brother or a sister of Christ, a member his body and church community.[4]

---

[1] From *Balthasar Hubmaier Schriften, Quellen zur Geschichte der Täufer, Gütersloh,* 1962.

[2] From the testimony of Ambrutz Spittelmayr, written in the castle prison at Cadolzburg in Franconia, October 25, 1527.

[3] *Von dreyerley Tauf. . .* 1527

[4] *Vom Geheimnus der Tauff,* ca. 1527.

"Believers wed and bind themselves to the Lord Jesus Christ, publicly, through the true sign of the covenant, the water bath of baptism," wrote Melchior Hofman.[5] And to this Menno Simons added, "When we are inwardly cleansed by faith we bind ourselves in the outward sign of the water covenant (*Wasserbund*). We bind ourselves to the Lord Jesus in his grace when we bind ourselves in baptism to live no longer in sin."[6]

Saved Through the Covenant

Within a few days of the first baptisms in Felix Manz's home at Zürich, dozens more "bound themselves in baptism" in that city and its surrounding countryside. Within a matter of months these had baptised hundreds and thousands more in the German cantons of Switzerland, in Austria, in Bavaria, in Württemberg, and down the Rhein into the Netherlands and Belgium.

Baptism followed teaching. But because they tied faith, repentance and baptism together, the first Anabaptists did not consider postponing one of the three. They did not wait to baptise until a convenient time after the new birth took place. There was no convenient time. They baptised at once—even though it might cost them their lives—because they took baptism for the sealing of their covenant with God.

Eucharius Binder, baptised and ordained by Hans Hut at Königsberg in Franconia in 1526, travelled at once through Nürnberg and Augsburg to Steyr in Austria, baptising hundreds of people along the way. The following year they caught him at Salzburg and locked him in a house with thirty-seven other Anabaptists. The authorities then set the house on fire and all of the prisoners perished in the flames.

Leonhard Dorfbrunner baptised more than three thousand people in less than a year's time after his conversion. Many young men like him travelled from city to city and from house to house, meeting with those who longed to follow Jesus, as described years later:

> Usually the service began with the reading of a passage from the New Testament and ended with the baptism of such as desired it, and with a general participation in the Lord's supper. Baptisms took place at any time and at any place, in the morning or in the evening, in the house or at the stream. The water was the symbol of the washing of repentance and the putting off of sin, the outward sign of the decisive entrance into a new and holy life. He who received it was henceforth no longer the master of his own life, but a servant of Jesus Christ, ready to do his will at whatever cost.[7]

---

[5] From *Die Ordonnantie Godts, De welche hy, door zijnen Soone Christum Jesum, inghestelt ende bevesticht heevt* . . . 1530.

[6] *Dat Fundament des Christelycken leers* . . . 1539

[7] Harold S. Bender, *Conrad Grebel*, (Goshen, 1950), pg. 138

In the Netherlands and northern Germany, spontaneous baptisms caused new congregations to spring up, as one historian put it, "like mushrooms."[8] Many Anabaptists testified on arrest that they did not know who baptised them. Those who baptised avoided revealing their names, and those who believed avoided it too, for safety's sake. But a few men like Leenaerdt Bouwens kept numerical records. For thirty years he baptised, on the average, more than three hundred people a year.

Too Young

The first Anabaptists asked people to wait for baptism only when they found the "document" to which the seal was to be applied incomplete.

In a letter "written in the dark with poor materials" in the dungeon of the castle at Gent in Belgium, Jannijn Buitkijns, burned at the stake on July 9, 1551, tells of nine other Anabaptists who were interrogated with him. One of them was an adolescent boy.

The boy confessed that he thought the baptism of believers was right and good. He had gone to the teacher once to be baptised, but he was not baptised yet.

"Why did the teacher not baptise you?" the interrogator asked.

The boy answered, "My lords, when the teacher explained the faith to me and asked me questions, he noticed that I was still immature in my understanding. He told me to go and search the Scriptures some more. But I wanted to be baptised. The teacher then asked me whether I knew that the world puts to death and burns those who are baptised. I told him that I knew that well. Then he said to me that I should be patient until he came the next time. He told me that I should search the Scriptures and ask the Lord for wisdom because I am still so young. Then we parted."

"Are you sorry that you did not get baptised?" asked the interrogator.

"Yes, my lords."

"If you were not imprisoned would you be baptised?" "Yes, my lords."

For these words they sentenced him to death, and Jannijn did not see him again.[9]

Not Ready

Lauwerens van der Leyen, imprisoned at Antwerp in 1559, faced the

[8] Carl Adolf Cornelius, the Roman Catholic historian.

[9] *Martelaers-Spiegel,* 1660

question: “Are you baptised?”

Lauwerens answered: “No.”

“Is baptism necessary then?” the interrogator asked.

“Yes,” said Lauwerens. “It is necessary for perfection.”

“Why then are you not baptised?” asked the interrogator.

“I was not good enough yet.”

“Why?”

“Because I was involved too much in this world. I was, and still am, deeply in debt. I thought that if I were caught, people could say I was a hypocrite. Many could be turned away from the truth. Therefore I declined to receive baptism. But I consider it good and right and I want to live and die in this belief. Though I have not yet become baptised, the Lord in his mercy will save me because of his sufferings and precious blood. I believe all that a Christian is bound to believe, and I will stand firm in it. You may do further with me as you please for I am in your power.”

They beheaded Lauwerens at Antwerp in Belgium on November 9, 1559.[10]

Antwerp, from the Scheldt (one of the mouths of the Rhein), home to a large “underground” fellowship of believers in the 16’th century. Many Anabaptist prisoners, including Lauwerens van der Leyen, lay in chains in Het Steen castle, centre foreground.

Exceptions to the rule were common in the sixteenth century. Some believers fell into the hands of the authorities before they got baptised. Some,

[10] *ibid.*

arrested during meetings, got converted during the incident or in prison. Some missed baptism for other reasons. But the question of their salvation did not become an issue. The Anabaptists had no doubts about God's mercy on the faithful.

Children

Roman Catholic and Protestant authorities often tried to rescue Anabaptist children from their "heretic" parents to baptise them. They accused the Anabaptists of murdering infants' souls. But the Anabaptists, resting on the Word of God, did not worry. Conrad Grebel wrote, "All children that have not come to know the difference between good and evil, who have not eaten from the tree of knowledge, are surely safe through the work of Christ."[11]

Menno Simons wrote:

> Little children, especially those born in Christian homes, have a special promise. It is a promise given to them by God with no rites involved. It comes to them through pure and abundant grace, through Christ who says: "Let the little children come to me and do not hinder them, for the kingdom of heaven belongs to such as these." This promise makes glad and assures all the saints about their children.
>
> Christian parents have in their hearts a sure faith in the grace of God concerning their beloved children. They believe that their children are sons and daughters of the kingdom. They believe that their children are under grace and have the promise of eternal life, not by any ceremony but through Christ. As long as they are mere children they are clean, holy, saved, and pleasing unto God, be they alive or dead.
>
> Christian parents thank God for his love to their children, so they train their children in godly ways. They correct, chastise, teach, and admonish them. They exemplify to them the irreproachable life until the children are able to hear the Word for themselves, to believe it and obey it. Then is the time, and not until then, that they should receive Christian baptism as Christ and the apostles practiced and taught. . . .
>
> If children die before coming to the age when they can decide between good and evil, before they have come to years of understanding and before they have faith, they die under the promise of God and that by no other means than the generous promise of grace given through Christ Jesus (Luke 18:16). If they come to the age where they can decide for themselves and have faith, then they should be baptised. But if they do not accept or believe the Word when they arrive at that age, no matter whether they are baptised or not, they will be damned, as Christ himself teaches (Mark 16:16).[12]

Infant Baptism

"*Simia semper manet simia, etiamsi induatur purpura* (a monkey stays a monkey even though you dress him in purple)," wrote Menno Simons. "In the same manner infant baptism will remain a horrid stench and abomination before God, no matter how finely the learned ones adorn it with garbled passages from the Scriptures."[13]

---

11 *Ein Brief an Thomas Müntzer,* September 5, 1524.

12 *Verclaringhe des christelycken doopsels* . . . ca. 1542

13 *ibid.*

Then, in a more serious tone he added:

> Because true Christian baptism involves such great promises, among them the promise of remission of sins (Acts 2:38, Mark 16:16, 1 Cor. 12:13, 1 Peter 3:21, Eph. 4:5), some would like to baptise their children. But they fail to notice that the above promises are given only to those who believe and obey the Word of God.[14]

Conrad Grebel wrote:

> The baptised are dead to the old life and circumcised in their hearts. They have died to sin with Christ, having been buried with him in baptism and arisen with him. . . . To apply such things to children is without and against the Scriptures.[15]

The Mode of Baptism

The first Anabaptists did not write about the mode of baptism. They baptised by pouring or immersion, in rivers or ponds, or in the houses, barns, caves, mills, or forests where they had their services. Shortly before Conrad Grebel baptised Wolf Ulimann in the Rhine River, Felix Manz baptized Hans Bruggbach[16] at a house at Zürich in Switzerland. This is the account:

After Hans confessed his sins and requested baptism Georg Cajacob (Blaurock) asked him, "Do you desire baptism?"

Hans replied, "Yes."

Then Felix Manz asked, "Who will forbid me that I should baptise him?"

"No one," answered Georg.

Then Felix Manz took a metal dipper (of the kind commonly found in Swiss kitchens) and poured water over Hans' head saying: "I baptise you in the name of God the Father, God the Son, and God the Holy Spirit."

The first Anabaptists saw no conflict between baptising by either pouring or by immersion. Menno Simons, who no doubt baptised mostly by pouring, freely spoke of "burial in baptism." Conrad Grebel, who baptised by immersion after the example of Christ and the apostles, wrote about the apostles themselves:

> After that, they were poured over with water. Just as they were cleansed within by the

---

14 *ibid.*

15 *op. cit.*

16 Hans Bruggbach (Brubacher) appears to have been the ancestor of Peter Brubacher of Wädenswil, mentioned in the *Ausbund* and in the *Martyrs Mirror*—and as such, of the Brubachers (Brubakers) now living in Pennsylvania and southern Ontario.

coming the Holy Spirit, so they were poured over with water, externally, to signify the inner cleansing and dying to sin.[17]

Einverleibung

Jesus is the head of the body of believers. The first Anabaptists believed that in water baptism we become members of that body. They called it an *Einverleibung*, literally a going into and connecting onto a body, or a growing into each other. That

An Ausbund writer wrote:

> Those of us who have been washed with the blood of Christ and made free from sin, are tied together in our hearts. We now walk in the Spirit who shows us the right way and who rules in us. The Spirit rules in our sinful bodies, that are now dead. And in Christ we become members of his body (einverleibt), and buried with him through baptism in his death. Now we live for him and keep his commandments.[18]

Menno Simons wrote:

> Those who hear and believe the Word of God are baptised into the body. They have a good conscience. They receive remission of sins, they put on Christ and become members of the most holy body of Jesus Christ. . . . All who hear the Gospel and believe in it, all those who are made alive by the Holy Spirit within them, no matter of what nationality or speech they are, Frisians, or Hollanders, Germans, Belgians, Jews, Gentiles, men or women, all are baptised into one spiritual body of which Christ is the head—that is, they are baptised into Jesus' church community (Col. 1:18).[19]

Noah's Ark and Jesus' Community

The story of the flood held symbolic significance for the first Anabaptists. Noah was Jesus. The ark was Jesus' church community, and the door into it was baptism. Jakob de Keersgieter, burned at the stake at Brugge in

Belgium wrote:

Baptism must be received upon faith for a burial of sin, a washing of regeneration, a covenant of the Christian life, and a putting on of the body of Christ. It is an ingrafting into the true olive tree and vine of Christ, and entrance into the spiritual ark of Noah, which belongs to Christ.[20]

After baptism the Anabaptists found themselves within the body of Christ, breaking bread together and sharing their material things. Whoever took part in the life of the body showed himself to be a member of it, but beyond this, "church

---

17 *Protestation und Schutzschrift,* 1524.

18 *Ausbund,* 114:4-5

19 *Verclaringhe des christelycken doopsels* . . . ca. 1542

20 *ibid.*

membership," in the beginning, did not exist.

Thousands of converts were baptised into the Anabaptist movement at meetings among people they never saw again. The believers (above all, the servants and messengers) moved about continually, and congregations that numbered several hundred people at one meeting might well number fifty or less in the next—and vice versa. Only in Moravia, at the beginning, did congregations become stable units. There they lived on the *Bruderhöfe* (also known as *Haushaben*, communal households in rented buildings in town) but their teaching on baptism remained the same. Messengers from the Bruderhöfe still baptised converts spontaneously wherever they travelled, and only those who decided to move to Moravia actually became part of the settled congregations there.

Bundesgenossen

Grown into each other through baptism into the body of Christ, the first Anabaptists called one another companions of the covenant (*Bundesgenossen*). To this teaching, Martin Luther and the translators of the first Dutch (Biestkens) Bible made a contribution. They translated 1 Peter 3:20-21 like this: "A few people, eight in all, were saved through water, and this water symbolises baptism that now saves you also—not the removal of dirt from the body but the *covenant* of a good conscience with God through the resurrection of Jesus Christ."

Baptism as a covenant and the resulting "society of the covenant" (*Bundesvereinigung*) brought the first Anabaptists to say like Jakob Kautz and Wilhelm Reublin in a letter to the town council of Strasbourg in 1529:

When the merciful God called us by his grace to marvellous light, we did not reject the heavenly message but made a covenant with God in our hearts to serve him in holiness all our days. . . . Then we reported our purpose to the companions of the covenant.

Pilgram Marpeck addressed his major book, published in 1542, to "the Christian society of the covenant (*Bundesvereinigung*) of all true believers."

Menno Simons' addressed his earliest Anabaptist writing to "all the true companions of the covenant scattered abroad."

Loyalty

Brothers and sisters deeply conscious of their covenant with Jesus become deeply loyal to him and to one another. In a letter to me, a friend once mentioned "the Anabaptist emphasis on corporate discipleship" as the "centrepiece of our great heritage." He was partially correct. The first Anabaptists spoke of corporate discipleship, but they revolved around Jesus, not around "corporate discipleship."

Jesus was the centrepiece.

The first Anabaptists did not bother writing about loyalty to the church, loyalty to the brotherhood, or loyalty to God-ordained leaders. They did not make two commitments, one to the head and one to the body. Their covenant with Jesus made all other relationships conditional.

The oneness, the love and the community that resulted from the Anabaptists' covenant with Jesus made their enemies suspicious. The Catholics and Protestants began to suspect that the Anabaptists had sworn themselves to one another with some secret and terrible oath. But when questioned about this, Ambrutz Spittelmayr said:

> I know of no other commitment we make to one another than the covenant we make in baptism. . . . We bind ourselves to God and become one with him in love, in spirit, in faith, and in baptism. At the same time God binds himself to us and promises to stay with us through thick and thin.[21]

Married to Jesus

The first Anabaptists spoke often of being "married to Christ." At baptism they did not bind themselves to a congregation or denomination, not to rules or constitutions or human authorities, but to Jesus—like a bride binds herself to the groom. Wherever their fellow believers followed Jesus, they were committed to supporting them. Wherever they did not, they were committed to oppose them. Hans Betz wrote:

> Faith comes from hearing Christian preaching, then when a person believes, he must be baptised. Baptism in Christ is the covenant of a good conscience. . . . the promise to live from this point onward in the will of God.
>
> We make a promise to God in baptism that we are bound to keep. Like a wife is subject to her husband here on the earth, so we become subject to Christ when we marry him in baptism.[22]

The "rose red blood of Christ" was unspeakably precious to the first Anabaptists. It released them from the debt of sin that they could not possibly have paid. But logic told them that Jesus who bought their debt had the right of claiming them as his bond servants.

This covenant with Jesus led them . . .

---

[21] From the written testimony of Ambrutz Spittelmayr, of October 25, 1527.

[22] *Ausbund,* 108:5-6

On to Communion

South of the baths at Ragatz and the Swiss village of Maienfeld, south of the snow-crowned peaks of Falkniß and Scesaplana where the setting sun lights up the snowfields of the Glarner and Rhaetian Alps lies the deep valley of the Domleschg. It lies in the part of Switzerland that is neither German nor French, but Romansh.

Romansh is the language of the Grisons (great grey mountains) of Switzerland. It is a Latin dialect, similar to Spanish or Romanian. It came to the Grisons with immigrants from Roman Italy who settled there, a thousand years before Georg Cajacob was born in the Domleschg in the village of Bonaduz.

Speaking Romansh, Georg found Latin easier to learn than German. But by 1513, when he was twenty-one years old, he finished his studies at the University of Leipzig in Germany and became a priest.[1]

He returned to the Grisons, and served for two years at Trins, across the river from Bonaduz where the Domleschg meets the canyon of the upper Rhein.

Georg said the *missa fidelium*. He baptised babies. He listened to confessions and absolved people from their sins. But he well knew that both he and the people whom he served lived in sin, and he did not feel forgiven. He was a tall, lively young man with a dark complexion. People called him "Strong Georg." But he was weak. He lived under the power of sin and had no strength to overcome it. He sinned time after time until he left the priesthood after two years and got married.

Getting married did not free Georg from sin. He still felt weak in temptation and longed to know Jesus, so he travelled north with his young wife to look for help in the Protestant city of Zürich.

The Protestants disappointed Georg. He could see they did not follow Jesus. But the Spirit of God moved his heart when he met Felix Manz, Conrad Grebel, and other seekers at Felix Manz's house on the winter evening of January 21, 1525. Georg asked Conrad to baptize him. Then Georg baptized the others, and they remembered Jesus by breaking bread and drinking wine together. Not long after this, the Protestant authorities caught Georg Cajacob, (by now nicknamed *Blaurock*[2]) and imprisoned him in the *Hexenturm* (witches' tower) prison at Zürich. He escaped several times, but they caught him again, and called him to answer

---

[1] Several writers speak of Georg Cajacob (of the house of Jacob) as "an ex- monk from Chur." Huldrych Zwingli seems to have thought he was one, but there is no historical evidence that he ever spent time in a monastery.

[2] Before he was well-known in Zürich, Georg attended a meeting and commented on what was said. One of those who attended the meeting asked who spoke, and someone answered: "The man in the blue coat." After that the people called him *Blaurock* ("blue coat").

before Huldrych Zwingli at the city court.

Zwingli called Georg a "great, foolish dreamer," too ignorant to read German correctly. He accused Georg and his companions of "mocking the church," of trying to "build a church within the church," and of overthrowing "divine and human authority." Especially offensive to Zwingli and the Protestant court was the way Georg baptised people and held communion services in ordinary houses, in secret, and without permission. To this, Georg replied:

> Christ the Lord sent his disciples out to teach all people and gave them power to grant remission of sins and, as an outward sign of forgiveness, to baptise them. When I taught this too, some turned in tears to me and asked me to baptise them. This I could not refuse. I baptised them according to their wish and called upon the name of Christ for them.
>
> I further taught them love and unity and to have all things in common, like the apostles commanded us. I taught them that they should always remember the death of Christ and his poured out blood. I showed them the practice of Christ in the nighttime meal. We broke bread and drank wine together so that they might remember that they are redeemed by one body of Christ and made clean by one blood, and that through this they were brothers and sisters one of another in Christ the Lord.[3]

A Nighttime Meal

On Feb. 5, 1525, Hans Ockenfuoss testified before the Protestant court at Zürich: "Two weeks ago I was in Zollikon in Jakob Hottinger's house. Conrad Grebel and some other men were there. They spoke of baptism and the nighttime meal. After that, Conrad took a loaf of bread and divided it among us. He ate from it too and said that from now on we want to lead a Christian life."

Leonhard Schiemer wrote from the prison at Rattenberg on the Inn:

> Those who have become one body and one loaf of bread in Christ—those who are minded alike (*gleichgesinnt*)—should keep the nighttime meal in remembrance of his death. Through this, everyone should be admonished to become like Christ, in obedience to the Father.[4]

Hans Betz wrote from the dungeon of the castle at Passau in Bavaria:

> Mark the counsel of God: Christ has set the pattern for a nighttime meal of bread and wine for his church community—the community that keeps itself from sin. If she eats the nighttime meal in remembrance of him, death will not overtake her.[5]

Huddled Around Jesus

When I began to read what the first Anabaptists wrote, two expressions

---

[3] From a letter Georg wrote to the city council of Zürich in the spring of 1525.

[4] *Eine Erklärung der 12 Artikel des christlichen Glaubens,* ca. 1526.

[5] *Ausbund,* 92:15

stood out to me. One was the mention of Jesus as our *Hauptmann* (captain or "head man"). The other was the term *kleiner Hauf* used for the followers of Jesus. *Kleiner Hauf* literally means a little heap or a huddle. At first I had a hard time picturing Jesus' followers like this. But when I began to see the place of Jesus in the Anabaptist movement, it became clear to me. Jesus is the captain, and his followers huddle around him. "Look to the captain. . . . Leap to your captain's side," wrote an Ausbund writer.[6] Those who follow Christ do this continually to get their directions from him.

The first Christians huddled around Jesus by breaking bread and drinking wine in remembrance of him whenever they got together. The first Anabaptists, out of love and necessity, did the same. In the first published statement[7] of the movement they wrote:

> Every time we meet as brothers, we should eat the nighttime meal together, to proclaim in this way the death of the Lord. In doing this we help one another to remember how Christ gave himself up and how his blood was poured out for us. In the same way we need to be willing, for Christ's sake, to give up our bodies and our lives for the brothers.[8]

The first Anabaptists could not have pictured a formal worship service without the breaking of bread. Christian worship without the Eucharist (the Greek word for thanksgiving, used by Paul in 1 Corinthians 10:16) was, before the sixteenth century, unknown.

Michael Sattler wrote:

> Do not forget the meetings, but put forth effort to have them regularly. Pray together, for all the saints, and break the bread together—so much the oftener (desto fleissiger) as you see the Lord's day approaching.[9]

When several Anabaptists were asked before the Dutch court in 1534 what they did in their meetings they replied: "In our meetings we read and discuss the Gospel, after which one of us breaks the bread and distributes it to all, that the bread is not able to save us, but it is only taken in memory of the suffering of our Lord."[10]

---

6 *Ausbund,* 78:1

7 This statement, prepared by the Anabaptists of Switzerland, possibly in 1526, was circulating before the *Brüderliche Vereinigung* of Schleitheim made its appearance. It corresponds closely to the first confession of the south German and Austrian Anabaptists, written by Leonhard Schiemer.

8 From *Christlicher Ordnung . . . damitt die lieb und einickeit erhalten wird*, Bern, ca. 1526.

9 From *An die Gemeinde Gottes zu Horb* . . . 1527

10 From a report of the Court of Holland to the Regent Maria of Hungary, then reigning at Brussels, dated February 17, 1534.

Both in the south (Switzerland, southern Germany, and Austria) and in the north (along the lower Rhein and in the Netherlands) the Anabaptists met for the nighttime meal at least once a week. "Small fellowships of Anabaptists sprang up like mushrooms everywhere," reads one report. "They moved from house to house for meetings in order to remain inconspicuous, where they read and studied the Scriptures and celebrated the nighttime meal."[11]

Conrad Grebel stated in one of his letters, "The nighttime meal shall be practiced often and used much."[12]

A Wedding Feast

In southern Germany the Anabaptists spoke of baptism as the sign of a believer's engagement (*Verlobung*) to Jesus, and of the nighttime meal as the marriage feast in which the bread and the wine were the rings.
In the Netherlands, Menno Simons wrote:

> Oh delightful assembly and Christian marriage feast! Feast commanded and ordained by the Lord himself. Bodily pleasure and bodily appetite do not belong here. But glorious and holy mysteries are set before and desired by true believers in bread and wine!
>
> Oh delightful Christian assembly! No senseless songs, but peace and unity among the brothers. Words of grace. Glorious benefits.
>
> Favour, love, service, tears, prayers, cross, and death are set forth with delightful thanksgiving and holy joy!
>
> Oh delightful Christian feast! The unrepentant are not invited. Harlots, rogues, adulterers, robbers, liars, tyrants, and those who shed blood must stay outside. But true Christians come. Born of God, walking with Christ, they come to love and believe. They are members of his body, flesh of his flesh, and bone of his bone.
>
> Oh delightful assembly and Christian marriage feast! No gluttonous eating and drinking. No vanity of pipes and drums. But hungry souls are filled with bread from heaven, the divine Word. They drink the wine of the Holy Ghost and sing and play in peace before the Lord.[13]

A Parable

The *Teaching of the Twelve Apostles* (Didache) written in the first century after Jesus said:

> As this broken bread, once dispersed over the hills, was brought together and became one loaf, so may your church be brought together from the ends of the earth into your kingdom.

---

[11] From C. A. Cornelius, *Historische Arbeiten vornehmlich zur Reformationsgeschichte,* (Leipzig, 1899).

[12] Letter to Thomas Müntzer, September 5, 1524.

[13] *Dat Fundament des Christelycken leers* . . . 1539.

This parable, known to the first Anabaptists, appears many times in their songs and writings. An Ausbund writer wrote:

> This is how Christ taught his disciples to keep the Passover in his flesh: He broke for them the bread and gave thanks. He gave them the cup and they drank. ... With the bread he showed that whoever has his Spirit belongs to him, becomes one flesh with him, a member of his body and of his church community for which he died. Like one bread is made from many grains, and one wine is made from many grapes, all true Christians become one bread and one wine in Christ the Lord. He sustains us and gives us true love in Gemeinschaft with him.[14]

Menno Simons wrote:

> Just as natural bread is made of many grains ground in the mill, kneaded with water, and baked over the fire, so is the Lord's Gemeinschaft. True believers are broken in their hearts with the mill of God's Word. Then they are baptised with the water of the Holy Ghost and formed by the fire of pure love into one body.[15]

Dirk Philips wrote:

> Indeed it is a marvellous and blessed union where all Christians are one bread and one body in Christ Jesus. They are one bread . . . baked by the fire of love. They are baptised by one Spirit into one body, and must like a natural body be one heart and one soul. They serve one another, help one another, and comfort one another, just like the members of a natural body.[16]

Before they beheaded him at Schwatz in Austria in 1528, Hans Schlaffer wrote:

> The body of Christ on the earth is the Gemeinschaft of those who believe on him. Whoever eats the bread of the nighttime meal expresses with that his desire to live in Gemeinschaft with this body and to be a part of it in all things—to stick with the Gemeinschaft though joy and sorrow, riches and poverty, honour and shame, mourning and rejoicing, death and life. He expresses his desire to give everything he has, both body and life for his brothers even as Christ gave himself for us.[17]

Inner and Outer Gemeinschaft

The first Anabaptists believed that the nighttime meal, like baptism, is an outer witness (Mitzeugnis) of inner Gemeinschaft with Christ. They believed that inner Gemeinschaft without the outer witness of bread and wine is incomplete. Jaques d'Auchy, killed at Leeuwarden in 1559, called those who spiritualised the meaning of the nighttime meal "heretics" and "destroyers of the breaking of bread." But the Anabaptists believed just as strongly that the outer witness without an inner sense of Gemeinschaft was incomplete, useless, and actually

---

14 *Ausbund*, 55:21-23

15 *Dat Fundament des Christelycken leers* . . . 1539

16 *op. cit.*

17 *Ein einfältig Gebet* . . . 1528

harmful.

"What does it help to eat of the holy meal if we do not enjoy the fruits it stands for, death to self, love and unity?" asked Menno Simons. "Outer communion profits nothing if we do not live in inner Gemeinschaft with the Lord and his body."[18]

In another article Menno wrote:

> Be they emperor or king, rich or learned, all who with a proud heart seat themselves at the Lord's table eat and drink to their own damnation. All who boast of the Lord's name but reject his commands and blameless example eat and drink to their own damnation. All who love houses and lands, possessions, friends, children, the world, favour, ease, and honour in this life more than they love Christ eat and drink to their own damnation.
>
> He who would sit with the disciples and guests of Christ at the Lord's table must be sound in the faith and blameless in conduct and life. Be he rich or poor, high or low, emperor, king, prince, earl, knight, or nobleman, none is excepted from this rule. The pious cannot partake of the nighttime meal with those who err in doctrine and whose lives are carnal. Such people are not in Christ. They must be kept outside until they repent and so become one in Spirit with Christ and his body.[19]
>
> Without penitence neither water, bread, nor wine avail in Christ, even if they were administered by the apostles themselves. That which avails before God is a new creature, a converted, changed and broken heart, a true fear and love of God, love for neighbours, a subdued, humble, sober, and peaceful life according to Jesus' example. Where there is such a new being there is indeed the true baptism and the true meal. To be baptised externally and to partake of the nighttime meal merely in Letter and appearance but not inwardly before God is to mimic God's work. It is hypocrisy and deceit. [20]

Without Superstition

The Anabaptists valued the nighttime meal so highly that they celebrated it together even if it cost their lives. But they rejected the superstitions that had grown up around the *missa fidelium* during the Dark Ages.

Amsterdam, centre of Anabaptist activity in the north, was only one of the many pilgrimage sites in the German countries of Europe. Thousands of pilgrims came to Amsterdam every year to visit its *heilige stede* (holy place) erected on the site of a miracle they said took place in 1345. A sick man there had received the host (the consecrated wafer of the mass). He vomited it up. His wife tried to burn it, but the flames would not consume it. Catholic leaders declared this a miracle and set loose a flood of pilgrims that greatly increased the prosperity and fame of

---

18 *Een lieffelijcke vermaninghe ofte onderwijsinghe wt Gods woort* . . . ca. 1558

19 *Dat Fundament des Christelycken leers* . . . 1539

20 *Een Klare beantwoordinge, over een Schrift Gellii Fabri* . . . 1554.

Amsterdam throughout the following centuries.

Dutch and German priests told stories of the host miraculously saving Christians from the Muslims and curing the blind, the sick and the crippled. A lamb could be saved from a wolf by the host. One priest put the host on the tongue of a sick cow and cured her. Many were the stories of how the host had turned into a child or bled when it was broken. People believed that one did not grow older while eating the host.

When the Anabaptists, in the middle of this, began to teach that the bread and wine stayed bread and wine, that Christ was to be found in spiritual Gemeinschaft but not in the elements of the nighttime meal, they brought Europe down upon them in wrath. An influential priest of Amsterdam compared the Anabaptists to the plagues of Egypt and called the people to pray at the *heilige stede* for a miracle to drive away these "devilish pigs and frogs."

Posters and pamphlets were used in the crusade against the Anabaptists. One picture showed the woman picking the vomited host out of the flames with a ring of angels kneeling around her in worship of it. It came with a text lamenting the fact that people were "losing respect for apostolic tradition, the ceremonies of the church, and the pronouncements of its holy fathers."

The Anabaptists replied calmly. Menno Simons wrote:

> We are not commanded in the Scriptures to argue about the tangible elements of the nighttime meal, for of what substance the bread and wine consist may be felt, seen, and tasted. We should strive rather to confirm ourselves to what the elements stand for.[21]

Conrad Grebel wrote:

> The mass is not to be reformed but abolished. The nighttime meal is to be restored as the apostles practiced it. Only the words of Christ are to be used, and they are not to be treated as having any magical meaning. In order to avoid a superstitious devotion and a falling away from the spiritual, everything out of the ordinary must stop. No special bread, no special cup, no priestly clothes and customs, and no special singing is to accompany the nighttime meal. It is a meal of Gemeinschaft and should not be taken alone, nor by dying persons. . . . All the details of the nighttime meal shall remind the believer of the body and blood of Christ and of the witness on the cross, so that he shall be willing to live and suffer for the sake of Christ and the brothers, the head and the members of the body.[22]

Communion with Jesus

After they beat him and drove him out of Zürich on the day they drowned Felix Manz, Georg Cajacob travelled through the mountains of Switzerland and

[21] *Dat Fundament des Christelycken leers . . .* 1539

[22] *op. cit.*

Austria, teaching, baptising, and breaking bread in the name of Christ. He returned to the Grisons and spoke to his own people, calling them to get up and follow the real Christ to find forgiveness of their sins. Many believed and great numbers gathered in secret to hear him speak—until the Austrian authorities caught him near Klausen (now the city of Chiusa in Italy), on August 14, 1529. There they tortured him at the Guffidaun castle, condemned him under a barrage of accusations, and burned him at the stake on September 6, 1529.

Before his death, Georg wrote:

> Prepare us for the nighttime meal, oh God, through Christ your beloved Son! Clothe us with your Spirit. Free us from death and suffering! When we shall eat at last of that nighttime meal, who shall wait upon us? The one who knows our hearts and redeems us from our sin!
>
> Blessed are those invited to the Lord's nighttime meal! Blessed are those who stay with Christ through all tribulation. He suffered. He hung on the cross, and those who follow him must suffer now. Oh Lord, give us pure love! Give us love to walk our way with joy! When our time comes to go, may we not, like the foolish virgins, find that the door to the feast has been closed. They cried, "Lord! Lord!" But their oil had run out while they were sleeping.
>
> Blessed is the one who watches with the wise virgins. He will inherit eternal possessions, and his eyes will see the clarity of God. The king will break out with a trumpet blast! The elect will join his parade! Therefore Zion, holy community of Christ, look at what you have received! Hold it and keep yourself pure. Then you shall inherit the crown![23]

In Jesus' communion, the first Anabaptists followed him…

---

[23] *Ausbund,* 5:22

On to Community

In the old city of Augsburg in Bavaria, Jakob Wideman decided to follow Jesus in 1527. Augsburg was a wealthy city. The Fuggers, Europe's richest and most powerful bankers lived there. But when Jakob found Jesus, he left money and earthly securities behind. Immediately after his baptism the authorities banished him from the city and he fled with others to Nikolsburg in Moravia.

The Anabaptist movement had swept through Nikolsburg a short time before. Perhaps as many as twelve thousand converts had been baptised. But Jakob Wideman and the refugees from Augsburg did not feel at home among them. Not all the Anabaptists of Nikolsburg had given up their possessions to follow Jesus. Some, like the lords von Liechtenstein, had kept their palaces, their servants, their swords, and their government positions. Jakob and other sincere seekers spoke against this, and within a year there were two Anabaptist congregations in Nikolsburg—the large *Schwertler* group (those who carry swords) and the *Kleinhäufler* (those of the little heap). In 1528 the Schwertler drove the Kleinhäufler, under the leadership of Jakob Wideman and Philip Plener, out of the city.

For a long time they walked, leading their children and carrying bundles of bedding and food on their backs. They numbered about 200 people, not counting the children. They walked north past Tannewitz in the direction of Muschau until they came to an abandoned estate called Bogenitz. There they camped for a day and a night.

At Bogenitz, after lifting their hands to heaven and calling on God for help, the Kleinhäufler chose Franz Intzinger, Jakob Mändel, Thoman Arbeiter, and Urban Bader to be their ministers of material needs. Jakob Mändel had been the general manager of the estates of the lords von Liechtenstein. Then these four men spread out a coat in front of the people "and everyone with a willing spirit, not out of obligation, threw onto it what he had."

From this time onward, the Kleinhäufler had their things in common. The lords von Kaunitz allowed them to settle in rented buildings in the Moravian town of Austerlitz. Jakob Wideman was their servant of the Word. Ulrich Stadler, another servant, joined him. Philip Plener settled with a community of brothers in the city of Auspitz. Jörg Zaunring and Jakob Hutter came with refugees from the mountains of Austria. Dozens, then hundreds and thousands upon thousands of new believers joined these Moravian communities—Rossitz, Lundenburg, Schäkowitz, Dämberschitz, Pausram, Pellertitz, Rampersdorf, Stignitz, Koblitz, Altenmarkt, Neumühl, Prutschan, Landshut, Nemschitz, and Maskowitz . . . a steadily growing list of communities, which in thirty years became the home of an estimated 60,000 new Christians.

Jesus the Founder of Community

Jesus Christ, who lived in community of goods with his disciples, prayed for them and all who would choose to follow him: "Holy Father, protect them by the power of your name— the name you gave me—so that they may be one as we are one .. . .May they be brought to complete unity to let the world know that you sent me and have loved them even as you have loved me" (John 17:11, 23).

The Castle at Mikulov (Nikolsburg) in Moravia, a province of the Holy Roman Empire that had as little to do with Rome as possible. Already inhab-ited by two non-Catholic groups, the Utraquists (followers of Jan Hus) and the Unitas Fratrum (Unity of Brothers), the town attracted Protestants as early as 1524, and during the 1530s about twelve thousand Anabaptists.

The first Anabaptists surrounded Jesus in community. They shared everything one with another—blessings as well as hardships—and the world saw in them the love of God.

Felix Manz, writing to the Zürich council in the early months of 1525 wrote that immediately after baptising new believers he "taught them further about love and unity and the holding of all things in common as in the second chapter of Acts."[1]

Johannes Kessler wrote about the first Anabaptist congregation in Switzerland:

> Now because most of Zollikon was rebaptised and held that they were the true Christian church, they also undertook, like the early Christians, to practice community of temporal goods (as can be read in the Acts of the Apostles). They broke the locks off their

---

1 *Quellen zur Geschichte der Täufer in der Schweiz, 1: Zürich*, ed. Leonhard von Muralt and Walter Schmid (Zürich: Theologischer Verlag 1952)

doors, chests, and cellars, and ate food and drink in good fellowship without discrimination.[2]

The joint council of Zürich, Sankt Gallen and Bern condemned the Anabaptists in 1527. One thing they held against them was their teaching on economics:

> They say that no Christian, if he is really sincere, may either give or receive interest on money. They say that all temporal goods are free and common and everyone has full rights to use them. We have been informed by trustworthy people that they often said this in the beginning of their movement, and in this way they got the poor and the simple to join with them.[3]

Sebastian Franck, while describing the Anabaptists, wrote:

> As far as one could see they taught nothing but love, faith, and the cross. They broke bread one with another as evidence of their unity and love. They helped each other faithfully as brothers, lending and giving, and they taught that all things should be held in common.[4]

The Anabaptists themselves wrote in their first statement of belief:

> The brothers and sisters of this church community shall have no property of their own. Rather, as in the time of the apostles they shall have all things in common. The property of the church community shall be considered one sole property, out of which the poor shall receive, every man according to his need. Like in the time of the apostles no brothers shall be left wanting.[5]

The first statement of belief of the Anabaptists in Austria, written by Leonhard Schiemer, includes this article:

> The brothers and sisters shall give themselves body and soul to God in his community. Every gift that God gives shall be held in common after the practice of the apostles and the first Christians. In this way the needy within the community will be taken care of.[6]

Peter Rideman, in a letter to the brothers in Austria wrote:

> Truly it is a sure sign—those who leave community of goods and go back to private property walk away from God. They lose their first love, and become enemies of God and thieves of what he gives to us.[7]

---

[2] *Sabbata* . . . ca. 1530

[3] From a mandate of the city councils of Zürich, Bern and Sankt Gallen against the Anabaptists, 1527.

[4] *Chronika, Zeybuch und Geschichtbibel,* 1531

[5] *Christlicher Ordnung . . . damitt die lieb und einickeit erhalten wird* (Bern, Switzerland, ca. 1526

[6] *Eine Erklärung der 12 Artikel des christlichen Glaubens,* ca. 1527

[7] *Peter Ridemans brief an die philippischen Brüder im land an der Ennß,* 1527

An outer testimony

Spirit baptism is an inner experience, taught the Anabaptists of Moravia. It is not complete until we receive the outer baptism of water. Communion is inner, spiritual union with God. It is not complete until we outwardly partake of the bread and the wine. In the same way, brotherly love is the inner, spiritual union of brothers and sisters in Jesus. It is not complete until we clasp our hands, embrace one another with our arms, and share our outward possessions in Christian community. Where such a materialisation of love takes place, the true Gospel of the kingdom has been preached.

Sebastian Franck, one of the Anabaptists' principle sources of information about the early Christians, helped them understand this type of love. He described how the early Christians lived:

> The bishop and his servants, the deacons, used to be their householders and stewards. They took care of both the spiritual and physical needs of the church. They distributed their possessions, which they held in common, to meet everyone's need. But after some time they began to get greedy. They began to turn common goods into private property and to use them for personal gain.[8]

Sebastian Franck stated his own opinion as well:

> To be fair, everything should be held in common. . . . Private property, like the use of worldly force, began when the wicked Nimrod stepped out of God's order after the flood. Not only the Apostles testified against this evil, but Plato and Epicurus as well.[9]

It is no wonder that the first Anabaptists, reading such information and committed to following Jesus at all costs, found themselves on a collision course with the ungodly capitalism of their day. Soon after the first adult baptisms in southern Germany Hans Römer directed a seeker, Ludwig Spon to Sorga, in Hesse: "There in a village near Hersfeld, called Sorga, there is a congregation that leads a good life. Everyone helps everyone else with goods and food when necessary. Forty or fifty people get together there."[10]

This particular group of Anabaptists at Sorga, after establishing relationships with Philip Plener in Auspitz, suffered a mass arrest. The authorities questioned the heads of the homes: "May a Christian own property?"

Answers received varied in detail but they were consistent: "A Christian may have property but in such a way that he has it not, and no one should call

---

[8] *op. cit.*

[9] *ibid.*

[10] *Urkundliche Quellen zur hessischen Reformationsgeschichte, 4: Wiedertäuferakten 1527-1626,* ed. Günther Franz (Marburg: N. G. Elwert 1951)

property his own. . . . Holders of property yet owning nothing, Christians use property only as long as it pleases God. Then, when a neighbour or when God needs it, they let it go. . . . Christians may have property but they should remain *gelassen* (unattached)."[11]

Other Anabaptists captured at the Hessian village of Berka said: "Everything except husbands and wives should be held in common. . . . Everyone who believes like us has just as much right to our belongings as we do, but those who don't share our faith do not."[12]

Heini Frei, captured and interrogated at Zollikon in Switzerland, said about the Anabaptists (after his recantation): They believed that everything should be pooled as common property, and whatever someone needed he should take from the common store.[13]

Love that Cannot Help but Share

Community, for the Swiss and South German Anabaptists, was not a legalistic obligation. It did not come from obedience to apostolic example, nor was it a penance. They shared their things in a spontaneous, joyful way because true love, they said, had unfolded itself in their hearts.

Gabriel Ascherham, trained as a furrier in the old Bavarian city of Nürnberg, became the leader of a large Anabaptist community at Rossitz in Moravia, in the late 1520s. Coming from Silesia, Bavaria and many parts of Switzerland and Austria, around one thousand two hundred brothers and sisters lived there in voluntary community of goods. Gabriel wrote:

> The apostles did not preach anything about community of goods nor order any one to keep it, in the first church at Jerusalem. But when they heard the good news of Christ and the kingdom of God the people believed and came to take part in the visible kingdom of the Holy Ghost. He filled them with joy and fixed their hearts upon heavenly blessings, so that they counted earthly possessions as nothing. Willingly, on their own and without being told, motivated only by the joy in their hearts, they went and sold their property, bringing the money from it to lay at the apostles' feet. Then they distributed to everyone according to his need. The first believers began community of goods without being told, everyone giving out of his own free will. Community of goods, as a result, was an open witness of the kingdom of God that had already come to them. It was not something commanded by men for the sake of the kingdom of God.[14]

Four hundred seventy years after the founding of the community at Rossitz, a nineteen-year-old Anabaptist—a boy who decided against becoming a Roman

---

11 *op. cit.*

12 Paul Wappler, *Die Stellung Kursachsens und des Landgrafen Philipp von Hessen zur Täuferbewegung* (Münster: Aschendorff 1910) 168-176

13 *Quellen . . .* Zürich, 48

14 From *Vom Unterschied Göttlicher und Menschlicher Weisheit*, first published in 1544.

Catholic priest and who joined the movement in Central America—put the same belief to words:

I believe that to live in community only to benefit from the blessings of it is wrong. Unless God has first called us to spiritual community and has placed community of goods into our hearts, all other motives or reasons for seeking community are wrong. Unless God has given us such a love that we cannot help but share our goods and our time with others, whatever we try is in vain.

I do believe that community should be optional, but why should it be optional? For one thing we do not want to force anyone into something that he or she has not been called to. But at the same time, if a person receives the call from God to live in community, then community is no longer an optional thing, but the will of God for that person. Now, my question is: Have we been called into community? If we have, then are we going to let preferences, likes and dislikes, etc. keep us from it? I surely would not consider going into community with others if this sense of belonging together is not there between us and them. This sense of belonging together is what holds people together as they work out their differences. As long as we can feel that, we should not be afraid of going ahead with whatever the Lord puts before us.

An Ausbund writer wrote:

To be like Christ we love one another, through everything, here on this earth. We love one another, not just with words but in deeds. . . . If we have of this world's goods (no matter how much or how little) and see that our brother has a need, but do not share with him what we have freely received—how can we say that we would be ready to give our lives for him if necessary?

The one who is not faithful in the smallest thing, and who still seeks his own good which his heart desires—how can he be trusted with a charge over heavenly things? Let us keep our eyes on love![15]

The Year of Release

The first Anabaptists found the promise of Christian community in the Old Testament year of release. Peter Walpot wrote:

For six years the Israelites could harvest their crops, every man for himself, but the seventh year was a year of release. It was proclaimed that the land should hold a solemn Sabbath unto the Lord.

On this seventh year the Israelites could not harvest their crops. Everything the land produced was to be held in common and enjoyed by everyone—by the father of the household and his servants, by the cattle and by the wild animals of the land. Slaves were to be released with all manner of gifts and presents, and whoever had lent anything to his neighbour was to cancel the debt in the year of release. It was to be a glorious time, like a wedding feast, and it was a picture of the time of the new covenant in Christ.

The true year of release is the acceptable year of the Lord, as the prophet himself interprets it. It is the year when those who all their lives have been slaves of the devil are released. We celebrate it by having all the goods that God has given us in common through Christian love, and by enjoying them with our neighbours, brothers, and households, not claiming anything for our own. We now live in a much more glorious and festive year of release than that of the Old Testament. We live in the year of grace.[16]

---

[15] *Ausbund,* 119:12-14

[16] *Von der wahren Glassenheit und christlicher Gemeinschafft der Güeter*, 1547

The Kingdom Community

The Kingdom of Heaven, the first Anabaptists believed, comes to earth in the community of those who follow Jesus. Ambrutz Spittelmayr, before he was beheaded for his faith in 1527, wrote:

> Nobody can inherit the kingdom unless he is poor with Christ, for a Christian has nothing of his own, no place where he can lay his head. A real Christian should not even have enough property on the face of the earth to stand on with one foot. This does not mean that he should lie down in the woods and not have a job, or that he should not have fields and pasture lands, or that he should not work. It simply means that he should not think that these things are for his own use and be tempted to say, "This house is mine. This field is mine. This dollar is mine." Rather he should say, "It is *ours*," even as we pray "*Our* Father."
>
> A Christian should not have anything of his own but should have all things in common with his brother, not letting him suffer need. In other words, I will not work that my house be filled, that my pantry be supplied with meat, but rather I will see that my brother has enough, for a Christian looks more to his neighbour than to himself.[17]

Wolfgang Brandhuber wrote in 1529:

> Watch out for false prophets who gather the money-hungry about them and resist the commands of Christ. They do not like to be told to live in the order of Christ. They become displeased upon discovering that every person in the church community cannot be his own treasurer (Secklmaister). They go around as hypocrites, contradicting the life of Christ and speaking against the order established by his beloved apostles. These false prophets say that it is not necessary to have all things in common. They say it is not necessary for every member to tell the others in love how much he has (or doesn't have). They do not want to have men made responsible by the community for everyone's money. Rather they want to keep their financial affairs to themselves and manage their own affairs. I call this wrong. Wherever God makes it possible for us to do so, we should have our things in common for his glory. If we share the most important things (our common faith in Christ), why should we not share that which is least important (our earthly goods)? I do not mean to say with this that we should carry everything together onto one pile. That would not even be proper in many situations. But the head of every home and everyone who has come to take part with him in the common faith should work together for the common fund (Seckl). This includes everyone: the married man, the young worker, the women, the girls, and whoever shares the faith. Even though every man earns his own wage (and Jesus said the labourer is worthy of his hire), love compels everyone to place his earnings into the common fund (den Seckl); yes, it is love that brings this about.[18]

Ulrich Stadler, servant of the Word at Austerlitz, who fled with a small group to when the *Kleinhäufler* were scattered for a time in the 1530s wrote:

> All gifts and goods that God gives to his own are to be held in common with all the children of God. For this we need sincere, resigned, and willing hearts in Christ. We need hearts who truly believe and trust God and are completely surrendered in Christ.
>
> People criticise us and say that the Lord never commanded us directly to have our goods in common and to appoint managers over the finances of the church community. But to

---

17 From Ambrutz's written testimony, October 25, 1527.

18 *Sendbrief*. . . 1529

live like this is to truly serve the saints. It is the outworking of love. In Christ we learn to lose ourselves in the service of the saints, to be and become poor if only others may be better off.

To hand over all lands and goods and to throw away our rights to private property takes true resignation (Gelassenheit) and a free giving of ourselves to the Lord and to his people. Each brother shall serve another. Each brother shall live and work but not just for himself.[19]

Linz, in Austria, where believers gathered here and there, in one another's homes at night. Living in a hostile city, not all of them could work, eat, and fellowship openly together, all the time, but their sense of Gemeinschaft with Jesus, and with one another remained strong. As persecution increased, it grew even stronger.

Berndt Rothmann, who wrote the main part of the *Verantwortung* published by Pilgram Marpeck and the south German Anabaptists, wrote:

We hope that the spirit of Gemeinschaft among us is so strong and glorious that community of goods will be practiced with a pure heart through the grace of God as it has never been practiced before. Not only do we have our goods in common under the supervision of the servants of material needs, but we also praise God with one heart and one inspiration through Jesus Christ, and we are inclined to serve one another in every way. All that have served their own materialism and the owning of property, such as buying, selling, and working for personal gain, interest, or speculation, even with unbelievers, and drinking and eating the sweat of the poor through whose labour we fatten ourselves—all this has disappeared completely among us through the power of love and community.[20]

Peter Walpot wrote:

To profess to believe in one holy Christian church and in the community of the holy ones is a main article of the Christian faith. This is not a profession of partial but of complete community, both in spiritual and material goods and gifts. The one who professes

---

19 From *Eine liebe Unterrichtung der Sünden halben, auch des Ausschlusses . . . und der Gemeinschaft der Güter halben*, ca. 1530

20 From *Eyne Restitution edder Eine wedderstellinge rechter unde gesunder Christliker leer gelovens unde*

to believe in the community of the holy ones, but who does not live in community of goods is a liar and not a true member of the Lord's church. How hard it is for the rich to enter the kingdom of God! It is easier for a camel to go through a needle's eye than for them to get in. If Christ would not require a total surrender and community of goods from all those who want to go in to eternal life and inherit heavenly goods, it would not be hard for the rich. It would be as easy for the rich as it is for the poor to enter the kingdom of God.[21]

Leupold Scharnschlager, servant of the brothers in Switzerland, wrote:

Some who profess the faith are neither hot nor cold. They say they have been baptised with the Holy Spirit and are members of the body of Christ. They are rich but do not know that they are miserable, blind, poor, and naked, and that the Lord will spit them out.

Some of these have gone back and allowed themselves to be taken up with the business and dealings (*Geschäft und Handel*) of this world again. They say they want to build up a business for the good of themselves and their children, but in doing so they fall back to loving the world from which they once turned away. By doing so they return to licking up what they have vomited out, and have given themselves over to foolish and hurtful lusts which drown men in destruction and perdition.

These who want to make money for themselves hinder and hold up the work of the Lord, and make it so that the knowledge of the truth does not grow. Instead of becoming rich in heavenly gifts and goods, they cause the church community to become drowsy and discouraged, weak in the faith and good works, and finally to go to sleep with the five foolish virgins.[22]

Greed and Property

Constantly on guard against the danger of "laying up treasure on earth" (Matthew 6:19), the Anabaptists of southern Germany and Austria condemned the twin evils of *Geiz* (greed) and *Eigenthum* (private property). No matter whether they lived in spontaneous or in total community of goods, the south German Anabaptists saw the holding of property only for oneself as sinful. They believed, like the early Christians, that everything we have belongs to God and our brothers.

Leonhard Schiemer, baptised and ordained by Hans Hut, wrote before they beheaded him at Rattenberg on the Inn:

Whoever gives himself to God under the cross is a child of God. But this is not enough. He must separate himself from all those who have not given themselves to God, and he must practice love and community with all those who have done so. For these are closest to him and with them he must hold in common all gifts received from God, whether instruction, abilities, property, money or anything else. What God lends to him, he must invest for the common good.[23]

Hans Betz wrote:

---

21 *Fünf Artikel*. . . 1547

22 From *Gemeine Ordnung der Glieder Christi in sieben Artikeln gestellt,* ca.

23 *op. cit.*

> God's church holds only to the customs of God. Her Gemeinschaft is in Jesus Christ and in his true peace. Like bread made of many grains that have all become one loaf, so is God's church community that has freed itself from private property.
>
> No person can live with a desire for wealth in God's community. Where there is greed the Lord Christ is not. Greed is of the devil. The devil was the first to take private property (*Eigenthum*) when he rebelled against God, the creator of life. For this reason God drove him out and consigned him to hell. The devil wanted to be like God (the true owner of property), but God could not tolerate that. . . .
>
> History tells us about greed. God gave the Israelites manna to eat. But those who gathered more than they needed found it full of worms. . . . Ananias, driven by greed lied to the Holy Ghost and God punished him. Judas, driven by greed, ended up hanging himself. In this way God punishes the greedy.
>
> Everything on this earth was created to be free. The one who claims it as private property breaks the command and robs the glory of God. For this reason he will receive his wages with the rich man in hell.
>
> God's church, washed in the blood of Christ is to be holy and pure. He who wants to be in it must purify himself by giving all he has to be used for the glory of God. He gives to his neighbor as he has freely received. . . . Oh how pleasant it is in Jesus Christ where brothers live together in unity and have all their property in common!
>
> The members of Christ share their spiritual and material gifts because they hold the kingdom of God in common. . . . They alone are the bride of Christ. . . . Oh church of God, keep your marriage pure! Do not let yourself be carried away!
>
> Turn from the enemy and his teachings. Do not let yourself be tricked like Eve who paid attention to his talk. Even if the serpent tries hard and long, do not let yourself be moved. Always follow Christ and you will live with him forever.[24]

The first Anabaptists could not continue, hand in hand, with the world's way of doing business. Hans Hut wrote:

> Everyone says that we should keep on in our business like we did before conversion. If this is so, why didn't Peter remain a fisherman, Matthew a tax collector, and why did Christ tell the rich young man to sell what he had and give to the poor? If it is right that our preachers may have great possessions, then the rich young man would have been in the right to keep his possessions too. Oh, Zachaeus, why did you give up your property so frivolously? According to those preachers' rule you could have kept it and still been a good Christian![25]

Equality

Powerful writers and leaders of the early sixteenth century, such as Thomas Müntzer in southern Germany and Michael Gaismair in Austria pointed the Anabaptists on to equality in Jesus. These men held a deep conviction that the hoarding of material goods was wrong. They believed that Jesus came to bring

---

24 *Ausbund*, 108

25 *Von dem geheimnus der Tauf*, ca. 1526

equality and material peace to men. Michael Gaismair wrote about Jesus' kingdom in 1526:

> All city walls, as well as all fortresses in the land shall be broken down, so that there will be no more cities but only villages. Then there will be no distinctions among men, and no one shall consider himself more important or better than anyone else. It is from differences of rank among men that dissension, arrogance and rebellion arise. But there is to be absolute equality in the land.[26]

The first Anabaptists made humble equality in Jesus their ideal. They rejected wealth, rank and power. Hans Hergot, executed at Nürnberg in Bavaria, in 1527, published a tract that described it.

Old Testament times, in Hans Hergot's tract, were the "age of the Father." New Testament times are the "age of the Son." And now, at the end of time, there is to be an age of the Holy Spirit (the millennium). Before this millennial age comes upon us, there are "three tables in the world. The first one is the table of superfluity. It is loaded and running over with too much on it. The second one is the table of moderation (comfortable poverty). It has just enough on it to meet necessity. The third one is the table of miserable poverty. It has hardly anything on it. But the people seated at the table of superfluity are still trying to grab what they can from it. Then a fight breaks out. God intervenes and both tables (the table of superfluity and the table of miserable poverty) are turned over. Then everyone must sit at the middle table of moderation."[27]

The first Anabaptists took Paul literally where he wrote::

> Our desire is not that others might be relieved while you are hard pressed, but that there might be equality. At the present time your plenty will supply what they need, so that in turn their plenty will supply what you need. Then there will be equality, as it is written: "He who gathered much did not have too much, and he who gathered little did not have too little" (2 Cor. 8:13-15).

After quoting this excerpt from 2 Corinthians, Peter Walpot wrote:

> By this the apostle makes it clear that the rich who come to the church should have no more than the poor, and the poor should have no less than the rich—but that among them there should be Christian community and equality.[28]

Peter Rideman wrote:

> Since all the saints have holy things in common, and since they all have Christ in common, they claim nothing as their own. God did not give his gifts to an individual, but to the whole body of believers. Therefore, they are to be shared with the whole body.

---

26 From the *Landesordnung* of 1526, a document that came from the Gaismair movement in South Tyrol.

27 From Hans Hergot's *Von der newen wandlung eynes Christlichen Lebens,* ca. Dec. 1526.

28 *op. cit.*

The same is true of natural things. They are not given to one man to enjoy, but to all men. Because of this the community of the holy ones shows itself not only in spiritual, but also in earthly things. Paul taught that one should not have an abundance while the other suffers a need, but that there should be an equality of goods. . . .

One can see in all things created that God, from the beginning, did not want things to be privately owned, but to be held in common. Only after man fell into sin did he claim things and make them his own. Then his possessions grew and he became materialistic. Through this collecting of created things, man has been led so far from God that he has forgotten him and has begun to worship created things instead of their Creator. . . .

Those created things that are out of man's reach are still held by all of us in common: the sun, the heavenly bodies, the light of day and the air we breathe. It was the will of God that his creation should be like this. But the only reason these things are still held in common is because they are out of the reach of man. So evil and so greedy has man become that if it were possible, he no doubt would have claimed these too.

That created things were not made to belong to man in private property is shown by the fact that when we die we leave everything behind for others. We can lay no permanent claim to anything. . . .

Because the things of this earth do not belong to us, the law said we should not covet them. They belong to someone else. We should not set our heart on earthly things because they are not ours. Whoever wants to follow Christ must forsake the ownership of created things and private property, as Christ said: "Whoever does not forsake everything he has cannot be my disciple." If a man is to be made new in the image of God, he must forsake all that draws him away from God—the lure of private property—for he cannot become like God if he is drawn away. Christ said: "Whoever will not receive the Kingdom of Heaven like a little child will not enter into it."

The one who has freed himself from earthly things lays his hands on what is true and what is of God. When he does this, it becomes his treasure. He turns his heart toward it. He empties himself of everything else, claiming nothing for his own, but regarding everything as belonging to God's children as a whole.[29]

Mine and Yours

When my older brothers got married my father told them, "Now you must stop saying this is *mine* and start saying it is *ours*." The first Anabaptists applied this principle, not only to marriage, but to baptism in the Lord's community. Peter Walpot wrote:

In the day of grace, men observe a great Sabbath. They observe one Sabbath after another and lead the most peaceful life on earth because they lay aside the words *mine* and *yours*, which do not belong to the nature of things. These words have been the cause of much warfare, and are still so today. Where do war and bloodshed come from? Where do contention and strife come from? Why is there so much disunity and division? All these things come from the desire for property and for claiming things as one's own.

Those who have become slaves of the words *mine* and *yours*, that is to private property, are friends of covetousness. The two daughters of shameful covetousness are called *Give me this* and *Bring me that*.

Just like the earth that can never soak up enough water, like the fire that never says, "It is enough," or like the one who suffers from dropsy and gets thirstier the more he drinks, the devil, death, and hell can never be satisfied. The more men have the more they want. He

[29] *Rechenschaft*, 1540

who wants much needs much. This is the greatest poverty and the most miserable bondage on the earth. It is that from which Christ saves us when we become part of his household—when we begin the true Sabbath, Pentecost, and Easter day.[30]

Communal dwellings at Velké Leváre (Großschützen), in Slovakia, still standing nearly five centuries after their construction by Anabaptist believers (Hutterites) who in Eastern Europe became known as *Habáni* from their life in the *Haushaben* (places where they all lived, ate, and worked together).

Temporal goods (*zeitliche Güter*) were seen as a necessary but dangerous thing to work with. Johannes Brötli, who had been the state church pastor of Zollikon in Switzerland wrote to his friends in that village before his execution as an Anabaptist messenger in 1530. He warned them that their love of material possessions made it hard for them to stay true to their baptismal vows: "Oh woe to temporal goods! They hinder you! Christ said it in his holy Gospel."[31]

Leonhard Schiemer spoke of those who loved and claimed temporal goods as their own:

> They pray: Give us this day our daily bread. But as soon as God gives it, they don't think of it as *ours* anymore but as *mine*. It isn't enough for them to concentrate on today, rather they are concerned about tomorrow, contrary to God's command. God commands us not to take thought for the morrow, but they take thought not only of tomorrow but for the whole year; not only for one year but for ten, twenty, thirty years. They are concerned, not only for themselves but for their children, not only when their children are young but also after they're grown up.[32]

Expressions of Community

Most early Anabaptists, even though they believed in community of goods and rejected private property, did not live in organised Bruderhöfe

---

[30] *op. cit.*

[31] *Quellen . . .* Zürich, 54

[32] *Quellen . . . 3*, Glaubenszeugnisse, 1: 70

(communal households). Persecution would have made that difficult. Even beyond this, there was a freedom in their Gemeinschaft which kept them from making laws exactly how it should be lived out.[33]

Leupold Scharnschlager wrote:

> The example of the first Christians is often misunderstood, and because of it some try to make laws, put on pressure, and get people into a corner with what appears to be a human or carnal way of becoming " righteous."
>
> We should remember that the community of the first Christians in Jerusalem was totally voluntary. Even after the Christians were scattered, Paul kept on teaching about giving over material things and community of goods (*Handreichung und Gemeinschaft der Güter*). We should seek to do this after the apostolic pattern, without forcing it upon anyone, but allowing people to be led into it. . . .
>
> Some say that since the Lord Jesus expects everyone to live in community of goods, we should boldly require it of everyone. But the Holy Spirit does not want it that way. It is not man's work to force others into community, just as community itself is not a work of the flesh. We should not go about it in a fleshly way but in a spiritual way, being careful not to violate the free will of the Lord's people (*dem Herrn sein Volk verstören in der Freiwilligkeit*).[34]

Balthasar Hubmaier wrote:

> A man should always have a concern for the next one, that the hungry be fed, that the thirsty get something to drink and that the naked be clothed. No one is really the owner of what he has, but the caretaker and distributer of it. But we should by no means take by force that which belongs to another and make it common. Rather we should be ready to leave our cloak along with our coat.[35]

Georg Blaurock, when questioned before the Protestant court in 1525, told Huldrych Zwingli that he "taught the believers to have all things in common after the example of the apostles." In a later court session he explained what he meant. He said that having all things in common was to share possessions freely with those who needed them. Felix Manz said the same.

Menno Simons lost a brother in the Münsterite revolts of the Netherlands, where economic communism and rebellion against the government went hand in hand. The peasants, stirred up by false prophets, had revolted against the wealthy and had taken their riches by force to distribute them to the poor. Against such an ungodly

---

[33] Jobst Möller, captured with his wife and fourteen others at an Anabaptist meeting at Frankenhausen in Thüringen, in 1534 professed before the Lutheran court that he believed it was wrong for Christians to own private property. He said the congregation to which he belonged taught community of goods. But the judges noted that he and the other members lived in individual dwellings, here and there throughout the area. Jobst explained that their goods were in private use but belonged to all the believers and were available to them as needs arose. This, no doubt, was the practice of most persecuted Anabaptist congregations in the early years of the movement.

[34] *op. cit.*

[35] From *Balthasar Hubmaier, Schriften, Quellen zur Geschichte der Täufer*, Gütersloh, 1962.

"community of goods" Menno was strongly opposed. But he wrote in 1552:

> We teach that all Christians are one body (1 Cor. 12:13). All partake of one bread (1 Cor. 10:18). All have one God (Eph. 4:5- 6). It is only reasonable that Christians care one for another. The entire Scriptures speak of mercy and love, the sign by which true Christians are known. "By this shall all men know that you are my disciples, if you love one another" (John 13:15).
>
> It is not normal for a person to care for one part of his body and leave the rest uncared for and naked. No. The intelligent person cares for all his members. It is this way in the Lord's church as well. All who are born of God and called into one body are prepared to serve their neighbours, not only with money and goods, but like Christ did, with life and blood. They show mercy as much as they can. No one among them is allowed to beg. They take strangers into their homes. They comfort the afflicted, clothe the naked, feed the hungry, and do not turn their faces from the poor.
>
> Such a community we teach and not that anyone should take and possess the property of others. . . . Our property has to a great extent been taken away from us. It is being taken away. Many a godly father and mother is put to the sword or burned at the stake. Obviously we cannot enjoy a free home life. Times are hard, yet none of those who have joined us, nor any of their orphaned children have been forced to beg. If this is not Christian practice, then we may as well forget about the Gospel. We may as well forget the holy sacraments and the Christian name, saying the life of the holy ones is all a fantasy or a dream.[36]

A great many Anabaptists never found their way into the Bruderhöfe, but those who did, built model communities that won the respect of contemporary society. An eyewitness described them in 1568:

> No one stood around with nothing to do. Everyone did what was asked of him, what he was able to do and what he knew how to do. It did not matter whether one was of noble birth, rich, or poor. Even the priests who joined the community learned how to work. . . . Everyone, no matter where they were from, worked for the common good and advantage of all. A helping hand was given where needed—it was nothing else but a complete body in which all the members served one another.
>
> It was like the works of a clock where every cogwheel drives another, and everything turns in an orderly way, or like a hive of bees where all work together, some making wax, some making honey, and some carrying nectar to the hive. . . .
>
> In all this there had to be order. Only through the keeping of order can a work go on—especially in the house of God where Christ himself is the one who says what needs to be done. Where there is no order things end up in chaos: God cannot live there and everything goes to pieces.[37]

Community under Test

Long after the Anabaptist movement began to decline elsewhere, the communities

---

36 *Een weemodige ende christelicke ontschuldinge . . . ouer die bitter nydige loegen, ende valsche beschuldinge onser misgonstigen . . .* 1551

37 *Geschichtbuech*

in Moravia kept on prospering in a phenomenal way. Messengers sent out every year brought back new believers. But the violence of the sixteenth century could not pass Moravia by. In 1535 King Ferdinand of Austria banished the Anabaptists. The community at Austerlitz fled. Ulrich Stadler and a number of families reached Poland. Jakob Wideman fled with a small group to Austria where he was captured, tortured and put to death in Vienna by the Roman Catholic authorities.

For two hundred years after this, the communities in Moravia and Slovakia passed through great tribulation. Roman Catholic, Protestant, and Turkish armies passed through the area time after time. They burned the communities. On one day the sky turned dark as twenty-five Bruderhöfe went up in flames at once. The soldiers slaughtered the men and chased the women and children from their homes in the dead of winter. They sought shelter in the woods and dug vast networks of underground tunnels to escape their enemies. Turkish soldiers grabbed their children, tying them together by their feet to sling them over their saddles, one on each side with heads hanging down, and galloped off to sell them as slaves. They violated the women, the children and the teenagers of both sexes in public. They undressed, tortured, and mutilated the men—singing off their hair, hanging them up by their genitals, beating them or cutting them to pieces in front of their wives and children until they died. They robbed the communities of their food, their animals, their tools and their clothing, until only a small remnant survived to flee across the mountains through Hungary and Romania to Russia.[38]

But in the face of the most brutal violence, the highest command of love did not die. As long as the Anabaptists lived in real Gemeinschaft with Jesus and with one another they shared what they had, and Jesus led them…

[38] This remnant survived as the Hutterite movement, still alive in hundreds of communities in North America and elsewhere, today.

On to Visible Order

Where the Werra flows between the Thüringer Forest and the highlands of the Rhön, the castle of the knights of Bibra- Schwebenheim overshadowed the little house of Johannes Hut, his wife, and his four children. Johannes (they called him Hans) bound books and sold them. He worked on a commission for the knights and travelled far and wide selling the books he bound.

In 1524, while passing through the city of Weißenfels in Sachsen-Anhalt, Hans Hut got into a discussion with a miller, a tailor, and a wool weaver. They talked about infant baptism. The longer they talked and compared what the Scriptures said, the better Hans could see that Christ wanted believers, not babies, to be baptised. When his wife gave birth to a baby shortly afterward, they decided to keep him at home.

The priest and the townspeople learned about this and called for a public dispute. The judges declared Hans the "loser" in the dispute and gave him eight days to leave Thüringen. With his wife and five children, and with their belongings tied up in bags on their backs, the Hut family set out for Nürnberg. There they met Hans Denck. They rented a house, and Hans Hut continued to travel around selling books. On May 15, 1525, he found himself in the city of Frankenhausen when the peasants, led by Thomas Müntzer, revolted and fell in bloody chaos before the armies of the German princes. Hans saw that armed revolt was not Jesus' way, and that Thomas Müntzer's followers had failed to build on earth a picture of the Kingdom of Heaven. So on May 26, 1526, in a little house by the gate of the Holy Cross in Augsburg, he asked Hans Denck to baptise him—and Jesus' cause in southern Germany gained one of its most enthusiastic promoters.

A Visible Church

Hans Hut began to baptise others wherever he went. Many of those he baptised, he ordained at once and sent out as messengers to keep on baptising. But he did not promote a vague, "spiritualistic" Christianity. Soon after he became part of the Anabaptist movement he wrote:

> When there are a number of Christians who have gone the way of the cross, suffering, and sorrow, and who have gotten tied together in a covenant, they become one congregation and one body in Christ—a visible church community.
>
> In the Lord's church all goodness, mercy, praise, glory, and honour appear in the Holy Spirit. All things are held in common: nothing is private property. . . . We prove our covenant by giving ourselves to Christ. We give ourselves to Christ by giving ourselves to the brothers and sisters. We give ourselves to them in body, life, property, and honour, regardless of how the world misunderstands us.[1]

[1] From *Quellen und Forschungen zur Reformationsgeschichte*, Leipzig, 1938

Hans Schlaffer, also baptised and ordained by Hans Hut, wrote:

> Because God, through his Son Jesus Christ, is again raising up a visible, holy, church community in these last and dangerous times, he wants it to become apparent in the world through the outward sign of water baptism.[2]

Menno Simons wrote:

> The visible community of the saints must be sound in teaching and sacraments. It must be irreproachable in life before the world, as far as man who is able to see only the outward, can tell. . . . The true community of Christ is made manifest among this wicked generation in words and work. She can no more be hidden than a city on a hill or a candle on a candle-stick.[3]

Dirk Philips wrote:

> God's church is not like Franck says, just an invisible fellowship of believers. The very term *ecclesia* (those who are called out) proves that. God's church is not invisible. The apostles, according to the command of Jesus and by the power of Christian baptism, gathered a community of believers out of all nations. Theirs was not an invisible community. The apostles did not address their letters in a general or indiscriminate way to all people. They specifically named the congregations and the people to whom they wrote.[4]

Paul Glock, Anabaptist messenger of southern Germany, fell into the hands of the authorities in Württemberg, where they imprisoned him for nineteen years in the Hohenwittlingen castle. They tortured him on the rack. They sent two priests to dispute with him. When Paul spoke of the community of the holy ones, the priests made fun of him. They said no man, only God, can know who belongs to that community and who does not. They said the true church is an invisible body of those who are right with God in their hearts, and that no one can point with their hands and say, "Here is the true church," or "There is the true church." But to this Paul Glock replied:

> Now it becomes clear that you are false prophets! When Christ was on the earth he pointed out the true church with his hands. He spread his hands out over his disciples and said, "These are my brothers, my mother, and my sisters." Everyone who does the will of Christ belongs to his family. Christ also said we would be the light of the world, and a city on a hill which cannot be hidden. He said we should love one another as he loved us so that the world could see this and know that we are his disciples. Peter said we should live an honest life among the gentiles so that they may be won without words. He also pointed to the Christian community. Since you are unable to do that, you are still children of the night and of darkness, and not members of the body of Christ. If you would be members of his body, you would certainly be able to point it out![5]

---

2 *Ein einfältig Gebet* . . . 1528

3 *Een Klare beantwoordinge, over een Schrift Gellii Fabri* . . . 1554

4 *Enchiridion*

5 *Geschichtbuech*

True Reality

The first Anabaptists spoke of inner Gemeinschaft with Jesus. They rejected the teaching that outer, visible rites and substances alone can save. Menno Simons wrote:

> Those who point you only to bread or water as something by which you are saved point you away from true reality. They point you to signs, from Christ back to Moses, and give you a vain hope and a false security so that you remain impenitent and without Christ all your life. You console yourselves so much with the signs that you remain without the signified truth, as may, unfortunately be seen in the case of the whole world. No matter how drunken, covetous, showy, vain, and untruthful the world's people are, they still boast of being Christians. They console themselves with this godless sealing by the idolatrous water. . . . and with the bread and wine of the preachers, to the extent that they walk without fear upon the broad way and remain without the Word of God.[6]

But the Anabaptists, with their emphasis on Gemeinschaft with Jesus, did not go the way of the spiritualists or the Pietists. They never rejected the outward sacraments. Instead, they taught that *true reality* is inner faith made complete by outer form.

The Struggle with the Spiritualists

The Anabaptists were not the left wing of the Reformation that some historians make them to be. They were not radical opponents to Roman Catholicism—doing things differently only to be different—but followers of Jesus. They followed his example in water baptism and in communion with bread and wine, no matter where that put them in the light of sixteenth century controversies.

Sebastian Franck, the scholar and historian, was a radical. So were Casper Schwenkfeld and later on the Quakers who rejected the visible sacraments altogether. Sebastian Franck wrote:

> I do not want to be a follower of the Pope. . . . I do not want to go with Zwingli… I will refuse to be an Anabaptist.[7]

He taught that the sacraments (water, bread, and wine) were given to the first Christians only because of their immaturity, and that it is no longer necessary to practice them.

To this, Dirk Philips replied:

> Something horrible is coming up like smoke from the depths of the pit to hide the brightness of the sun. This is Sebastian Franck's teaching that the holy rites instituted by Christ are no longer important, and that they are like a baby's things and child's play. Franck says the visible sacraments are weak elements, and no longer necessary. . . . To this coarse blasphemy I reply: Who has ever written so shamefully of the holy rites as Sebastian Franck? Shall God permit the devil to do with the sacraments whatever he wants?

---

6 *Een Klare beantwoordinge, over een Schrift Gellii Fabri* . . . 1554

7 From *Von vier zwiträchtigen Kirchen, deren jede die ander verhasset und verdammet,* ca. 1530.

> It is an unendurable blasphemy for Sebastian Franck, a scorner of God and the sacraments, to look upon the first Christians as children who played with rag dolls, while he claims to have reached spiritual manhood. As if Jesus Christ, the apostles, and the first Christians did not have the Holy Spirit because they used outward elements in connection with faith! What abominable presumption and blindness! A man contradicting Christ and rejecting his rites. What foolishness of heart![8]

Pilgram Marpeck took a firm stand against the spiritualists in southern Germany. His book, the *Verantwortung*, is directed against the error of rejecting or minimising the importance of the sacraments—like Thomas Müntzer and Casper Schwenkfeld did. Conrad Grebel and the Swiss Brethren, the Anabaptists of Austria, and those of the Bruderhöfe in Moravia felt likewise. "On the question of baptism," wrote one historian, "the Zürich brethren and Thomas Müntzer went opposite directions. For Grebel, baptism had increasing significance, and proper baptism was emphasised as part of the obedience required by the church. Müntzer, however, developed more and more in the direction of a mystical spirituality in which outward forms such as baptism had no place or meaning."[9]

Visible Limits

Jesus church community can be nothing other than fully visible. We cannot follow him in secret. Either we show by our actions that we belong to him, or we show by our actions that we do not. Either we belong to his body and function as members of it, or we are not part of the body.

The first Anabaptists recognised these clearly visible limits of the Lord's church community. They baptised with water those who belonged to Jesus. They separated from their communion those who did not. They believed that this binding in baptism and this loosing in separation was the binding and loosing of which Jesus spoke in Matt. 16:19.

Leonhard Schiemer wrote:

> All who have not thrown themselves with all their possessions underneath the cross of Christ and into the community of the holy ones, all who have not been unbound from their sins (entbunden) by the Lord's church are of the devil and of the antichrist.[10]

Peter Rideman wrote:

> Since man's sins are left behind and forgiven in baptism, and since the Lord's church community holds the key (to remit or retain sin), baptism should take place before the brothers. The whole community should kneel together with the convert before his baptism takes place, asking God to forgive his sins. But if this cannot be, and if the brothers cannot be

---

[8] From *Een verantwoordinghe ende Refutation op twee Sendtbrieven Sebastiani Franck, cortelijck uyt die heylighe Schrift vervaet*, ca. 1535.

[9] Harold S. Bender, *Conrad Grebel*, Goshen (1950), pg. 116

[10] Quellen und Forschungen zur Reformationsgeschichte}, Leipzig, 1938

present, the baptiser may baptise the convert apart, or alone.[11]

Menno Simons wrote:

> Do not say, "Let the church community put me out. Their putting out will not hurt me," and other such lighthearted things. I tell you the truth, I would rather be cut into pieces than to allow myself to be separated for a valid reason from the Lord's church. Brothers this is serious!
>
> In the Old testament they burned evildoers with fire. That is a small thing compared to our day when evildoers are delivered unto Satan in the name of Christ and in the binding power of his Holy Word. Let everyone be careful to conduct himself wisely before God and his church community so that he may never be smitten with such a curse by Christ—so that he may never be placed outside of the holy congregation by Christ and his church community. All who are outside of Christ's congregation must be in that of Antichrist. Oh children, take care! Watch, pray, and be on guard. It is a fearful thing to fall into the hands of the living God.[12]

Who Should Be Put Out

As soon as he believed and was baptised, the Anabaptist convert began to enjoy the blessings and order of the Lord's church community. He became a disciple and friend of Jesus. He remained on intimate terms with Jesus and his body as long as he obeyed him. But these blessings ended when he disobeyed Jesus, and if he persisted in that disobedience.

A person could be baptised, become part of the body of Jesus and be separated from it shortly afterward. But he could not be baptised, live in sin, and keep on belonging to it. If he disobeyed Jesus and returned to living in sin, Jesus and the members of his body had to separate themselves from him.

The first Anabaptists spoke of two reasons for this separation (*Absonderung*) from the body of Jesus. The first and greatest reason was to awaken the disobedient to the reality of their condition and to bring them back to repentance. The second reason was to protect the health and testimony of the body of Jesus itself.

Menno Simons explained who should be put out and why:

> Christ says, "If your brother sins against you, but will not hear you, nor the witnesses, nor the church, then let him be to you as a heathen man and a publican." Paul says that if a brother turns out to be a fornicator, covetous, idolatrous, an accuser, a drunkard, or a cheat, then we should not eat with him. To this class belong all who openly walk in the damnable works of the flesh which Paul names elsewhere. Lazy people who become busybodies must be put out. Divisive people, all who argue against the teachings of Christ and his apostles must be put out.
>
> All who lead carnal lives or persist in false teachings must, as a last resort, be put

---

11 *op. cit.*

12 *Een gans grontlijcke onderwijs oft bericht, van de excommunicatie*. . .1558

out of the Lord's church community in the name of Christ. By the power of the Holy Ghost and by the binding Word of God, they must be put out, marked and avoided until they repent.[13]

A City without Walls

Menno Simons wrote:

> As long as the Israelites dealt with evildoers among them, they remained upright and pious. But when they neglected internal discipline, they fell into all kinds of wickedness and idolatry. . . . This is also the way it went in the first Christian community. As long as the overseers required a godly life, as long as they baptised and gave the nighttime meal only to the penitent, as long as they put sinners out, according to the holy writings, they were Christ's church community. But as soon as they sought a carefree life without the cross, they laid aside the rod of discipline and preached peace. In this way they established an anti-Christian Babel, which has existed by now for many centuries. . . . A community without discipline and a separation from sinners is like a vineyard without trenches, like a city without walls or gates. Enemies freely come to plant their weeds within it.[14]

An Act of Love

The first Anabaptists believed in being firm but not harsh. Menno Simons, although he went along with unsound teachings on excommunication in his later years, did what he could to keep separated members from harsh treatment. He wrote:

> No one is separated from the communion of the brothers except those who have already separated themselves by false doctrine or improper conduct. We do not want to put anyone out. We want to receive. We do not want to amputate but to heal. We do not want to discard but win back, not grieve but comfort, not condemn but save. Whoever turns from evil and comes back to the Gospel into which he was baptised cannot and shall not be put out.[15]

In another tract he wrote:

> We should not deny necessary services, love, and mercy to those who have been separated from communion. Separation is a work of divine love, not of unmerciful, heathenish cruelty. True Christians love, help, and pity everyone, even their most bitter enemies. True Christians hate cruelty. They have a nature like God of whom they are born. God makes his sun to rise on the evil and on the good and sends rain on the just and unjust. If we are of a different nature, we show that we are not his children. . . . We do not separate people from the church community to destroy them but to help them.[16]

Holy but Human

Even though they believed in a visible church community with visible limits, and even though they believed in keeping the Lord's church holy and

---

[13] *op. cit.*

[14] *Een Klare beantwoordinge, over een Schrift Gellii Fabri* . . . 1554

[15] *Een lieffelijcke vermaninghe,* ca. 1558

[16] *Grondelijk onderwijs oft bericht van de excommunicatie* . . . 1558

separated from sin, the first Anabaptists did not boast, as some accused them of boasting, that they were a perfect brotherhood. They knew that they were still human. Dirk Philips wrote:

> Several Gospel parables describe the Lord's church community. One parable is that of the net cast into the sea which drew up all kinds of fish (Matt. 13:47). The other is the parable of a king who made a wedding for his son and invited both the good and the bad (Matt. 22:2). Christ speaks in these parables of the kingdom of heaven, that is of his church.
>
> After hearing these parables we must admit without arguing that not only the God-fearing but the wicked come into the church community of Christ. But the wicked are not to stay there. We are to separate them from our communion as far as we are able, already here on this earth. Then in the future, the work will reach completion when Christ separates the sheep from the goats on the youngest day.[17]

Kortrijk (Courtrai), in Flanders, Belgium, home to a large, active fellowship of believers during the sixteenth century—nearly all of them involved with the town's cloth weaving industry. Jacques van der Mase, a leader among them, turned from armed revolution (at Münster in Westfalen) to the simple, peaceful way of Christ. Spanish authorities caught and burned him at the stake in the 1530s. Twenty-three others met the same fate, and still more believers from Kortrijk got drowned or burned in other Flemish cities. The church at Kortrijk was crushed. The believers scattered, but the seed they carried with them survives in church communities around the world.

Menno Simons wrote:

> We teach that the nighttime meal is to be observed as the Lord Jesus himself observed it, that is, with a church community that is outwardly without spot or blemish—without open transgression and wickedness. The church can judge only that which is visible. What is inwardly evil but does not appear outwardly, God alone will judge. God alone, not the community of brothers, can discern the hearts and minds of men.[18]

The Cost of Visibility

The visible sacraments of baptism and the nighttime meal brought

17 *op. cit.*

18 *Opera Omnia Theologica*, Amsterdam, 1681

unspeakable suffering upon the Anabaptist movement. But Dirk Philips wrote:

> We are not weakened or confused by those who ask us what benefit baptism has. They ask us why we suffer persecution to be baptised when we ourselves say that salvation is not dependant upon outward signs. They say that faith and love can override all outward institutions such as baptism and the nighttime meal. They point to Moses who discontinued circumcision in the wilderness when it was not convenient, and say that Christians may now leave off from baptising believers or do as they please about it. But we pay no attention to them. . . . They have the nature of spiders turning everything good into evil, yes, even honey into poison.[19]

Hans Hut of Thüringen discovered the high cost of following Jesus in a visible way. After baptising an untold number of converts into the Lord's church community, they arrested and tortured him. One night, lying unconscious in his cell after an especially severe torturing session, his foot overset his candle. The straw in the cell caught fire and burned him. Eight days later he died. They drowned his daughter at Bamberg in Franconia and his son Philip fled to Moravia where he joined an Anabaptist Bruderhof.

But walking in the light, "shining as stars in the universe among a crooked and depraved generation," those whom Hans had baptised into a visible church community followed Jesus . . .

---

[19] *op. cit.*

On with the Message

Oid, oid, lo que nos manda el Salvador. Marchad, marchad,
y proclamad mi amor. Pues he aquí, yo con vosotros estaré
Los dias todos hasta el fin os guardaré.

Id, id por el mundo. Id, Id y predicad el evangelio, Id, id va adelante
el todopoderoso Salvador.
¡Gloria, gloria aleluya a Jesús!
¡Gloria, gloria aleluya a Jesús!
Nuestras almas él salvó, nuestras manchas él lavó,
¡Proclamemos pues, a todos su amor![1]

The mighty strains of a missionary hymn stopped me beneath the window of the chapel where my students were in chorus practice. In passing I had caught the words and they held me transfixed.

Mirad, mirad, la condición del pecador,
¡Qué triste es! ¡Qué llena de dolor!
Sin luz, sin paz camina hacia la eternidad, Y no conoce el
gran peligro en que está.[2]

The message gripped my heart, as always. Only this time more so. It was a missionary hymn. Dry leaves swirled through the dead grass of December. The hills of Santa Ana, El Salvador stood above great spreading trees along the road through Zacamil. I thought of the bombs we had heard at close proximity a few nights before. (They had bombed a bank close to the mission in the capital city.) I thought of the rattle of machine gun fire, bullet-pocked bunkers on flood-lit bridges, helicopters flying in formation at tree-top level, heavy artillery pointing down on all sides, buses with tires shot out and laden with bombs set across the highway, and tiny houses flying white flags.

Salid, salid, embajadores del Señor, Buscad, buscad el
pobre pecador. Aprovechad el tiempo que el Señor nos da,
Pues pronto el día de salud acabara.[3]

---

[1] Take heed, take heed to the Saviour's command! March on, march on, proclaiming his love! He said he would be with us and keep us unto the end of the world. Go out, Go out into the world! Go out and preach the Gospel! Glory hallelujah to Jesus! He saved our souls, he washed away our sins. Let us proclaim to all the world his love!

[2] Look, look at the condition of the sinner! How sad it is! How filled with pain! Without light, without peace he walks toward eternity and does not know the danger he is in!

[3] Go out, go out, ambassadors of the Lord! Search for the poor sinners. Make good use of the time the Lord gives you, because the day of salvation will soon be over!

I knew that the young people singing this song were conscious of its words. Many came from non-Christian homes. A number of them were orphaned in early childhood. Numerous boys had been inducted into the army and had either escaped or explained their way out of boot camp by proving to the generals their Christianity.

Id, id por el mundo. Id, id y predicad el evangelio. Id, id va adelante, el todopoderoso Salvador. . .[4]

So soon they would be back in the cities to put this song to practice. First-generation Anabaptists singing a missionary hymn—how I loved the spirit of these Salvadorean and Guatemalan young people! Theirs was the spirit of Christianity's oldest extant missionary hymn, written by an Anabaptist in Moravia in 1563.[5]

"The Swiss Brethren movement began," observed a scholar, "because Conrad Grebel had the courage to make an unreserved personal commitment to this ideal (the ideal of a voluntary Christian community) regardless of the consequences. Where others shrank from adoption of the full New Testament ideal because of fear that it could not be carried through in practice, as for instance, Luther, Grebel acted. He chose to follow the vision without calculation of possibilities or practicalities, believing that the truth commands: it does not merely advise."[6]

The Anabaptists sent out *Sendboten* (messengers) at once, even though the task of evangelism has never been carried out under greater difficulty. An eye-witness of the beginning of the Anabaptist movement in Switzerland wrote:

> Suddenly one saw a great many people, as though ready for a journey, girded with ropes, passing through Zürich. In the marketplaces and squares they stood and preached a better life, conversion, freedom from guilt and brotherly love.[7]

Every Anabaptist messenger, if caught, faced torture and death. No roads were safe. They travelled on foot, through forests and mountain ranges, and preached by night. They were the only evangelical missionaries of their time. Every European country prohibited them. Coming from underground churches that had little or no money, they could not depend on regular support. But they "steadfastly witnessed to the Word of the Lord, by life and work, by word and deed. They spoke with power of the kingdom of God. They called all men to repentance, to turn to

---

4 Go out, go out into all the world! Go out and preach the Gospel! Go out and follow your Saviour who goes before you. . .

5 *Die Lieder der Hutterischen Brüder*, pp. 650-652

6 Harold S. Bender, *Conrad Grebel*, (Goshen, 1950) pg. 213

7 From Joseph von Beck, *Die Geschichts-Bücher der Wiedertäufer in Oesterreich-Ungarn* . . . (Vienna, 1883).

God from the vanity of the world and from a sinful and wretched life. God gave his blessing to this work and it was carried out with joy," wrote Kaspar Braitmichel of the Bruderhöfe in Moravia, in the mid-1500s.

The messengers went out with joy, but many did not return. Sent out two by two, they took leave of their wives and children, hoping but not really expecting to see them again on the earth. They simply went out and preached at the cost of their lives. Menno Simons wrote:

> We desire with burning hearts that the true Gospel of Christ would be preached throughout all the world. We desire that it may be taught to all men as Christ commanded, even at the cost of our life and blood.[8]

Kaspar Braitmichel wrote:

> We practice the sending out of Christian messengers like the Lord commanded, saying: "As my father sent me, so send I you. I have chosen you and ordered you to go out and bring in a harvest." To carry this out we send servants of the Gospel every year to all the countries to which we have a reason to send them. These men visit those who desire a better way of life, who eagerly seek and ask for the truth. Spies and hangmen notwithstanding, we visit those who seek, by day and by night, at the cost of the messengers' necks, their bodies, and their lives. In this way, the Lord, like a good shepherd, carries his flock together.[9]

Roman Catholic authorities accused Josef Schlosser, Anabaptist messenger imprisoned in Poland in 1579, of being a deceiver of the people. "If you would be a good man," the authorities said, "you would stay in your own country and leave other people alone."

To this Josef replied, "I deceive no one. The reason we go out into all countries is to obey the command of Christ to call people to repentance and to help those who want to lead a better life."

So great was the hunger for the Gospel in Poland that they had to hide Josef in stocks in the castle dungeon to keep people away from his cell. In spite of the authorities' dire threats, these people had been coming in a continuous stream to hear what he had to say.

Filling the Lord's house

Hieronimus Kräl, Anabaptist messenger imprisoned in a dungeon in Austria until his clothes had completely rotted away and he had only his shirt collar to send to his friends as a sign of his continued steadfastness, wrote:

> We are not sent out for anyone's harm or disadvantage. Rather we are sent out to seek the salvation of men and to show them the way to repentance and conversion.[10]

---

8 *Die oorsake waerom dat ick M. S. niet of en late te leeren, ende te schrijuen. . .* ca. 1542

9 *Geschichtsbuech,* ca. 1570

10 *ibid.*

This sending out, in obedience to the command of Christ, continued year after year. Not only the men went. Leonhard Dax, a converted priest of München in Bavaria, joined the communities in Moravia. On the Sunday before St.~Martin's day in 1567, they sent him out with his wife Anna, Ludwig Dörker, Jakob Gabriel Binder, Jörg Schneider, and a sister called Barbara from a new Bruderhof at Tawikovice near Mährisch-Kromau. Not long afterward they fell into the hands of the Protestant authorities at Alzey on the Rhine, 500 miles away.

Political unrest did not stop the messengers. In 1603, after years of oppression, plundering, and terror during the Hungarian revolution, the Anabaptist communities of that country sent six messengers to East Prussia on the Baltic Sea. Sailing from Denmark, they were captured by a Swedish ship and taken to Sweden. Only after much difficulty did they reach their destination—a group of seekers in the Vistula Delta.

"We preach where we can," said Menno Simons toward the end of his life, "both by day and night, in houses and in fields, in forests and wastelands, in this country and abroad, in prisons and bonds, in the water, the fire and on the scaffold, on the gallows and upon the wheel, before lords and princes, orally and by writing, at the risk of possessions and life. We have done so for many years without ceasing."[11]

Invited or not invited, the Anabaptists preached the truth. Klaus Felbinger, a south German messenger wrote:

> Some have asked us why we entered the territory of the duke of Bavaria. I answered: "We go not only into this land but into all lands as far as our language extends. We go wherever God opens a door. We go wherever God directs us to hearts who earnestly seek him and who are tired of the ungodly life of the world. We go to those who wish to amend their lives. To all such places we go and will go.[12]

Kaspar Braitmichel wrote:

> Since God the Almighty desired to build his house and cause his community to increase, he always provided a way of grace that more souls found their way out of the desolate and apostate nations into the brotherhood so that the Lord's table and house were well filled.[13]

The World Upside Down

The greater the first Anabaptists' joy in the Lord and in one another, the greater their desire to bring souls into Gemeinschaft with Christ—and the worse the persecution they faced. Luther called them *Schwärmer* (swarmers). Both

---

[11] *Opera Omnia Theologica,* (Amsterdam, 1681)

[12] *Abgeschrift des Glaubens welchen ich, Klaus Felbinger, zu Landshut den Herrn daselbst für mich und statt meines mitgefangenen Bruders zugestellt habe,* 1560

[13] *Geschichtsbuech,* ca. 1570

Protestants and Catholics called them vermin, gangsters, and thieves. Sebastian Franck wrote in 1531:

> The Anabaptists spread so rapidly that their teaching soon covered the land... They soon gained a large following and baptised thousands. . . . They increased so rapidly that the world feared an uprising by them, though I have learned that this fear had no justification whatsoever.[14]

The Gospel of the Kingdom spread throughout Europe in the 16th Century, as on this back street in Strasbourg, through aggressive person to person contact, and prayer.

Heinrich Bullinger, Reformed clergyman of Zürich, and bitter opponent of the Anabaptists reported that "people run after them as though they were living saints." Feared, admired, or cursed, the Anabaptist movement could not be ignored. Wolfgang Capito, a Protestant leader in Strasbourg, wrote in 1527:

> I frankly confess that in most Anabaptists piety and consecration may be seen. They are zealous beyond any suspicion of insincerity. What earthly advantage could they hope to gain by enduring exile, torture, and unspeakable punishment of the flesh? It is not because of a lack of wisdom that they are somewhat indifferent toward earthly things. It is because of their divine motivation.[15]

Listening to Christ's command to go out and preach the Gospel to all nations, the first Anabaptists followed him . . .

---

[14] *Chronica, Zeytbuch und Geschychtbibel*, (Strasbourg, 1531)

[15] Quoted in C. A. Cornelius, *Geschichte des Münsterischen Aufruhrs* (Leipzig, 1860).

On to Witness

Among the dairy farms at Goes on the Dutch island of Zuid Beveland, Joost Joosten grew up singing. He excelled in Latin at school, but his heart was in the songs he sang, and his parents found a place for him in the choir of the village church.

People noticed him when he sang—fair-haired boy with a clear voice—and liked him. In 1556 King Philip II of Spain visited the Netherlands. They gave him a high mass at Middelburg and called upon the choir from Goes to sing. Joost had turned fourteen. The king saw and heard him. After the mass he said: "Bring me that boy. He must go back with me to Spain!"

But Joost did not want to go to Spain to live in the richest royal court in Europe. He wanted something far better. He hid for six weeks until they gave up looking for him and the king was safely gone. Then, when he was out of school, he made known his desire to follow Christ. An Anabaptist messenger baptised him in a secret meeting, and the king's officials started looking for him again.

They caught Joost in 1560 and put him in jail. Four interrogators from the Holy Office of the Inquisition came to question him. On five sheets of paper Joost wrote for them what he believed. He also wrote songs and sang in jail.

The inquisitors had Joost pulled on the rack. They had hot steel rods turned through his knees and pushed through his legs until they came out at the ankles. But his heart could not be moved. Then the court convicted him and sentenced him to death.

They made a little house of straw on the town square. The people came by boat, on horseback, and on foot to see. They lined the streets and the sides of the square, surrounded by soldiers to hold them back . . . and waited.

The village of Goes, in Zeeland, as seen from the church tower, today.

The soldiers brought him in chains. The people had not seen him so pale or so thin before. Then suddenly, what was that? He was singing!

Joost Joosten was singing again…the same clear voice…a man's voice now…and some of them recognised the song he sang. It was one he had written as a new Christian: "Oh Lord Christ, in my mind I see you standing always before me!"

They put him inside the little house of straw. He was still singing when the flames roared up. It was the Monday before Christmas, 1560, and Joost Joosten was eighteen years old.

Witnessing

"Hans Koch and Leonhard Meister witnessed at Augsburg, Anno 1524 . . . an old man and a youth witnessed at Amsterdam . . . Thomas the printer witnessed at Köln am Rhein, Anno 1557."

Witnessing to whom? Of what?

At first glance these *Ausbund* song headings may bring to mind the Anabaptists' witnessing in court, or their willingness to speak with others of what they believed. But on second glance it becomes clear that "witnessing" in the sixteenth century involved more than it usually does today.

The Mennonite church into which I was baptised went "witnessing" once a month. My first turn came on a warm July evening in 1977. I travelled to London, Ontario, with a group of brothers in my friend's Monte Carlo. Soft Evangelical music from the rear speakers calmed my trepidations as we entered Highbury Avenue and neared the intersection of Richmond and Dundas streets in the heart of the city. It was Friday evening. Tracts moved fast among throngs of pedestrians while the lights came on. Some sneered. Some asked questions. Most people respectfully took our *Just for You* tracts. A Jewish college professor asked us thoughtful questions. His wife, he said, was a Mennonite from Manitoba. Then, after we ran out of literature, we shared our impressions on the long ride home.

This, for us, was "witnessing."

The first Anabaptists did it otherwise. An eye-witness account from the mid-1500s reads:

> The nine men knelt on the green meadow. Blood flowed over the sword. Three women were drowned. One laughed when they put her into the water. Then we buried them all together in one deep grave. . . . There was much weeping. Many people cried to God that he would give rest to the departed souls. But others mocked, saying they were the devil's horde and served the Antichrist. . . .
>
> This was done on Friday morning. Many important people had come riding in. They came lightheartedly, but we all went home in tears. I cannot describe everything I saw.[1]

[1] *Ausbund*, 26

Menno Simons wrote:

> If Socrates could die for his beliefs, if Marcus Curtius and Gaius Mutius Scevola could die for the city of Rome and the good of the state, if Jews and Turks brave death for the laws of their fatherland, why should I not offer my soul for heavenly wisdom? For the brothers? For what Christ has established?[2]

"Witnessing" to the first Anabaptists was to give one's life for what one believed.

Christ the Faithful Witness

Following Christ the Amen, the faithful and true witness (Rev. 1:5 and 3:14), the Anabaptists became witnesses with him. Holding to the testimony of Jesus (Rev. 12:17 and 19:10), the Anabaptists overcame their fear of death. Their highest honour became the privilege of testifying for Christ at the cost of their lives (Rev. 20:4).

Menno Simons wrote:

> The heavy cross of Christ is the mark of the true church, the cross which is carried for the sake of his Word. Christ said to his disciples, "You will be hated of all nations for my name's sake." Paul wrote: "All that will live godly in Christ Jesus will suffer persecution. . . . " The cross was the mark of the first church.
> Now it is that again, here in the Netherlands.[3]

All who wish to go in by the right door, Christ Jesus, must sacrifice all they have. They must take upon themselves the heavy cross of poverty, of distress, of disdain and sorrow and sadness. They must follow the rejected, the outcast, and bleeding Christ . . . until through great tribulation they enter the kingdom of God.[4]

Preaching and the Cross

"The yoke of Christ is easy and his burden is light," taught the Anabaptists, "but his cross is heavy."

Preaching that does not involve cross bearing looks suspicious. Menno Simons wrote:

> Do not hope that the time will come when the Word can be preached without the cross. Oh no! It is the Word of the cross and it will remain that to the end. The Word has to be preached with much suffering and sealed with blood. . . . If the head had to suffer torture and pain, how shall his members expect peace? If they called the master of the house a devil, will

---

[2] *Christelycke leringhen op den 25. Psalm*, ca. 1538

[3] *Een Klare beantwoordinge, over een Schrift Gellii Fabri*. . . 1554

[4] *Eyne troestelijke vermaninge van dat lijden, cruyze, vnde veruolginge der heyligen* . . . 1558

they not do so to those of his household? Christ said, "You will be hated by all men for my name's sake."[5]

Conrad Grebel wrote:

> Christians who believe right are sheep in the midst of wolves— sheep for butchering. They must be baptised in fear and distress, sorrow, persecution, suffering, and death.[6]

A large part of the *Ausbund* consists of encouragement for Christians carrying the cross. One of Menno Simons' most meaningful books is *The Cross of the Holy Ones* published in 1554.

Hated Without a Cause

Persecuted but not forsaken, troubled on every side yet not distressed, perplexed but not in despair, cast down but not destroyed, the first Anabaptists believed it necessary to bear in their bodies the dying of the Lord Jesus so that his life might become apparent in them (2 Cor. 4:8-11).

Menno Simons wrote:

> With my wife and children I have endured misery and persecution for 18 years. . . . While they (the Protestant preachers) repose on beds with soft pillows, we hide in out-of- the-way corners. While they listen to music at weddings and banquets, we listen for dogs to bark, warning us of impending arrest. While they are greeted as Doctor, lord, and teacher, we are called Anabaptists, night preachers, deceivers, and heretics. People salute us in the name of the devil. While they are handsomely rewarded for their services with large incomes and good times, we get fire, sword, and death.[7]

Leonhard Schiemer wrote:

> We are scattered like sheep without a shepherd. We have left our houses and lands and have become like owls of the night, like game birds. We sneak about in the forest. Men track us down with dogs, then lead us like lambs back to town. There they put us on display and say we are the cause of an uproar. We are counted like sheep for slaughter. They call us heretics and deceivers.[8]

Christoph Bauman, a Swiss Anabaptist wrote:

> Where shall I go? I am so ignorant. Only to God can I go, because God alone will be my helper. I trust in you, God, in all my distress. You will not forsake me. You will stand with me, even in death. I have committed myself to your Word. That is why I have lost favour in all places. But by losing the world's favour, I gained yours. Therefore I say

---

5 *Dat Fundament des Christelycken leers . . .* 1539

6 *Ein Brief an Thomas Müntzer,* September 5, 1524

7 *Een Klare beantwoordinge, over een Schrift Gellii Fabri. . .* 1554

8 *Ausbund,* 31:4-5

to the world: Away with you! I will follow Christ.

It was long enough, world, that I floated about in you, oh treacherous sea. You deceived me long enough. You detained me. While I was a slave to sin, and wronged God, you loved and honoured me. But now you hate me. I have become a spectacle to the world. Everyone in every place shouts "Heretic!" after me, because I love God's Word. But I have no greater treasure than God's Word, so I will not allow myself to be turned from it—to be turned away from my God and my Lord. I will keep on being "obstinate."

I have no place left to me on the earth. Wherever I go I must be punished. Poverty is my fortune. Cross and sorrow have become my joy. Bonds and imprisonment have become my garment. Such is the heraldry of my king!

Even among animals of the forest I find no rest. People chase me up and drive me away. I cannot come into any house. People drive me out. I must duck and dodge and creep about like a mouse. All my friends have forsaken me. All streets are barred for me. The people are determined to capture me as soon as they find me. I suffer at their hands. They rough me up and beat me. They hate me without a cause.

The people begrudge me the crumbs from their tables. They are unwilling to let me drink water from their wells, and they do not want me to enjoy as much as the light of the sun. I have no peace among them. They will not let me enter their doors. They are ashamed of me because I choose to follow Christ.

I am sold into the hands of my enemies and betrayed above all by those to whom I have done the most good. I served them cheerfully by day and by night. But now they lead me like a lamb to the slaughter. I sought their salvation but they rejected my efforts. They curse me for it and drive me away. They drive me into distress. . . out of their houses, their fields, their woods, and their forests. Wherever I lodge they chase me out. They treat me brutally. They hunt me like a man hunts a deer. They set traps for me and search for me, ready to hit me over the head, stab and bind me. I am forced to forsake my shelter and go out into the rain and the wind.

Even those who want to be Christians condemn me. Because of God's name they expel me out of their church. The hypocritical masses make a fool out of me. They say I belong to the devil and that I do not have a God. They do all this because I hate their sectarian and treacherous ways, and because I avoid the way of sin people raise a great cry after me: "Heretic, get out of here!" They throw my past sins before me and say: "Let the hangman dispute with him!" They put me on the rack and torture me. They tear my body apart.

God, will you not kindly look into this and see what the people are doing? I commend myself to you and leave myself in your hands.[9]

The cross was heavy, but the Anabaptists gladly endured it to gain eternal joy. Leonhard Schiemer ended his description of the Anabaptists' tribulation with these words:

Oh Lord, no tribulation is so great that it can draw us away from you. . . . Glory, triumph and honour are yours from now into eternity. Your righteousness is always blessed by the people who gather in your name. You will come again to judge the earth![10]

Christoph Bauman's account ends likewise with words of mercy and hope:

God, I pray from my heart that you would forgive the sins of those who trouble

---

[9] *Ausbund*, 76

[10] *op. cit.*

me. And do keep all your children safe, wherever they are in this valley of sorrows—driven apart, tortured, imprisoned, and suffering great tribulation. Father, most precious to my heart, lead us into the promised land. Lead us out of all pain and martyrdom, anguish, chains, and bonds into your holy community. There you alone will be praised by the children you love: those who live in obedience to you! Amen.[11]

What About the Children?

Every parent who joined the early Anabaptist movement knew what his decision would bring upon his family: poverty, suffering, and most likely flight. Parents knew at baptism that their finding peace with God could well leave their companions in a widowed state or their children as orphans. Along with the joy of seeing sons and daughters baptised came the dread of seeing them burned at the stake.

Menno Simons wrote:

> Believing parents are minded like this about their children: they would a hundred times rather see them in a deep dark dungeon for the sake of Christ, than sitting with deceptive priests in an idol church, or in the company of drunken dolts in a tavern. A hundred times rather would they see them bound and dragged before the court, than to see them marry rich companions who do not fear God—feted in dances, song and play, pomp and splendour and musical instruments. A hundred times rather would they see their children scourged from head to foot for the sake of the Lord than to see them dressed in silks, jewellery, or costly trimmed and tailored clothes. Yes, a hundred times rather would they see them exiled, burning at the stake, drowned, or being pulled apart on the rack for righteousness' sake than to see them live apart from God—than to see them be emperors or kings only to end up in hell.[12]

The Flame of God

Martin Luther and his colleagues met at Speyer on the Rhein in 1529. They gathered to define the evangelical liberties of the new Protestant states of Germany, and to establish the Protestant church in "peace, liberty, and the blessing of God." At the same meeting they passed a resolution: "Every Anabaptist, both male and female, shall be put to death by fire, sword, or in some other way."

But Martin Luther and his colleagues could not carry out their plans at once. Neither could the Roman Catholics, Huldrych Zwingli, nor John Calvin. The flame of the Anabaptist movement, instead of flickering out, grew brighter.

Kaspar Braitmichel wrote:

> The authorities wanted to extinguish the light of truth, but more and more kept getting converted. They caught men and women, young men and girls—everyone who gave himself up to the faith, and who separated himself from the ungodly affairs of society. In some places all the prisons were full. The persecutors wanted to frighten them. But they sang in prison and were so joyful in their bonds that the prison keepers feared instead. The

---

[11] *op. cit.*

[12] *Van dat rechte christen ghelooue . . .* ca. 1542

authorities no longer knew what to do with them all. . . .

> The Kurfürst arrested—due to the emperor's mandate—around 450 believers. His subordinate, the Lord Diedrich von Schönberg had many Anabaptists beheaded, drowned, and killed in other ways at Alzey. His men searched for them, dragging them from the houses of the city and leading them like sheep to the slaughter in the city square.
>
> Of these believers, not one recanted. They all went joyfully to their death. While some were being drowned and beheaded, the rest sang while they waited their turn. They stood strong in the truth they professed and sure in the faith they had received from God. A few of them whom they did not want to kill right away they tortured by chopping off their fingers, by burning crosses into their foreheads, and through many other evil means. But the Lord von Schönberg finally asked in despair: "What shall I do? The more I sentence to death the more there are!"[13]

The stronger the winds of persecution the higher leaped the flames of the Anabaptist revival. German courts soon discovered that the joyful testimony of Anabaptist believers during public executions stirred the masses. This led to the gagging of the condemned and in some cases the screwing of their tongues to the roofs of their mouths or the calling in of military bands to keep the crowds from hearing what they said. But the first Anabaptists' witness could not be extinguished. Even with their tongues cut out, their hands tied behind them, and a bag of gunpowder pulled up beneath their jaws, they could lift a finger and smile.

Companies of mounted solders authorised to kill Anabaptists on the spot roamed through southern Germany. At first there were four hundred soldiers, but the number soon had to be increased to a thousand. The chronicle of the brothers in Moravia, at the end of a report of 2,173 people put to death for what they believed said:

> No man was able to take out of their hearts what they had experienced. . . . The fire of God burned within them. They would die the most violent death, in fact they would have died ten times rather than forsake the truth to which they had married themselves. . . . They drank from God's fountain of the water of life and knew that God would help them to bear the cross and overcome the bitterness of death.[14]

Powerless Against the Truth

The first Anabaptists comforted one another with the promise that men are "powerless against the truth" (2 Cor. 13:8), and that no enemy could do to them what God would not allow.

Kaspar Braitmichel wrote:

God said through the prophet that whoever persecutes his people pokes him in the eye. God allows such people to make many plans, but he does not allow them to carry them all through. David sang: "The kings of the nations rise up and rulers take counsel with one another against the Lord and his Anointed One. But he who lives in the heavens will laugh at them and will frighten them with the pouring

13 *Geschichtbuech*, ca. 1570

14 *Geschichtbuech*, ca. 1570

out of his wrath."

God lets those who persecute his children dig their own grave. He lets the stone they throw up fall down onto their own heads. God meets those who make plans against him in such a way that it becomes clear what is happening—for glass cannot smash the rock. Neither can a flying piece of paper or a bit of straw withstand a roaring flame.

Many times God allows those who persecute his children to go ahead with their plans for a while in order to prove the faithful. The faithful need to drink from the cup of suffering until it is empty. But in the end, those who persecute God's children must drink their own mud soup and crunch down the bits of broken glass they have prepared for others.[15]

When they beheaded the seven Anabaptists at Schwäbisch- Gmünd Berthold Aichele, provost of the Swabian League, was the man in charge. Berthold was a ruthless killer, the man who ordered the massacre of the believers at the Mantelhof in Württemberg who got caught in a meeting on New Year's day, 1531.

By the mid-1530s Berthold could boast of having killed at least forty messengers and one thousand, two hundred other "Anabaptist heretics." But God spoke to him through the lives of his defenseless victims. He saw their faces as they died and heard their testimonies, including that of the miller's son.

Finally, after the public execution of the messenger Onophrus Griesinger[16] at Brixen in South Tyrol, he could take no more. Convicted mightily, he lifted his hands toward heaven and cried to God for mercy. In a loud voice for all those assembled to hear, he promised before God never to lay hands on an Anabaptist again.

The lamb, Christ Jesus, overcomes!

Where, O death, is Your Sting?

Johannes Faber, Dominican friar of Heilbronn in Baden-Württemberg wrote:

> How does it happen that the Anabaptists so joyfully and confidently suffer the pain of death? They dance and jump into the flames. They see the flashing sword without dismay, and speak and preach to the spectators with big smiles on their faces. They sing

---

15 *op. cit.*

16 Onophrus Griesinger, beheaded on October 31, 1538, had, before his conversion, been the clerk of a mine in the archbishopric of Salzburg. He led large numbers to the Lord throughout the Austrian Alps. Caught several times, eluding spies and with the price of eighty guilders on his head, he held large unexpected meetings in public places and directed refugees to the Bruderhöfe in Moravia. After a three-day communion service in the jurisdiction of Schöneck in 1538, they caught him and threw him into the castle dungeon at Brixen. Tortured on the rack and by other means, he wrote six hymns before his death.

> psalms and hymns until their soul departs. They die with joy, as if they were in a merry company, and remain strong, confident, and steadfast until their death. Persisting defiantly in their intention, they also defy all pain and torture.[17]

Johannes Faber concluded that the Anabaptists' courage must be the result of "a powerful deception from hell's dragon." But the Anabaptists knew better.

South German authorities beheaded Gotthard of Nonnenberg and Peter Krämer at the Windeck castle in 1558. A song in the *Ausbund* tells about their deaths:

> The people were surprised. They said, "What is this? They go to death willingly, even though they could be free." Gotthard answered, "We do not die. Death just leads us to heaven where we shall be with all of God's children. We have this as our sure hope. Therefore we enter the gates of death with joy!"[18]

Witnessing fearlessly to their faith, the Anabaptists followed Christ . . .

---

17 From *Von dem Ayd Schwören. Auch von der Wiedertauffer Marter. Und woher es entspringe, dass sie also fröhlich und getröst die pein des Tods leiden. Und von der Gemeinschaft der Wiedertäufer*, published in Augsburg in 1550.

18 *Ausbund*, 21:12

On to Peace

More than the pungence of curing meat and wood smoke greeted those who entered the back room of Matthias Fischer's house in Augsburg, on August 24, 1527. Matthias was a butcher. But on this day he had no meat to trim nor sausages to stuff. With his wife and children he had cleaned up his shop and gotten ready for an Anabaptist meeting to take place in his house. Little did he know that it would be the most important and longest remembered meeting of Anabaptists in southern Germany.[1]

Jakob Kautz, the ex-Protestant preacher, came from Worms. Hans Hut, Jakob Wideman and Hans Schlaffer came. Eucharius Binder and old Eitelhans Langenmantel came, with Hans Denck, Jakob Dachser and around sixty other messengers from the mountainous forests and walled cities of central Europe.

Anabaptists from Augsburg, in Bavaria, quickly carried Jesus' good news of peace through southern Germany, Austria and beyond. But city authorities (under the Reformer, Urbanus Rhegius) allowed them no peace at home. After many arrests, public floggings, and executions, the believers' community dispersed—while their witness for peace lives on.

Some of those who came had been scholars or priests. Some had been wealthy land owners. But among all those assembled, none had left a more illustrious career behind him than Leonhard Dorfbrunner, a Teutonic knight from Weissenburg in Franconia.

Trained to fight, Leonhard Dorfbrunner's future in the Emperor's army had seemed secure—until the Spirit of God spoke to him and another fight began: A fight between good and evil in his soul. Leonhard, in the early 1520s turned to God and decided to become a priest. But the priesthood did not satisfy him. The more he learned of Christ's gospel, the greater became his desire to follow him in the way of peace. He began to read the Gospel and preach to the people in German, but they threw him into prison. Then, rejecting his knighthood, Leonhard learned the knifesmith's trade and found his way to Steyr in Austria. There, in the summer of 1527 Hans Hut baptised him and sent him out as a messenger.

---

1 The meeting that has come to be known as the "Martyrs' Synod."

An Unarmed Knight

No longer on horseback, nor with sword, halberd, or dagger in his belt, Leonhard Dorfbrunner set out on the most dangerous mission of his life. He set out unarmed to teach people a strange new way of life.

Travel through the forests of central Europe required preparation in the sixteenth century. Just after the peasants' war, with freeloaders and highwaymen on the loose, one had to travel armed. But Leonhard, choosing the way of Christ, determined to offer the other cheek and to return good for evil.

By August he got to Augsburg and attended the meeting in Matthias Fischer's house. The brothers gathered there sent him and Hänslin Mittermeier of Ingolstadt on a teaching journey to Linz and the bishopric of Salzburg. Everyone got an assignment. Brothers left two by two in every direction, and within three months the flames of their martyr's fires began to light up the town squares of Salzburg, Rattenburg, Brunn in Moravia, Schwatz, Weissenburg, Vienna, Augsburg, Passau, and Linz.

Leonhard Dorfbrunner, before setting out for Linz, spent some time with persecuted Anabaptists in the city of Augsburg itself. All the leaders of the little congregation by the gate of the Holy Cross were in jail. The authorities did their best to stop further activities. They arrested all Anabaptists they could get their hands on. They shouted at, hit, and tortured brutally whoever did not escape. Elizabeth Hegenmiller had her tongue cut out, and they burned Anna Benedikt's cheeks through before they drove her out of the city in the spring of 1528. But Leonhard Dorfbrunner, trained in the martial arts, did not fight back. He simply left. Within a few weeks they caught him at Passau on the Danube. Pulled on the rack, Leonhard Dorfbrunner suffered in silence. A new Christian baptised less than a year earlier, he had already baptised three thousand others. He was a strong man, on fire with the zeal of youth. But, like Christ, he "turned the other cheek" to his tormenters and forgave them. They burned him at the stake in January, 1528. Then, a short while later, a new book appeared in Augsburg.

Vengeance is of God

The new book, published by Philipp Ulhart, was an Anabaptist statement on why Christians do not fight. Because of dangerous times, the author's name did not appear in it.[2] But it was the definite testimony of women like Elisabeth Hegenmiller and Anna Benedikt, and of men like Leonhard Dorfbrunner, who gave up their lives rather than defend themselves. It was the testimony of the whole church at Augsburg that suffered with Christ in the process of getting to know him, and that became like him in his death.

The little book from Augsburg begins with a reference to what the Protestants taught about bearing arms:

---

[2] Research has pointed, in recent years, to Pilgram Marpeck's authorship of the booklet.

> Luther and his men use the Scriptures to persuade the common people to take up arms and to defend themselves. They get the people to trust, body and soul, in the force of arms, and they cause lords and cities to rise up against the emperor. What a terrible shedding of blood when false prophets and their followers begin to fight in the name of God! (Jeremiah 6, Ezekiel 22, 23).[3]

God has appointed no power or rulers on the earth except Caesar. Caesar and his worldly government will rule on the earth until their time is up, as predicted by Daniel (Daniel 11), when the wrath of God will come upon all men (Isaiah 24). All flesh needs the power and control of Caesar.

Jesus Christ, however, does not rule or judge in earthly matters or in earthly kingdoms. No matter whether his followers get treated good or evil, they pay back nothing but patience and love. They are willing to submit everything they have, even their bodies and their lives, to earthly powers, that is, everything which has to do with what they believe. No man may use force or rule over others in matters of faith in Christ, for it is not earthly lives but eternal life which is at stake. God himself will not take eternal life away from any creature in heaven or on earth (Romans 8, Matthew 10).

Nothing but Christ

The writer of the Augsburg booklet stated his purpose clearly:

> I want to present to you professing "evangelicals," you teachers and preachers, nothing else but the crucified, patient, and loving Christ.

Then the writer described how knowing Christ frees us from the love of possessions, and thereby from the very source of strife and self defence:

> To know Christ and his teaching is to live no longer after the flesh. It is to hang no longer onto our possessions, and to be born again, through which we die to all earthly things. He who hangs onto his old life and possessions will lose them. But he who gives them up comes to possess eternal life (Matt. 19). He puts every thought of self-defence behind his back, offers to carry the cross for his master and Lord, Christ, and does this faithfully with all meekness, love and patience (Matt. 11) like the lambs of God. . . .
>
> Where Christ's teaching and life take over, fleshly rule and power ends. Where people, on the other hand, are ruled by the flesh, Christ must leave, like he left the land of the Gadarenes (Matt. 8). Christ had to leave the land of the Gadarenes because his work affected their business (their hog operation), something which needs to be taken into account if we want to be saved. . . .
>
> The loss of property is a small thing to give up for the love of God and our fellowmen. But it is the fear of losing possessions that deceives the whole world. It is that which binds the love of God and the love of man on the earth.
>
> If Christ must leave, like he left the village of the Gadarenes, unrighteousness takes over. Love grows cold (Matt. 24). Selfishness (*Eigennützigkeit*) takes over and all men suffer. It is easy to see how blind, senseless, selfishness destroys the whole world, but

[3] All excerpts from the Augsburg booklet taken from the *Aufdeckung der Babylonischen Hurn und Antichrists alten unnd newen gehaimnuß und grewel* . . . ca. 1530

men would much rather tolerate it than they tolerate sincere, loving Christians. They hate those who try to free them from the devil's destructive power. Oh blind Gadarenes! The whole world is blind!

Self-Defence and *Eigentum*

The writer of the Augsburg booklet wrote:

Those who think they possess their goods (Eigentum) want the government to protect them. They think it necessary to use force to keep peace, to protect their own possessions and the possessions of others. In fact, all use of force comes from the possession of property. From the holding of property comes all government and force in the world. But the communities of Christ (*die Gemeinen Christi*) are not based on the holding of property, but on Christ. They are subject to Christ before all else.

Therefore, those who are spiritual concern themselves with keeping spiritual peace, and those who are of the flesh concern themselves with holding onto their possessions in a fleshly peace.

God only permits, he does not promote the use of worldly force. The use of force does not come from that which is good, but from that which is evil, and God only tolerates it out of necessity. God knows that if he would take the use of ungodly force out of the world, society would become totally chaotic. So, for the good of his children who must also live in the world, he lets it go.

A Better Peace

For the sake of peace among the rebellious children of Israel, God gave the sword to Moses, to enforce his laws. Joshua, David and others were given the sword for the same reason—to keep an outward, temporary peace among unconverted men. But Christ and his followers have another calling. Christ does not bring the peace of Moses, nor an outward peace of the flesh. Rather, he calls his followers to have peace one with another and says: "I give you peace. I leave it with you, not as the world gives" (John 14). . . .

The Lord Most High, Christ Jesus, did not come to rule, force, judge, accuse, or have anyone accused before him. Rather he came to serve, and to allow himself to be ruled over, forced, accused, judged, condemned and mistreated. He is the mirror into which we must look if we want to see whether we resemble Christ or not. If we would do so, the question of whether we should take part in worldly government would soon be resolved!

The selfish also try to justify themselves with love for their neighbours. They ask: "Shouldn't we defend our neighbours when they are in danger, if we can do so? Hasn't God made us responsible to do this? God told us not to ignore our neighbours when they are in need, and to treat others like we want them to treat us.

Using such human logic, Simon Peter took it upon himself to defend Christ. But listen to what Christ did: He reached out and healed the man whom Peter, using worldly force, had struck (Luke 22). Christ does not want the kind of love that causes others to get hurt or despised. Rather he wants to see us loving and not hating our worst enemies (Luke 6), no matter what they do to us. . . .

True Christians help whom they can, whether friend or foe, as long as no one gets hurt by their help. The spirit of brotherly assistance will never be wanting among them. In fact, Christ's followers are so dedicated to help others that they would be ready to die for them. Complete love in Christ reaches out to friends and enemies. It is the result of freedom in Christ and spiritual union with him.

Three Swords

The first Anabaptists believed God gave three kinds of authority to three groups of people. The first sword was that of the world. The second was that of the Israelite nation, and the third was the spiritual sword of the Christian community.

Clemens Adler, from Austerlitz in Moravia, wrote:

> Since Christians are to forgive all misdeeds, why should it be necessary for them to exercise capital punishment? It is a matter for the heathen to sit in judgement over people's lives. Yet some have the notion that we should do this, either by authority of the law of Moses or of the worldly government, neither of which are of any concern to Christians. . . . From all of this it is easy to judge who are Christians and who are not. For our neighbours, those that carry swords, have the notion that they are Christians too, but their actions prove otherwise. . . . Indeed they are neither heathen, Jews, nor Christians; they do not themselves know what they are but confuse the sword of the world, Moses and Christ and patch them all together—like mixing cabbages, peas and turnips. Oh the blindness![4]

Hans Denck wrote:

> So it is with the teaching and work of Moses, David and all the patriarchs. However good they may be, where the love of Christ has outshone them with something better it is necessary to regard them as bad. . . . So the zeal of Moses, when he slew the Egyptian who did violence to the Israelite, was in a sense good, because he struggled for the right against the wrong. But, had Moses understood, or genuinely possessed, perfect love, he would have rather let himself be killed on behalf of the Israelite, his brother, than to have murdered the Egyptian, his brother's enemy.[5]

The Augsburg booklet stated:

> To God, all earthly kingdoms and estates are nothing but pens full of pigs—pigs that root up and destroy his vineyard (Psalm 80). And all those who rule over, protect and manage these pig pens are nothing but swineherds, because outside of Christ there is no faith, neither among Jews, Gentiles or professing Christians (John15, 2 John 1, 3 John 1).
>
> To the evil world belongs the evil sword. Evil rulers in the world must rule in their evil way to protect the evil of private property. In this way, a semblance of peace is maintained among the ungodly, for Christ can have nothing to do with Belial (2 Cor. 6). But the peace of Christ is something totally different. It has nothing to do with satisfying the flesh or hanging onto property. Rather it is that which allows us to live great joy and peace in the midst of our friends and enemies, no matter how things go. This is the peace of Christ of which he spoke: "I give you my peace, not as the world gives it."

Neither sword nor worldly force was used by the first Christians until the days of the emperor Constantine. Christians did not believe in using the sword and Christ had not given permission to anything more than the sword of the Word. Whoever went beyond that,in the days of the early church, was considered a heathen or an infidel. But the pope, as a servant of the church, married the church to

---

4 From *Das urteil von dem Schwert mit unterschidlichem gewalt dreier fürstenthum der Welt, Juden und Christen*. . . (Austerlitz, 1529).

5 From *Von der Wahren Liebe* . . . 1527.

the Leviathan of carnal power—supposedly doing Christ a service. Then the Antichrist was born and the mystery of iniquity began to appear (2 Thess. 2), which had been hidden for a long time previously.

The Peace of Christ

The first Anabaptists did not use the negative term nonresistance. They spoke only of *Wehrlosigkeit* (being without defence) and it was this defenceless response of men like Leonhard Dorfbrunner, the converted knight, that struck other knights and military men to the heart. Truly, it "heaped coals of fire" upon their heads as Paul had predicted (Romans 12:20-21). And it clearly revealed who was on which side of the struggle. "A lamb does not bite a wolf," declared the Anabaptist Adrian Henckel when they arrested him in the Hartz Mountains of Central Germany.

From the beginning of the movement, most Anabaptists did not question what Christ wanted them to do about war. They refused to fight. In 1530 Hans Herschberger, a young Swiss believer was called upon to defend his Protestant canton. Hans stoutly refused: "I would not fight against anyone, not even against the Turks."[6]

The road to Schleitheim (Schlatten), on what is now the border between Switzerland and Germany, held real dangers for those attending the meeting of believers on February 24, 1527. Many were promptly arrested and killed. Others fled to Moravia. But Anabaptists continued to gather in secret, hurrying up what is still called the *Täuferwegli* into the woods, for another 150 years.

Anabaptists meeting at Schleitheim, Switzerland, in 1527, believed the sword was for the world and the Word of God for the church. They wrote:

> We are agreed as follows concerning the sword: The sword is ordained of God outside the perfection of Christ. It punishes and puts to death the wicked, and guards and protects the good. In the law the sword was ordained for the punishment of the wicked and the same sword is now ordained to be used by worldly rulers.
> In the perfection of Christ, however, only the ban is used for a warning and for the excommunication of the one who has sinned, without putting the flesh to death—simply the warning and the command to sin no more.

6 From the *Basler Aktensammlung,* IV p. 337

> Now it will be asked by many who do not recognise this as the will of Christ for us, whether a Christian may or should employ the sword against the wicked for the defence and protection of the good, or for the sake of love.
>
> Our reply is unanimously as follows: Christ teaches and commands us to learn of him, for he is meek and lowly in heart and so shall we find rest to our souls. . .
>
> Secondly, it will be asked concerning the sword whether a Christian shall pass sentence in worldly dispute and strife such as unbelievers have with one another. This is our united answer: Christ did not wish to decide on or pass judgement between brother and brother in the case of the inheritance, but refused to do so. Therefore we should do likewise. Thirdly it will be asked concerning the sword: Shall one serve as a civil authority if called on or elected to the office? The answer is as follows. They wished to make Christ king but he fled and did not reject the ordinance of his father. We should do as he did and follow him so that we shall not walk in darkness. . . .
>
> Finally it will be observed that it is not appropriate for a Christian to serve as a worldly ruler because of these points. The government rules according to the flesh, but the Christian according to the Spirit. Their houses and dwelling remain in this world, but the Christians' citizenship is in heaven. The weapons of their conflict and war are carnal and against the flesh only. But the Christians' weapons are spiritual, against the fornication of the devil. The world's people come around with steel and iron, but Christians with the armour of God, with truth, righteousness, and the Word of God.[7]

Hans Hut, and many Anabaptists with him, thought Christians would take up arms after the Lord returned. But whatever would happen then was not of primary importance. Menno Simons expressed a more characteristically Anabaptist feeling when he wrote:

> Antichrist wants to defend and assert his cause with the Sword, but Christ Jesus has no sword or weapon other than suffering with his Holy Word. Oh bloody cruelty, which exceeds the cruelty of unreasoning animals! For man, the reasoning creature shaped in the image of God, born without fangs, claws and horns with a sickly tender flesh... as a sign that he is a creature of peace and not of conflict, is so full of hatred, cruelty and bloodshed that it can neither be conceived, spoken nor written. How far, how far, have we departed from the teaching and example of our Master who taught and sought only peace, saying: "Peace I leave you, my peace I give unto you."[8]

In the same writing Menno Simons summed up the Anabaptist nonresistent position when he wrote:

> Our wagon fortress is Christ, our weapon of defence is patience. Our sword is the Word of God and our victory is free, firm and undisguised faith in Christ Jesus. Iron, metal, spears and swords we leave to those who (alas) consider men's and pigs' blood of about the same worth!

Converted like Leonhard Dorfbrunner to the way of peace, the Anabaptists moved. . .

---

7 *Brüderliche Vereinigung* . . . 1527

8 *Dat Fundament des Christelycken leers* . . . 1539

On to an Ethical Way of Life

As a child, Ursula Hellrigl had to leave her home in the deep valley of the River Inn. Travelling fast, at night, through the forests and along mountain trails from Austria, she arrived with her parents at Auspitz in Moravia. There, upon reaching her early teens, she decided to follow Christ and joined the community through baptism. When the families from Auspitz needed to flee, in 1535, Ursula and a company of refugees fell into the hands of the police at Passau in Bavaria. She was fifteen years old.

Ursula steadfastly resisted the tortures through which the authorities tried to get her to recant. Even though she rarely caught a glimpse of him, she knew that the young man she admired, the "lively and quick-witted" Hans Fuchs who had travelled with the group from Moravia, was also in prison. He was sixteen years old. But they sent him to Venice as a galley slave, and transferred her to the dark, evil, castle of the Vellenberg, above the city of Innsbruck in Austria.

Ursula was grief-stricken, homesick and lonely. Her mother had died in prison, and two older brothers were also imprisoned, but she no longer knew where. Then, after five years of miserable confinement she learned of another Anabaptist in the castle.

Austrian authorities had thrown Jörg Liebich, an Anabaptist messenger, into the dungeon of the Vellenberg after they caught him preaching in the upper Inn Valley. People said the place was haunted and on several occasions evil apparitions rose up in his cell. The devil tempted him in visible form. But after Jörg had suffered months of mental and physical agony, the lord of the castle suddenly put Jörg into a comfortable room and gave him good food to eat. They brought Ursula into the same room and chained her one foot to one of his. Then they left them alone day after day. Kaspar Braitmichel wrote:

> What the devil and his children wanted to see is easily apparent. But they kept themselves pure and feared God. They did not allow themselves to be led astray by any temptation.[1]

Both Jörg and Ursula spent their time with Christ. While the days grew long, Ursula wrote a song:

> Eternal Father in heaven, I call to you from my innermost being. Do not let me turn away from you, but keep me in your truth until the end. Oh God, keep my heart and my mouth. Watch over me every hour. Do not let me turn away from you because of anxiety, fear or distress. Keep me steadfast in your joy. . . . I lie here in chains, waiting on you God, with a

---

1 *Geschichtbuech,* ca. 1570

very great longing (*mit sehr großem Verlangen*) for the time when you will set me free.[2]

Hope and Ethics

The Roman Catholic authorities of the Vellenberg, knowing human nature, expected to see Jörg Liebich and Ursula Hellrigl fall into sin. But they did not understand the prisoners' great longing to see Christ, and how that longing purified them as Christ is pure.

Menno Simons wrote in 1541:

> The Word of God is stirring up our German countries with its teachings. The finger of God can be felt in this while the Word becomes daily more powerful and clear. The haughty are humbled. The greedy learn to share. Drunkards become sober. The immoral become pure. Men fear to think a thought or do a deed contrary to God's Word and will.[3]

Shining Lights

"Walk worthy of the Lord and the Gospel," wrote Menno Simons. "Do whatever God asks of you without complaining. Act so that none may truthfully accuse you. Be sincere. Be blameless in this crooked and perverse generation. Shine like beautiful lights, like torches in the dark night of this evil world."[4]

Hans Denck wrote in 1525:

> All unbelief is sin. . . . Only when the law has done its work in us and when we stop seeking our own good can the Gospel find room in our hearts. We get faith by listening to the Gospel.
>
> Where there is faith, there is no sin. Where there is no sin, there the righteousness of God dwells. The righteousness of God is God himself. Sin is that which is contrary to God. All believers were at one time unbelievers. To become believers their old man had to die. They had to stop living for themselves (like they did in unbelief), and they had to let God begin to live in them through Christ. They had to stop living in an earthly way and start living in a heavenly way.[5]

Anabaptist leaders meeting at Schlatten in Switzerland clearly separated the works of darkness from the works of light:

> Things that are not united to God cannot be other than abominations from which we must flee. By this we mean all Roman Catholic and Protestant activities, such as church services, public meetings, politics, the swearing of oaths, and drinking houses. . . . From all these things we shall be separated. . . . Neither will we use unchristian, devilish weapons such

---

[2] *Ausbund,* 36. In the *Ausbund* the song is mistakenly attributed to Anna of Freiburg.

[3] *Van dat rechte Christen ghelooue* . . . ca. 1542

[4] *Een lieffelijke Vermaninghe aen den verstrooyden, en onbekenden kinderen Gods, Anno LVI.*

[5] From the confession Hans presented to the court at Nürnberg in Bavaria in January, 1535.

as swords and armour, for Christ said "resist not evil."[6]

The Ethic of Decency

Menno Simons wrote:

> We know that he who fears the Lord is honest, chaste, and sober. He will never drink, talk, sing, and dance with frivolous women.[7]
>
> Keep strict watch over yourselves, both outwardly and inwardly. Trim, teach, purify, warn, and chasten your hearts with the Word of God. Curb your thoughts. Subdue and distinguish your evil desires in the fear of the Lord, for blessed are the pure in heart.
>
> Just as there are many wicked men who violate poor simple, women, so on the other hand we find shameless women and girls. Many times they are the reason that such disgrace is sought and practiced upon them. Although many are not guilty of the deed, they are guilty of having too much to do with male companions. By their bold singing, dancing, drinking, kissing, flirting, primping and fixing up, they kindle the fire of base passions, which continue until they are consumed.[8]

Ethics and Education

The educated scoffed at the first Anabaptists for following unlearned men. But they were mistaken. Numerous early Anabaptist leaders had studied at the best universities in northern Europe, and even those of humble origin soon became "learned" in the Scriptures. Felix Manz read and interpreted the Hebrew Old Testament to a study group in his home. Conrad Grebel, writing to his brother-in-law and former teacher in the University of Vienna, Dr. Joachim von Watt, told of his Bible class where they were studying the Gospel of Matthew in Greek. A Latin poem by Conrad Grebel appeared in a book published by Huldrych Zwingli.

The first Anabaptists, although they disapproved of much that went on at the universities, did not in any way disapprove of learning. Their children learned to read well and much. Menno Simons, who wrote a great amount in Dutch and Latin wrote:

> I have never disdained education, nor proficiency in languages. In fact I have honoured and coveted both from my youth. But unfortunately I have never attained to them. I am not so bereft of common sense that I should disdain the knowledge of languages (Hebrew and Greek) through which the precious Word of Grace has come to us. Rather, I wish that I and all the godly ones would be at home in these languages, if we would employ them in genuine humility to the glory of God and the service of our fellowmen.[9]

Education for the Anabaptists involved the learning of both spiritual and elementary

---

6 *Brüderlich Vereinigung etzlicher Kinder Gottes sieben Artikel betreffend* February 24, 1527

7 *Dat Fundament des Christelycken leers* . . . 1539

8 *Van dat rechte Christen ghelooue* . . . ca. 1542

9 *Eyne klare vnwedersprekelike bekentenisse vnde anwijsinge* . . . ca. 1554

facts. They learned not to exalt themselves but to use their learning for the good of others. Especially in Moravia the education of children become an important work of the Lord's community.

The Ethic of Selflessness

The first Anabaptists, following Christ, lived for others. Hans Leupold, beheaded at Augsburg in 1527, said:

> If we know of anyone who is in need, whether or not he is a member of our church community, we believe it our duty, out of love to God, to help him.[10]

Speaking about the state churches, Menno Simons wrote:

> These people boast of being true Christians in spite of the fact that they have lost the sign of true Christianity altogether. Many have plenty of everything. They wear expensive, stylish clothes. They ornament their houses with costly furniture. They have money and live in luxury. But they allow their own members— those who have been baptised and who have partaken of the same bread with them—to beg. They allow the poor, the hungry, the suffering, the old, the lame, the blind, and the sick to beg for bread.[11]

A Protestant attending an Anabaptist meeting near Strasbourg in 1557 reported the questions put to the converts who were baptised:

> Are you ready if necessary to give all your possessions to the service of the brothers? D[12]o you promise not to fail any brother that is in need if you are able to help him?

For many Anabaptists the evidence of selflessness was freedom from private property in total community of goods.

Business Ethics

Conrad Grebel had a special problem with Christians charging interest on loans. He and most other Anabaptists taught that charging interest was of the devil, and they did not believe that Christians could be bankers, financers, or owners of large businesses.

---

[10] Hans Leupold, who wrote the triumphant song *Mein Gott dich will ich loben . . .* (*Ausbund*, 39) shortly before his death, was arrested with 88 others in the home of the sculptor Adolf Doucher, in Augsburg, on Easter Sunday, 1528. After his trial in which he gave a clear and complete testimony he was sentenced "from life to death" by the city court. Hans cried out at once: "No indeed, gentlemen of Augsburg, but from death to life!" causing great fear to come upon the people. They beheaded him on April 25, 1528 and after burning holes through their cheeks they banished the rest, including his wife and two children, the youngest of which was five months old. Hans was a young man and a leader in the church community. He had been baptised for almost a year.

[11] *Opera Omnia Theologica,* Amsterdam, 1681

[12] From A. Hulshof *Geschiedenis van de Doopsgezinden te Straatsburg van 1525 tot 1557*, Amsterdam, 1905.

Peter Rideman wrote:

> We allow none of our number to work as a dealer or a merchant since this is sinful. The wise man says, "It is almost impossible for a dealer or a merchant to keep himself from sin. Like a nail sticks between the door and the hinge, so does sin stick between buying and selling." Therefore we allow no one to buy to sell again as the dealers do. But to buy what is necessary for the needs of one's house or craft, to use it and then sell what one produces, we consider right and good.[13]

Daily Ethics

For a thousand years the church of the Dark Ages had taught people that only a few (the "religious"), could live an ethical life, and that the great majority of Christians (the "secular") needed to live in sin. A truly ethical lifestyle, they taught, was characteristic of religious orders, but apart from them it could not be expected.

The Reformers saw it differently. They did away with monasteries and religious orders and believed that all men should live right—at least on the Lord's day.

But the first Anabaptists did not involve ethics with place nor time. In touch with the Lord Jesus they lived to please him every day of the week. For this reason, the keeping of a "Sunday-Sabbath" held no significance for them.

Mang Karger, converted in South Tyrol in Austria (now northern Italy) testified before the Roman Catholic court in 1529:

> In the beginning God made the earth in six days, then he rested on the seventh. This is where the keeping of the Lord's day came from, and this is where I will leave it. The Scriptures do not forbid working on Sunday and it is not a sin, but one should celebrate it and keep it holy, unlike the priests who spend their Sunday forenoons in idolatry and their Sunday afternoons in adultery.[14]

Benedikt Kamperer's wife, Agathe, also interrogated in 1529, said:

> Concerning the keeping of special days, there is no day more holy than another. Sunday is the day appointed to get together, preach the Gospel, and discuss it. But people are misusing it now and spending the day as free time to do evil deeds.[15]

Wolfgang von Moos, testifying at Vill near Neumarkt in South Tyrol, simply said he believed nothing about keeping special feasts, Sundays, and holidays other than what is written about them in the New Testament.

---

[13] *Rechenschaft*, 1540

[14] *Geschichtbuech*

[15] *ibid.*

Ethics on Test

Jesus warned his disciples against doing good works to be seen of men. At the same time he told them to do good works so that others would see them and glorify God. The Anabaptists, facing both challenges, drew unusual observations from their enemies. Ulrich Zwingli, after calling the Anabaptists *satanas in angelos lucis conversos*,[16] wrote in 1527:

> Their life and conduct seems at first impression irreproachable, pious, unassuming, attractive, yes above this world. Even those who are inclined to be critical will say that their lives are excellent.[17]

A Reformed pastor of Appenzell in Switzerland said:

> The Anabaptists are people who at first had been our best propagators of the Word of God.[18]

Other reformed preachers from the canton of Bern informed the Swiss court in 1532:

> The Anabaptists have the semblance of outward piety to a far greater degree than we and all the churches that unitedly confess Christ with us. They avoid offensive sins that are very common among us.[19]

These facts disturbed Heinrich Bullinger, a leader of the Swiss Reformed church, very much. He wrote several books against the "shameless rabble" (the Anabaptists) in which he said:

> Those who unite with them will be received into their church by rebaptism for repentance and newness of life. Then they lead their lives under a semblance of a quite spiritual conduct. They denounce covetousness, pride, profanity, the lewd conversation, and immorality of the world. They shun drinking and gluttony. In short, their hypocrisy is great and manifold.[20]

The Jesuit priest, Christoph Andreas Fischer, leader of the Counter-reformation in Austria spoke of the Anabaptists:

> They call each other brothers and sisters. They use no profanity nor harsh speech. They do not swear nor carry weapons. In the beginning they would not even carry

---

16 devils transformed into angels of light

17 From *In Catabaptistarum Strophas Elenchus*, 1527

18 Walter Klarer, quoted in J.J. Simmler, *Sammlung alter und neuer Urkunden,* (Zürich, 1757)

19 W. J. McGlothlin, *Die Berner Täufer bis 1532*, (Berlin, 1902)

20 From *Der Widertöufferen Ursprung, fürgang, secten, wäsen, fürnemme und gemeine . . .* 1535

knives. They are modest in eating and drinking. They do not wear stylish clothes. They do not go to law before the magistrates, but they suffer everything in make-believe patience.[21]

In 1582, Franz Agricola, Roman Catholic theologian of the Dutch province of Limburg, wrote in his book *Against the terrible errors of the Anabaptists*:

> Among the existing heretical sects there is none which in appearance leads a more modest or pious life than the Anabaptists. They are irreproachable in their outward public life. They do not say lies. They do not deceive, swear, fight nor speak harshly. They avoid intemperate eating and drinking. No personal outward display is found among them, but humility, patience, uprightness, neatness, honesty, temperance and straightforwardness in such measure that one would suppose they had the Holy Spirit of God![22]

Following Christ into an ethical lifestyle, the first Anabaptists moved . . .

---

[21] Some of the books written by this man against the Bruderhöfe in Moravia are *Von der Wiedertauffer verfluchtem Ursprung, gottlosen Lehre, und derselben gründliche Widerlegung*, 1603 (The cursed origin of the Anabaptists, their godless doctrine and its thorough refutation), *Der Hutterischen Wiedertauffer Taubenkobel in welchem all ihr Mist, Kot und Unflat zu finden ist. . .* 1607 (The Hutterite Anabaptist pigeon house in which all their manure, mud, and garbage is to be found . . .) and *54 erhebliche Ursachen warum die Wiedertauffer nicht sein im Lande zu leiden . . .* 1607 (54 valid reasons why the Anabaptists cannot be tolerated in the land).

[22] From *Erster evangelischer Prozess wider allerlei grausame Irrtümer der Wiedertäufer*, (Köln, 1582).

On to Modesty

"*¿Serán monjas*? (Are they nuns?)" the old woman at the fruit stand asks in a low voice, her attention fastened on two girls coming up the cobblestone street.

"No," replies her granddaughter with a smile. "They are Patricia Ramirez and Elena Chavez. They have joined the Mennonites."

Twin towers of the church at San Francisco de Borja cast long shadows across the plaza. The two girls with white veilings fluttering in the breeze, modest skirts and net shopping bags find their way through town. New Christians in Mexico, near the end of the twentieth century, they are in an old situation— Anabaptists in a Roman Catholic town.

"*¡Qué lindo!* (How pretty!)" says the old woman at the fruit stand. "When I was young everyone wore dresses like that."

Simple Clothes

Those who follow Christ wear simple clothes. Peter Rideman wrote:

Since their citizenship is in heaven, Christians put on heavenly jewels. They learn from the world. Worldly people, no matter where they live, try to dress themselves as much as they can according to the custom of their land. They do this to please the world. How much more should Christians observe and imitate the ways of the land to which they belong: heaven! How much more should they adorn themselves according to the custom of heaven, to please God! Christians forget all other adornment to obtain the jewel of godliness. Those who desire this jewel are adorned by God with holy virtues. Holy virtues look better on them than gold chains around their necks. Those who recognise this forget about pearls and silk and gold.[1]

Menno Simons wrote:

> The writings say that the just will live by faith, and that a good tree will bring forth good fruit. We know that a humble person will never come around in jewellery or costly clothing. . . . He knows God and his Word. His fear and love for God forbid him to do such things.[2]

Then speaking about the state churches, he wrote:

> They say they believe, but oh, there are no limits to their accursed haughtiness, to their foolish pomp and pride. They go about in silks and velvet. They wear costly clothes. They put on gold rings, chains, silver belts, pins, and collars, veils, aprons, velvet shoes, slippers, and who knows what all else for foolish finery. They never stop to think that Peter

---

1 *Rechenschaft*, 1540

2 *Dat Fundament des Christelycken leers* . . . 1539

> and Paul have forbidden all this to Christian women. And if it is forbidden to women, how much more is it forbidden to the men who are their leaders and heads! Everyone owns as much finery as he can afford, and sometimes more than that.
>
> Everyone wants to outdo the rest in this cursed folly. They do not remember that it is written: "Love not the world, neither the things that are in the world" (1 John 2:15-17).[3]

Practical Clothes

The first Anabaptists, following Christ, avoided extremes in clothing styles. They avoided impractical and uncomfortable clothes. But they did not design new distinctive garments. The messengers Veit Grünberger and Veit Schelch, sent out by the Bruderhöfe in Moravia, are one example among many.

Travelling through Waldt in Pintzgau in northern Austria, the two men fell under suspicion of being Anabaptists. But the people of the town had no way of knowing for sure until they followed them into a hotel and watched them as they received their food. No sooner did the messengers bow their heads in prayer than the cry "Anabaptists!" reached the constable's ears, and they were promptly arrested and put in chains.

A court description of Philip Plener, elder of the Anabaptist community at Auspitz in Moravia, describes him wearing a grey riding jacket with blue sleeves, a black beret and red trousers. This was in keeping with the Anabaptists' practice of wearing loose-fitting, solid-coloured clothes, "according to the manner of the land." Men usually wore knee pants tied around the waist with a sash. Women and girls, even little girls, wore head coverings.

Anabaptist men considered shaving a perversion. When Albrecht, the lord of the Waldstein castle in Moravia, received Anabaptist messengers from the Bruderhof at Wätzenobitz and "in great wickedness cut off their beards," the entire brotherhood suffered their disgrace. Already in the 1520s Thomas Müntzer taught that wearing the beard was a part of following Christ. Leaders at Strasbourg forbade the trimming of the beard according to worldly fashions, in 1568, and Hans B[4]etz of Znaim in Moravia called the shaving of the beard (as practiced by both Roman Catholic priests and the Protestant Reformers) a "sure sign of the Antichrist."

Johannes Kessler of Sankt Gallen in Switzerland described the Anabaptists in the 1520s:

> They shun costly clothing and despise expensive food and drink. They clothe themselves with coarse cloth and cover their heads with broad felt hats. Their entire manner

[3] *Van dat rechte christen ghelooue . . .* ca. 1542

[4] The first Anabaptists, like their Hutterite descendants, wore both beards and moustaches. Two hundred years later, after the Napoleonic wars of the early 1800s, the Amish began to shave the moustache to protest French militarism. Some Amish groups did not stop wearing the moustache until after they were in America.

of life is completely humble. They bear no weapon, neither sword nor dagger, but only a short bread knife.[5]

Modest Clothes

Because the Anabaptists were slow to follow changes of style, they did eventually stand out somewhat. Thieleman J. van Braght compared the world's fashions about him with the changing phases of the moon.

An Anabaptist, describing life on the Bruderhöfe in Moravia in the 1560s, wrote:

> Dancing, playing and drinking are not to be seen among us. No fancily cut, stylish, or immodest clothing is worn. . . . But the one who leaves what is good and returns to the world . . . the one who reappears with a stylish collar around his neck, big floppy pants and checkered garments becomes instantly popular among sinners again. . . . The people of the world commend him for abandoning the brotherhood and for having become a "true Christian."[6]

Anabaptist leaders, gathered at Strasbourg in 1568, wrote:

> Tailors and seamstresses shall stick to the simple and modest customs of the land in regards to clothing. They shall make nothing new for pride's sake.[7]

Peter Rideman wrote:

> We serve our neighbours with all diligence, making all manner of things to meet their needs. But that which serves pride, style, and vanity, such as elaborate braiding, floral designs, and embroidery on clothing, we make for no man. We want to keep our consciences unspotted before God.[8]

New Christians entered the Anabaptist movement from all walks of life. They entered by the hundreds and thousands. It would have been neither practical nor possible to help all of them into a new set of clothes. But the brotherhood did give practical direction. Peter Rideman wrote:

> The person who comes from the world does not sin when he wears out his clothing after coming to the knowledge of the truth. But he should avoid misusing his conventional attire and should not let it hinder him from finding divine adornment. If it hinders him, it would be better to throw his clothes into the fire than to keep on wearing them. . . . We do not permit our brothers and sisters to make or purchase stylish clothing. Satan might take an opportunity in that to betray us again.[9]

---

5 From the diary of Johannes Kessler which he wrote during the early 1500s

6 *Geschichtbuech*, ca. 1570

7 *Artikel und Ordnungen der christlichen Gemeinde in Christo Jesu,* 1568

8 *op. cit.*

9 *ibid.*

Modesty and Conviction

> Innerly convicted to dress modestly, the first Anabaptists of all walks of life dressed as common peasants. In a meeting at Köln am Rhein in 1591, some of their leaders warned against "the wearing of fancy clothes, which speak more of worldly styles than they do of Christian humility." But they concluded that "it is impossible to prescribe for each individual what he shall wear."[10]

In the beginning the Anabaptists did not regulate specific dress patterns. When such regulations first appeared among groups with Anabaptist background (such as the Old Flemish Mennonites and the Amish), many leaders warned against them.

The Dutch artist, Rembrandt van Rijn, painted this picture of Cornelis Anslo, Mennonite minister of Amsterdam, with his wife, in the early 1600s. Even though Dutch Mennonites were the first to take an active part in commerce and industry (Cornelis was a cloth merchant) many dressed in plain clothes until well into the 1800s.

Gerrit Roosen, author of the confession of faith of the Anabaptists in northern Germany, and of the *Christliches Gemüthsgespräch* was a leader among European Anabaptists in the seventeenth century. On December 21, 1697 he wrote:

> I am truly sorry that you have been disturbed by people who exalt themselves and make rules about things not clearly laid down in the Gospel. If the apostles had told us exactly how and with what the believer is to clothe himself, then we would have a case to work on. But we dare not contradict the Gospel by forcing men's consciences about certain styles of hats, clothes, shoes, stockings or haircuts. Things are done differently in every country. We

---

10 At this meeting, attended by a large number of Anabaptist leaders fromGermany and the Netherlands, the Spirit of Christ led to unity and peace. Those present from the Netherlands lamented the fact that they had misused church discipline and the ban. They came to see that excommunicating people over details of application was wrong, and all those assembled prepared a statement of faith (the Concept van Keulen) together.

dare not excommunicate people just because they do not line up to our customs. We dare not put them out of the church as sinful leaven, when neither Jesus nor the apostles bound us in matters of outward form. Neither Jesus nor the apostles made rules or laws about such things. Rather, Paul said in Col. 2 that we do not inherit the kingdom of heaven through food and drink. Neither do we inherit it through the form and cut of our clothes.

Jesus did not bind us in outward things. Why does our friend Jakob Amman undertake to make rules, then exclude those from the church who do not keep them? If he considers himself a servant of the Gospel but wants to live by the letter of outward law, then he should not have two coats. He should not carry money in his pocket nor shoes on his feet. If he does not live according to the letter of Jesus' law, how can he force the brothers to live by the letter of his own laws? Oh that he would follow Paul who feared God, who treated people gently and who took pains not to offend the conscience of the weak. . . . Paul did not write one word about outward forms of clothing. But he taught us to be conformed to those of low estate and imitate only that which is honourable. We are to do that within the manner of the land in which we live. We are to shun styles and proud worldliness (1 John 2). We should not be quick to change our manner of dress. Fashion deserves rebuke. New articles of dress should not be accepted until they become common practice in the land, and then only if they are becoming to Christian humility.

I do not walk in the lust of the eyes and worldliness. All my life I have stuck to one style of dress. But suppose I should have dressed myself according to another custom, the way they do it in another land? Should I then be excommunicated? That would be illogical and against the Scriptures.

The Scriptures must be our guide. We dare not run ahead of them. We must follow them, not lightheartedly, but in carefulness and fear. It is dangerous to step into the place of God's judgement and bind on earth what is not bound in heaven.[11]

Not in extremes, not in worldly fashions but modestly dressed, the first Anabaptists followed Christ . . .

[11] *Abschrift von Gerhard Rosen von Hamburg. Den 21. Dezember, 1697*

On to Christian Families

On the Koppenstraat in the Dutch city of Briel, Anneken Jansz led a sheltered life in the large house of her parents. They had money and she was their only child.

Anneken, in the flower of her youth, met a young man called Arent. He was a barber-surgeon and their love led to marriage. They should have been happy. But money, parties, nice dresses, and expensive wines did not meet the longings of their hearts. Then one night another youth came to the Jansz home. His name was Meynaert and he spoke of following Christ.

Before he left, he baptised Arent and Anneken upon the confession of their faith.

Because they got baptised, Arent and Anneken had to flee. They left her parents' home and escaped across the English Channel to London. There a baby, Esaias, joined their family, but Arent took sick and died. Anneken packed her few belongings and returned to be with believers in the Netherlands.

Back in the Netherlands, on a wagon loaded with people travelling from Ijsselmonde to Rotterdam, Anneken and a companion, Christina Michael Barents, sang Christian songs. It was a cold morning in December. A passenger suspected that they were Anabaptists and reported them as soon as they got to the city. The police arrested them as they boarded a boat to Delft.

For one month the women were in jail. Anneken cared for Esaias, now a year and three months old, and wrote a confession of faith. Then they sentenced the two women to die.

On the morning of the planned execution day, Anneken woke up early and wrote a letter:

> Esaias, receive your testament:
>
> Listen, my son to the instructions of your mother. I am now going the way of the prophets, apostles, and martyrs to drink from the cup from which they drank. I am going the way of Christ who had to drink from that cup himself. Since he, the shepherd, has gone this way, he calls his sheep to come after him. It is the way to the waterspring of life.
>
> This is the way the kings from the land of the rising sun came to enter the holy age. It is the way of the dead who cry from beneath the altar: "Lord how long?" It is the way of those who are sealed in their foreheads by God.
>
> See, all these had to drink from the cup of bitterness like the one who rescues us has said: "The servant is not greater than his Lord, rather it is good enough for him to be made equal to him." No one comes to life except through this way. So go through this narrow gate and be thankful for the Lord's chastening.
>
> If you want to enter the holy world and the inheritance of the saints, follow them! The way to eternal life is only one step wide. On one side is the fire and on the other side the

> sea. How shall you make it through? Look my son, there are no short cuts. There is no easier option. Every alternate route leads to death. The way of life is found by few and walked upon by fewer yet.
>
> My child, don't follow the crowd. Keep your feet from the way of the majority because it leads to hell. But if you hear of a poor, needy and rejected little group that everyone makes fun of and hates, go there! When you hear of the cross, there is Christ!
>
> Don't draw back from the cross. Flee the world. Hold to God and fear him alone. Keep his commandments. Remember his words. Write them on your heart and bind them to your forehead. Speak of them day and night, and you will become a fruitful plant. Keep your body holy for the Lord's service so that his name will be made great in you. Do not be ashamed to confess him before men. Do not be afraid of men. Rather leave your life than depart from the truth.
>
> My son, struggle for what is right, unto death! Put on the armour of God. Be a true Israelite. Kick injustice, the world and all that is in it away with your feet and love what is from above. Remember that you do not belong to the world, just like your father and mother did not belong to it. Be a true disciple of Christ and have no community with the world.
>
> Oh my child, remember my instructions and do not leave them. May God let you grow up to fear him. May the light of the Gospel shine in you. Love your neighbours, feed the hungry, and clothe the naked. Do not keep two of anything because others are sure to need what you do not. Share everything God gives you as a result of the sweat of your brow. Distribute what he gives to you. Give it to those who love God and hoard nothing, not even until the next morning; then God will bless you.
>
> Oh my son! Lead a life that fits the Gospel, and may the God of peace make you holy in body and soul! Amen.
>
> Oh holy Father, sanctify the son of your maidservant! Keep him from evil for your name's sake.[1]

After writing the letter, Anneken folded it and tied it up in a piece of cloth along with a few coins she had left. She dressed Esaias and at nine o'clock, in the white winter sunlight, they led her and Christina down the street of Delft toward the city gates and the River Schie.

Crowds of people lined the streets. On the way, Anneken called out: "I have a baby five quarters of a year old. Who will take him?" A baker, a poor man and father of six, reached out and took Esaias. Anneken gave him the folded piece of cloth with the coins and the letter. Then they tied the women up, broke the ice, and threw them into the river to drown.

It was January 24, 1539.

A Spiritual Family

During the violent years of the Anabaptist revival, ordinary family ties took second place. Many, like Anneken Jansz, suffered the rejection of well-to-do families for their decision to follow Christ. Many, like her, also lost their marriage partners and

---

[1] Abridged from *Der blutige Schauplatz oder Märtyrer-Spiegel der Taufgesinnten* (Scottdale, 1915). The English *Martyrs Mirror* does not include the complete account of Anneken Jansz.

needed to give up their children. But they willingly suffered the grief of giving up earthly family ties for the joy of belonging to the family of God. Even the joy of marriage gave way to the "union between God and man that weighs a thousand times more than the union between men and women."[2]

Peter Rideman wrote:

> Marriage takes place in three grades or steps. The first grade is the marriage of God with the soul of man. The second grade is the marriage of the spirit with the body. The third grade is that of one body to another, that is, the marriage of man with woman. Bodily marriage is not the first, but the last and lowest grade. It is visible and serves as a picture of that which is invisible, that of
> the middle and highest grades. Just as man is the head of the woman, so the spirit is the head of the body and God is the head of the spirit.[3]

Natural Families

God's adopted children become one spiritual family. But within this spiritual family there are natural families too.

The one who follows Christ is ready at all times to give up natural family ties—parents, children, or marriage partners—for his sake. But Jesus Christ did not reject or minimise family life. He obeyed his parents, respected the families of his followers, and blessed their children. In all this the Anabaptists chose to follow him instead of the Church of the Dark Ages.

For a thousand years the church of the Dark Ages had taught that the relationship between men and women was evil, that it was holier to stay single than to marry, and that the Holy Spirit left the room during the act of marriage. The marital relationship was forbidden on Sunday because it was the day of the resurrection, on Monday in honour of the faithful dead, on Thursday because of Jesus' arrest, on Friday for the crucifixion, and on Saturday for the virgin Mary. That left only Tuesday and Wednesday. But even then, Catholic couples needed to confess what they did in private. The "sin" of the marital relationship was put nearly on the same level as adultery or immoral perversion.

The Reformers did not break with this position altogether, nor with Augustine of Hippo's ideal of marital relationships without passion. Martin Luther in his book *The Estate of Marriage* wrote:

> Intercourse is never without sin; but God excuses it by his grace because the estate of marriage is his work and he preserves in and through the sin (of intercourse) all that good which he has implanted and blessed in marriage.

The first Anabaptists could not accept such a dual position. They saw enforced celibacy and a frowning on the act of marriage as another "sure sign of the

---

2 *Die Fünff Artickel darmb der Größt Streit ist Zwischen unns und der Wellt,* 1547.

3 *Rechenschaft*, 1540

Antichrist." They believed that Christian marriage is God's order and design. Large families of home-educated children, wives who found joy in submission to their husbands, grandparents, handicapped and older single people who received loving acceptance became part of their way of life.

Hans Betz wrote:

> The Scriptures tell us that every man should have a wife for his body, a wife to bear him children so that they can be multiplied on this earth. God already commanded Adam and Eve to get busy in this way in the Garden of Eden. Marriage should be held in the same honour today, in purity and according to God's command. Marriage is honourable and good for all. The bed of the married couple is not defiled. In fact, God takes pleasure in it.[4]

Due to persecution there were many Anabaptist widows and orphans, but there were also many weddings. Some people who lost their partners soon married again to care for their children. But others lived for years without knowing whether their partners were dead or alive.

Celibacy

Those who lived in an unmarried state received the full support of the Anabaptist brotherhood. In fact, the first Anabaptists saw value in celibacy, even though they did not think it should be enforced. They were quick to appoint single brothers as servants of the Word and to send them out as messengers to preach and baptise. Single sisters stood out for their dedication to the work of the church community, and many witnessed to their faith at the price of their lives. Jakob Hutter, before they burned him at the stake on February 25, 1536, at Innsbruck in Austria, wrote to the believers in the Tirol:

> I also need to speak to you about marriage because there are so many single brothers and sisters among you. My desire is that every one of them would know how to handle and keep themselves.[5]

Celibacy, when practiced among the Anabaptists, took place in the wholesome context of the Christian home and community, never in separate institutions. The Anabaptists expected men and women, both single and married, to uphold the New Testament ideal of moral purity.

Wholesome Teaching on Marriage

The first Anabaptists did not think, like Luther, that everyone should get married to put an end to sexual immorality. Rather, they taught the necessity of following Christ in a holy walk of life both within and without marriage. Marriage is not a concession to man's evil nature. It is a holy institution, a picture God gave to

---

4 *Ausbund*, 102:7-8

5 From *Jacob Hueters Schreiben an die gmain im oberland*. . . ca. 1535

show his love for the church.

Swiss Anabaptists published a booklet on marriage as early as 1527. Dirk Philips later wrote another book on the subject. Godly marriage and home life were put into proper perspective by many other Anabaptist writers such as Peter Walpot, who wrote:

> It is a command of God to honour father and mother and to keep marriage intact, and it is natural to love one's children and one's wife. But Christ said: "The one who loves these more than me is not worthy of me. . . ."
>
> Christ says that what God has joined together, man should not take apart. It is important that we investigate carefully whether it is God who has led a man and a woman together or if they simply came together in the world. Many come together as prostitutes and rascals and have a priest (who is usually a rascal too) marry them. Can this be God's work?
>
> Those who have been brought together by the devil live under the devil's power. Where greed and money have led to marriage, shall such a marriage be of God? The one who separates himself from an evil marriage to follow Christ is not separated by man but by Christ and his Word. Even though we may call it a marriage separation (*Ehescheidung*), it really is no separation of a marriage. . . . But those who get divorced apart from Christ and his Word, simply on human grounds like the rascals of this world get divorced, do what is wrong and sinful.[6]

The first Anabaptists looked at marriage vows like they looked at baptismal vows. They believed that there was no way of breaking them without incurring condemnation. Anabaptist couples committed themselves to each other for life and worked out problems as they came along. Divorce was not an option for believing couples. Menno Simons in his book *The True Christian Faith* wrote:

> I write this so that everyone might wake up, repent, and lament before God his past disgraceful conduct. I write it that they may defile no longer their neighbours' beds, nor violate young women. Let everyone live in honour, each with his own wife, the unmarried keeping from all immorality. If an unmarried brother cannot restrain himself, let him seek a godly wife in the fear of God. If he has committed fornication but not yet married another, let him honour the girl he disgraced. Let him lift her up from shame, marry her with Christian love according to the word of God and teach their children and children's children what Tobias taught his son: "Beware of all harlotry and take not a strange woman. Keep to your own wife."

Directions for Young People

"Those who give themselves in marriage," counselled Anabaptist leaders in Strasbourg, "shall do so with the counsel and knowledge of the elders. They shall begin marriage in the fear of God and inform their parents of their plans."[7]

> "The church community will not marry young people of believing parents without their parents' consent," decided the leaders of the Dutch Anabaptists. "But parents must have a valid reason to refuse consent. In the case of young people who have unbelieving parents, they shall seek their advice and honour them. But if their parents

---

[6] *Fünff Artickel* . . . 1547

[7] *Artikel und Ordnung* . . . 1568

refuse to give consent for marriage, the believing young people will submit themselves to the judgement of the brothers."[8]

The Place of Children

Even in heavy persecution, the first Anabaptists dedicated much time to their children. Menno Simons wrote:

> Admonish your children daily with the Word of the Lord. Set a good example. Admonish them to the extent of their understanding. Constrain and punish them with discretion. Use moderation, without anger or bitterness, so that they do not get discouraged. Do not spare the rod. Use it when necessary and think on what is written: "He that loves his son spanks him often so that he may have joy in the end. But he who is too lenient with his child takes his side and is frightened whenever he hears a cry." An unrestrained child becomes headstrong like an unbroken horse. Do not turn him loose when he is young, or he will be stubborn and disobedient when he grows up. Correct your son. Keep him from idleness or else you will be put to shame on his account.
>
> If you believe that the end of the righteous is everlasting life, and if you believe that the end of the wicked is eternal death, then do your utmost to lead your children right. Pray to God for grace. Pray that he would keep them on the straight path and lead them with his Spirit. Watch over your children's salvation like you watch over your own souls. Teach them. Show them how to do things. Admonish them. Warn, correct, and punish them as occasion requires. Keep them away from undisciplined children from whom they hear only lying, cursing, fighting, and mischief. Direct your children to reading and writing. Teach them how to spin and do other useful jobs suitable to their age. If you do this, you will live to see much honour and joy in your children. If you do not do these things, heaviness of heart will consume you. A child left to himself disgraces both his father and mother.[9]

A Married Monk?

Many loving letters written by Anabaptist prisoners to their husbands or wives have been preserved. And the great love they shared becomes apparent in the accounts of wives and husbands encouraging one another before or during their executions.

Michael Sattler and his wife were a case in point. Michael had been prior of a Benedictine monastery and his wife had been a Beguine nun. But on May 15, 1527 he told the German court:

> When God called me to be a witness to his Word, I left the monastery and took a wife according to God's rule. I did so when I contemplated the unchristian position in which I was, and when I saw the monks and priests in such great pride and luxury, seducing this man's wife, that one's daughter, and the other one's maid. Paul said that in the last days men would forbid to marry and command to abstain from foods which God has made to be enjoyed with thanksgiving.[10]

---

[8] *Besluyt tot Wismar*, 1554

[9] *Kindertucht*, ca. 1557

[10] From the eye-witness account of the trial by Klaus von Graveneck.

Michael Sattler and his wife, travelling home together from a meeting of Anabaptist leaders, fell into the hands of the authorities. After they burned Michael at the stake, they turned their full attention on his wife, coaxing, threatening, and pleading with her to recant. But she refused to listen to them. She kept the type of Christ and his church unbroken until they drowned her in the Neckar eight days later.

Willing to build with Christ, or if necessary, to forsake with Christ their family ties, the first Anabaptists moved . . .

On to Christian Service

The Mennonite church called my father into the *Dienst* (service) when I was five years old. After that he went to sit with four other *Diener* (servants) and one elder behind a bare wooden pulpit along one side of the meetinghouse, and my brother David took charge of me in the young boys' corner. Our oldest *Diener*, Elam Martin, was a full servant (*voller Diener*). He did the baptizing and the marrying in our congregation. Sometimes we called him our bishop, although he was not ordained to any special office. Our one elder, my great-uncle Samuel Horst, took care of the church's money.

My wife first attended meetings among the Old Colony Mennonites at Chortitz, Manitoba. There, speaking Low German, they had a *Lehrdienst* (teaching service). The *Lehrdienst* included all the ordained men of the congregation who as individuals were often called *Lehrer* (teachers).

Both traditions, I learned later, are of Anabaptist origin: servants and teachers, the teaching-service of the Lord's church. Menno Simons explained them in his *Brief and Clear Confession* of 1544:

> The apostles ordained bishops and teachers wherever they established congregations. They ordained men who were sound in the faith and did not want pay. These were men of God, servants of Christ who laboured, taught, sought out, pastored, and kept watch only through love. They did not do this only one or two hours a week. They did it at all places and at all hours in synagogues, streets, houses, mountains, and fields.

As freely as they had received the Gospel they were ready to give it. But the new congregations, driven by love and the Spirit of God supplied the watchers of their souls with all the necessities of life. They assisted them and provided everything the servants of Christ could not obtain themselves.

Training for Service

In the same tract, Menno Simons continued:

> Brothers, humble yourselves and become blameless disciples so that you may become servants called by the church community. Try your spirit. Prove your love and your life before you begin to teach. Do not go on your own account. Wait until you are called by the Lord's church. Once you are called by the Spirit and constrained by love, then watch diligently over the sheep. Preach and teach valiantly.[1]

The brothers who gathered at Strasbourg in 1568 gave direction for training:

> Let the servants of the Word travel through the communities to prevent, as much as possible, any spiritual lack. Let them comfort the brothers and sisters with wholesome teaching. Let ordained servants accompany the younger ones on these journeys so that the

[1] *Een korte ende klare belijdinge . . . van der mensch-werdinge onses lieven Heeren Jesus Christi . . .* 1544

young may be instructed in the ways of the household.[2]

Who Calls the Servant?

"The calling of servants, according to the writings, takes place in two ways. Some are called by God alone without any agent," wrote Menno Simons. "This was the case with the prophets and apostles. Others are called through the Lord's church as may be seen from Acts 1:23-26."

Pilgram Marpeck, who lived in this house (on the left, with the bay window) held a good job at Rattenburg on the Inn. A mining engineer and government official, he lived far more comfortably than most people of his time. But when he turned to Jesus and became a servant of his church community, he lost everything he owned. Not just once, but time and again, as he moved from place to place to tend to Jesus' flock in need.

Dirk Philips wrote:

> God punished Korah, Dathan, and Abiram who undertook to do things to which they were not called. God will punish all men likewise who go forth without being sent by him. Let everyone see to it that he does not run ahead on his own before he is called of the Lord or by his church community in the right way.[3]

Anabaptist leaders meeting at Wismar in Mecklenburg decided in 1554:

> No one is to undertake of himself to go from church to church, preaching, unless he is sent and ordained by the congregation or the elders.[4]

---

[2] *Artikel und Ordnung. . .* 1568

[3] *Enchiridion*, 1564

[4] *Besluyt tot Wismar*, 1554

A Servant's Work

"A servant is to preach the gospel and feed the flock," wrote Dirk Philips. "Preaching is more important than feeding the flock with the sacramental signs. But in this passage the Lord puts them together."

At Strasbourg, the Anabaptist leaders defined the servant's work:

> Servants and elders are to take care of the widows and orphans among us. They are to visit and watch out for the physical needs of families in danger, especially where men are in prison. They are to bring them food if necessary and comfort them so that everyone may feel secure in the love of the brotherhood, and so that the men suffering in prison may have rest in regard to their families.[5]

Signs for Service

Some people in the sixteenth century said they would believe the Anabaptists if they could prove by special signs that they were called of God. To this Dirk Philips replied:

> To require signs and not be satisfied with the Word is an evidence of unbelief. Jesus did not praise the Pharisees for wanting a sign. He praised the centurion for his humble attitude.
>
> Suppose these people would see us doing miraculous signs. Would they not follow the Pharisees' example and ascribe our abilities to the devil? The Jews require a sign and the Greeks seek wisdom. But we preach Christ crucified. . ..
>
> Paul explicitly describes how a bishop shall be qualified. But he does not say that a bishop has to perform miracles. Nor do we read that Timothy, Titus, or other godly leaders of the early church did miracles. A man may be a bishop and not perform any sign, but he must preach the Gospel and feed the flock of Christ (Acts 20:28 and 1 Peter 5:2). It is true that miracles testified to the Gospel in the beginning. They confirmed and verified the Gospel because the Gospel was new. But signs are no longer needed. The law was also given with miraculous signs. But when Josiah found the book of the law, nothing extraordinary happened. He just read it and carried out what it said. In the same way we must be satisfied with the Gospel that has now come to light. We must rest in this and remember that it is an "evil and adulterous generation that looks for signs."
>
> Those who insist on signs and wait on workers of miracles are in error. They should watch out lest they accept and receive Satan, mistaking him for Christ. Satan is very clever and a good hypocrite.[6]

The Servant's Dues

The first Anabaptists opposed the state church idea of supporting religious leaders with taxes and obligatory tithes. Simon Stumpf and Felix Manz both admonished Zwingli that servants of the Gospel were "not to live from tithes and wages," but were to be supported by voluntary gifts from the church community.

---

5 *op. cit.*

6 *op. cit.*

Conrad Grebel wrote the same in his letter to Thomas Müntzer.

Menno Simons counselled servants to despise money and if necessary to "do manual labour like Paul: rent a farm, milk cows, or learn a trade if possible. Then whatever you fall short of will doubtlessly be given to you by the brothers, not in superfluity, but as necessity requires." The elders at Strasbourg wrote:

> Servants of the Word cannot fulfil their calling without neglecting their earthly labour. They have great responsibilities and are often gone from home for several days and sometimes weeks at a time. Therefore it is right and proper that we supply them with perishable and earthly goods. Especially responsible are the members of the congregations that they serve.[7]

The first Anabaptists considered the work of preaching and establishing congregations so important that they did not want their servants tied down with material responsibilities. At the meeting in Schleitheim, in Switzerland in 1527, the leaders decided that "the shepherd shall be supported by the community that has chosen him. He shall be given what he needs so that he may live of the Gospel as the Lord has commanded."

Dangerous Service

The challenge faced by Anabaptist messengers and servants of the Word were well illustrated by the meeting at Schlatten. During the meeting they had decided:

> When a shepherd is banished or martyred another man shall be called right away so that God's little flock may not be destroyed.

Right after the meeting Michael Sattler with his wife, as well as Wilhelm Reublin and his wife, Matthias Hiller, Veit Verringer, and a number of other Anabaptist men and women fell into the hands of the police. They lay in prison until one by one they either recanted or were drowned or burned at the stake. Those were the options faced by servants of the Word in the sixteenth century.

But in weakness and great tribulation the work of Christ went on . . .

---

[7] *op. cit.*

In Spite of Terrible Mistakes

Nearly everyone at the Sankt Pelagius school of the Chorherrenstift in Bischofszell in the Thurgau liked Ludwig. He was a quiet well-mannered student. Like many Swiss boys of his age who came from wealthy homes, he studied Latin, Greek, and Hebrew. His teachers saw in him the makings of genius, and by the time he was seventeen he matriculated in the philosophical faculty of the University of Basel.

In his studies of the classical works, including the New Testament, Ludwig became steadily more fascinated with the life of Christ. By the time he was twenty, he had decided to become a priest, and they ordained him in the beautiful city of Konstanz, down by the lake where the bishop lived.

While serving as chaplain at Wädenswil, south of Zürich, Ludwig found his longing to know Christ leading him closer to events taking place in that city. In 1523 an article of his, against the use of images in worship, fell into the hands of Huldrych Zwingli who published it. With this, Ludwig Haetzer, the young priest from the Thurgau, became a Reformation personality.

The leaders of the Swiss Reformation respected Ludwig's command of languages and his talent for writing. In 1524 they gave him his first commission, the translation of a Latin book for the evangelization of Jews. Ludwig did an excellent job.

Before he was altogether done, the Reformed leaders began to involve him in a much greater work, the translation of the Scriptures into German.

As a translator of the Old Testament, Ludwig travelled to Augsburg in Bavaria to work with scholars there. They had him work on the Psalms. It was an exciting job. Ludwig bypassed the Latin Vulgate and worked directly from handwritten Hebrew manuscripts. He met all the important people of Augsburg and accepted an invitation to stay with a couple, Georg and Anna Regel, on their country estate, the Lichtenberg, not far from the city.

Georg and Anna accepted Ludwig and loved him as their son. Anna, especially, who spent many hours with him while he worked at his papers in the house, developed a close relationship with him. But the Regels had unusual friends. It wasn't long until Ludwig discovered that Anabaptists visited the Lichtenberg. Then, one night the armed guard of the Duke of Bavaria came galloping in. They surrounded the house and arrested Georg and Anna for questioning while Ludwig escaped and found his way back to Zürich.

During the fall and winter of 1524 Ludwig worked with teams of translators, many of them highly educated men much older than he, in Swabia and Bavaria. Then they sent him to work on the book of Isaiah in Basel. It was in Basel that his polite, thoughtful ways led him into trouble. A girl who did the cleaning at the house where he stayed fell hopelessly in love with him. At first Ludwig tried not to pay her special attention. But little by little he felt stirrings in his own heart, and when she asked him to come to her room one night, he went.

It was so easy. No one found out about it, and no one suspected anything. But Ludwig felt terrible. He felt sinful and contaminated—a translator of the Scriptures, an earnest Christian, one regarded highly by everyone—and now a fornicator. He could not stand it and asked for leave to go to Strasbourg.

Little by little as he grieved for his sin, Ludwig felt the peace of God returning. In Strasbourg he met Hans Denck, and they became close friends with much in common. Their education and interests were alike, but Hans Denck was an Anabaptist. When the news came of Felix Manz's drowning in Switzerland, the Protestant authorities expelled Hans Denck from Strasbourg, and Ludwig decided to follow him.

They travelled through Bergzabern and the Kurpfalz to Worms on the Rhein and worked on translating the minor prophets. When the evangelical preacher, Jakob Kautz, tacked his theses to the door of the church and called for a public debate, Hans and Ludwig took part. But the authorities expelled them from the city, and Ludwig returned to Strasbourg.

To his surprise, the Reformed leaders at Strasbourg had found out what took place that night in Basel. The girl had confessed it, and when they questioned him, Ludwig could not deny it. Then, out of a job and out of favour with nearly everyone (including the Anabaptist congregation at Strasbourg), he followed Hans Denck to Augsburg and Nürnberg in Bavaria.

Ludwig studied and wrote. He kept in touch with Georg and Anna Regel at the Lichtenberg, which he considered his home. Two years later at Regensburg in Bavaria, he baptised several people, and the Anabaptist movement took root in that city. Then, back in the Thurgau in Switzerland, he married a young woman who had worked for the Regels and who had since joined the Anabaptists.

More and more, as Ludwig studied the life of Christ, he turned against his university education. After publishing a book against the foolishness of much learning, and while working on a translation of the Apocrypha, the Protestant authorities caught up with him at Konstanz on November 28, 1528. They charged him with disturbing the peace and with living in adultery with Anna Regel.

Ludwig did not deny it, and her name was discovered as an acrostic in one of his hymns. But he spent his time in prison profitably. He prayed and wrote songs. Convinced at last of the Lord's mercy, even in this time of humiliation and distress, he wrote eight hymns. The brothers in Moravia used most of them in their hymn collections, and the Swiss Anabaptists included his poetic version of 1 Cor. 13 in the *Ausbund.* It ends with the words:

> Love will never come to nothing. Everything has an end but love. Love alone shall stand.
>
> Love clothes us for the wedding feast because God is love and love is God. He helps us out of all distress, and who shall take us far from him? Knowledge swells but love builds up. Everything done without love comes to ruin. Oh love! Oh love! Lead us with your hand and bind us together. False love is that which deceives us. Amen.[1]

On February 4, 1529, they led Ludwig Haetzer to the town square of Konstanz. He walked calmly to his death. In clear words he spoke to the crowds who had gathered, warning them to repent and turn to God. The people felt sorry for him. He was young and good-looking. Of his extraordinary intelligence they had no doubt. But they could do nothing more than watch through tears as he knelt, willingly, for the executioner's sword.

A Counterattack

The Anabaptists, like Samson, were a threat to the enemies of God. Their movement was a spiritual attack on those enemies and, like Samson, they suffered the effects of a massive, spiritual counterattack.

The Anabaptists didn't fall into just a few errors in passing, just a few misjudgements quickly corrected. Like Samson, they committed all-involving, history-changing blunders that all but wiped them from the face of the earth.

Ludwig Haetzer,[2] who translated the prophets into German, yielded to temptation. Hans Pfistermeyer,[3] who gave his testimony before the Protestant court, recanted when they put him under pressure. So did Jakob Kautz,[4] the man who tacked the theses onto the church door at Worms. But even beyond the effects of these personal failures were the effects of the terrible mistakes the Anabaptists made together.

Mistaken Teachings

Apart from the Scriptures, the Anabaptists had no literature in the beginning. Neither did they have established teachings. But as the movement grew and their literature and teachings took form, mistakes became apparent in both.

---

1 *Ausbund*, 57:6-7

2 Quoted in chapter eight of this book.

3 Hans, who had been an outstanding leader among the Anabaptists of Switzerland, is quoted in chapter nine of this book. After he recanted, he became a tool of the Reformers to bring those who had been his fellow- Anabaptist prisoners back to the state church. He was not as successful in this as the once widely used Anabaptist messenger and author, Peter Tasch, of Hesse, who recanted in 1536. Peter convinced hundreds to come back to the state church before he died in immoral disgrace.

4 Quoted in chapter seven.

The Dutch and north German Anabaptists did not believe that Jesus got his flesh and blood from Mary, or that he had an ordinary human body. They believed that Mary was only a recipient of the Holy Spirit's work within her and that his body, as a result, was totally celestial. They (especially Menno Simons) defended this view at length, using unscientific "facts" to prove themselves right. This mistaken teaching, and the emphasis placed upon it, discredited them with the state churches and kept sincere seekers from joining them.

Other Anabaptists strongly believed in keeping the Sabbath,[5] or else in not keeping any day special at all. Some believed in paying military taxes, while others, notably the brothers in Moravia, strongly opposed it. But in few areas did the Anabaptists differ more from their descendants than in their teaching on divorce and remarriage.[6]

It was not uncommon for Anabaptists to lose their married companions when they decided to follow Christ. Unbelieving husbands disowned their wives, and unbelieving wives deserted Anabaptist men. After discussing what to do about it, Menno Simons, Dirk Philips, Leenaerdt Bouwens, Gillis of Aachen, and three other Anabaptist leaders decided in 1554:

> If an unbeliever wishes to separate for reasons of the faith, then the believer shall conduct himself honestly. He shall not marry again as long as the unbeliever remains unmarried. But if the unbeliever marries or commits adultery, then the believing mate may also marry, subject to the advice of the elders of the congregation. . . .
>
> If a believer and an unbeliever are in the marriage bond together and the unbeliever commits adultery, then the marriage tie is broken. If the unbeliever says it was an accident and desires to mend his ways, then we permit his believing wife to return to him and admonish him—if conscience allows it and in light of the circumstances of the case. But if the man is a bold and headstrong adulterer, then the innocent party is free. She shall, however, consult with the congregation and remarry according to their decisions in the matter.[7]

In other writings Menno Simons reinforced this teaching:

> Divorce is not allowed in the Scriptures except for adultery. Therefore we shall not to all eternity consent to it for other reasons. . . . We acknowledge no other marriage than that which Christ and the apostles taught in the New Testament: that of one man with one woman (Matt. 19:4). A married man and woman may not be divorced except in case of adultery (Matt. 5:32), for the two are one flesh.[8]

---

5 Notably Oswald Glait, prominent and widely respected Anabaptist messenger in Moravia and Silesia. Glait published a tract on keeping the Sabbath. A song in his memory *Ein anderes Lied von Bruder Oswald den man zu Wien heimlich ertränkt hat um der göttlichen Wahrheit willen* is preserved in the *Lieder der Hutterischen Brüder*.

6 Sixteenth century polemics against the Anabaptists mention their teaching on divorce and remarriage as another example of their "heresy."

7 *Besluyt tot Wismar,* 1554

8 *Grontlijcke onderwijs oft bericht, van de excommunicatie* . . . 1558

The Swiss Anabaptists in a booklet on marriage stressed the fact that the union of believers with Christ is more precious than the union between husbands and wives. They taught the permanence of marriage, and that it shall not be broken except in case of adultery. But then, with the counsel of the congregation, they did allow the "innocent party" to marry again.

The Anabaptist leader, Rauff Bisch of the Kurpfalz, said at the Frankenthal disputation in 1571:

> We believe that nothing may terminate a marriage except adultery. But if the unbeliever wants to divorce because of the faith, we would let him go as Paul says in 1 Cor. 7. We believe that the cause for divorce should never be found in the believer.[9]

The Anabaptists of Hesse, in central Germany, stated in 1578:

> We believe and confess that a man and woman who have by divine foreordination, destiny, and joining in marriage become one flesh may not be divorced because of excommunication, belief or unbelief, anger, quarrelling, hardness of heart, but only in the case of adultery.[10]

The Anabaptists in Moravia included the following among their five articles of faith in 1547:

> If the unbelieving one departs let him depart. . . . A brother or sister is not under bondage in such a case.[11]

Most Anabaptists emphasised the fact that "nothing can break the marriage bond except adultery." But the presence of divorced and remarried couples among them caused personal hardship and earned them much criticism. On at least one occasion a brother who had remarried, Klaus Frey of Ansbach in southern Germany, was executed for bigamy.

After the sixteenth century the Anabaptists' descendants gradually changed their position. By the end of the 1800s (and the rise of Fundamentalism in America) the Mennonites, the Amish, and the Hutterites all took a firm stand against a second marriage or living with another partner after a divorce.

A Mistaken Emphasis

Even though Christ was not an ascetic as were some of the first Christian religious orders, a trend toward asceticism developed early in the Anabaptist movement. It was the trend that eventually came to pattern the lives of their Old Colony, Amish, and Old Order Mennonite descendants. *Is 's nett zu scheh*? (Isn't it

---

[9] From *Protocoll, Das ist Alle handlung des gesprechs zu Franckenthal inn der Churfürstlichen Pfaltz, mit denen so man Widertäuffer nennet}, first published at Heidelberg in 1571.*

[10] From *Das Bekenntnis der Schweizer Brüder in Hessen*, 1578.

[11] *Fünff Artickel* . . . 1547

too nice?) was a question I heard innumerable times during my growing up years in southern Ontario. Anything from dress material to living room stoves to lawn chairs and painted barn siding could be condemned by the brotherhood simply because it was "too nice."

To associate what is nice with what is evil happened easily in the sixteenth century. Comfortable houses, nice clothes, and orderly, easy lives belonged to the "world" and only dungeons, flight, torture, grief, and anxiety remained for the true followers of Christ. The Anabaptists, living in such an other-worldly atmosphere of persecution, had no time for humour or recreation. At first from necessity, but soon from a brotherhood emphasis on strict asceticism, they ruled out many normal comforts of life. In Switzerland the Anabaptists even condemned congregational singing as a frivolous concession to the senses.[12]

Most early Anabaptist leaders had studied in the universities of central Europe. But they rejected their education, and with it their knowledge of the fine arts, philosophy, and culture. At the same time they made sure that their children had no access to them.

The Anabaptists became pilgrims and strangers—literally. Following Christ, nothing earthly mattered anymore. Driven out of the cities, their children grew up far removed from central European society. They slept on straw on the earthen floors of mountain homes. They spoke the coarse dialect of the peasants and dressed in homemade clothes. Within a few generations this austerity narrowed them—especially those of Switzerland and the moors of Friesland, Groningen, and around the Baltic Sea— into such closed-minded, rural, ethnic groups that it became hard for new converts to know or join them.[13]

Mistaken Prophecies

Free to read and understand the Scriptures for themselves, the Anabaptists began at once to study the prophecies of Daniel and the book of Revelation. Many of them concluded that the coming of Christ, the defeat of the wicked, and the peaceful reign of a thousand years was soon to begin. Nowhere did this belief gain a more firm ground than in southern Germany under the teaching of men like Hans Hut and Melchior Hofman.

About the same age as Conrad Grebel, Melchior Hofman spent his boyhood in the German city of Schwäbisch-Hall. He liked to read. For hours he would sit and

---

[12] Conrad Grebel, in his letter to Thomas Müntzer, gave the following reasons why it is wrong to sing in a worship service: There is no example for it in the New Testament. It does not edify. Paul forbids it (Eph. 5:19 and Col. 3:16). We are forbidden to practice what the New Testament does not command. Christ requires preaching, not singing. Human beings may not add to the words of Christ. Singing is not ordained by God and must be rooted out by his Word.

[13] With this it must be said that between 1675 and 1720 nearly twenty five percent of the names in police records regarding Anabaptist arrests in the Canton of Bern, Switzerland, were new family names, suggesting that they were still winning a substantial number of converts to the church.

read the mysterious books of Johann Tauler, Meister Eckhart, and Heinrich Suso, his favourite authors. But his father apprenticed him to a furrier in a city coat maker's shop.

Before Melchior turned twenty, his employer sent him north to buy furs. Once he knew the trade well, he travelled to East Prussia, Scandinavia, and Livland (modern Estonia) to look for them.

In the 1520s Livland was an unhappy, strife-torn place. Between the Baltic Sea and the great forests of Russia, it was a Slavic country "christianised" by the Roman Catholic order of the Brothers of the Sword. The bishops of the conquering church and the knights who protected them struggled for control of the rich grain lands of Livland, while the common people worked for them from dawn to dusk with little pay. Melchior Hofman soon saw the injustice, felt the tension, and began to point men to the teachings of Christ to find a better way.

At first Melchior thought Martin Luther could help. But when his studies of prophecy and his call for righteous living led him into conflict with Luther's followers, he saw that he had to take his own way. The authorities of Livland deported him, and in 1525 he moved on to Stockholm in Sweden.

In Sweden (a good place to find and work with furs) Melchior published his first book, a study on Daniel, chapter 12. It upset the city authorities, and he left for Kiel in Danish Holstein. By now a regular speaker in Protestant churches, he spoke often on the last days and on the prophetic symbolism of the tabernacle and the ark of the covenant. Little by little he developed a three- dispensational theory of end-time events. He taught that the first end-time period was the age of the early church. The second period was that of the power of the popes (the various beasts of Revelation). The last period was to be the one of Enoch and Elijah, the two witnesses, in which evil would be overcome and Christ would return to reign on the earth for a thousand years.

As in Sweden, Melchior's teachings made trouble in Danish Holstein, and in June, 1529, he with his wife and baby arrived as refugees in the Protestant city of Strasbourg.

In Strasbourg Melchior joined the Anabaptists and found enthused listeners to his prophetic explanations. One couple in particular, Leonhard and Ursula Jost, gave him their loyal support. Both of them claimed the gift of prophecy and spoke about the visions they had seen. Melchior published their prophecies in two books, and after many in northern Germany and the Netherlands had read them, he travelled to those regions himself to visit interested contacts.

Everywhere he went, Melchior found open ears for his good news of the coming kingdom of Christ. In the East Friesian city of Emden he baptised over three hundred people in a few weeks' time. Then, travelling back to Strasbourg through the valley of the Rhein, he welcomed more and more converts into the Lord's *Bundesgemeinde* (fellowship of the covenant). The year following he visited Amsterdam, baptizing fifty people, and Leeuwarden in Friesland, where Obbe Philips joined the brotherhood. Filled with prophetic zeal, Melchior Hofman became the Lord's instrument to transplant the Anabaptist movement from central Europe to the lands along the North Sea.

As the Anabaptist movement grew in the Netherlands and northern Germany, the prophetic teaching of Melchior Hofman came to incorporate a social problem of long standing. For many years the common people of the region had lived on vast estates of the landed gentry. Year after year the lords of these estates saw their wealth increase, but the common people who worked for them got poorer as their numbers multiplied. To them, the hope of Christ's prompt return, the overthrow of the rich and the establishment of justice and equality in a kingdom of peace seemed like promises too good to be true. But, as Melchior pointed out, they stood in the Scriptures, and all it would take was faith and a willingness to act upon these promises for them to become reality. First dozens, then hundreds and thousands of people, their eyes bright with the hope of imminent relief and glory, joined the new Anabaptist movement in the low countries.

Nowhere did the message of Melchior Hofman find a better hearing than in the old city of Münster in Westfalen on the lowland plains along the Rhein. The people around Münster spoke Plattdeutsch. For years they had watched heavily laden barges bring trade goods into the city. Then, on long muddy roads between clumps of dark forest and scattered farmsteads across the plain, merchants left with horses and mule trains to carry their goods into the uplands of Germany.

Münster was a trading city under the charter of the Hanseatic League. Its weavers' guild and even its industrious monasteries were some of the wealthiest in northern Germany. But in spite of the city's wealth, many of its residents were poor. When the poor people of Münster heard of the peasant's revolt in the south and of the Anabaptist's message of a coming kingdom of peace, they responded with their whole hearts. They began to seek for the truth, and Berndt Knipperdolling, a cloth merchant who lived near the Sankt Lamberti church, became their leader and spokesman.

In 1531 a new priest came to Münster. He was Berndt Rothmann, a young man educated in the school of the Brethren of the Common Life at Warendorf in Westfalen.[14] He spoke well and with Berndt Knipperdolling defended the cause of the people.

Berndt Rothmann's teaching awakened within the people a great desire to know the real Christ. Soon after coming to Münster, he published a resumé of the

[14] The Brethren of the Common Life lived in religious communities throughout northern Europe. Founded in the 1370's by Gerrit Groote they developed a reputation for honesty and spirituality. They held all their things in common like the early Christians. The deeply spiritual writings of Gerrit Groote and Thomas a Kempis (who lived in a community of the Brethren at Zwolle in the Netherlands) still speak to those who seek Christ.

teachings of the Gospel,[15] and by 1532 the people threw the images out of the Sankt Lamberti church and declared it an evangelical meeting place. Then two Anabaptist messengers, Bartholomeus Boeckbinder and Willem de Cuyper, converts of Melchior Hofman arrived. On January 5, 1534, they began to baptise the believers of Münster.

Things went fast. A young Anabaptist from the Netherlands, Jan van Leyden, came to assist Berndt Rothmann and Berndt Knipperdolling in the leadership of the new congregation.

Within a short time he married Berndt Knipperdolling's daughter. Then, believing that Christ was soon to come (Melchior Hofman had predicted he would arrive already in 1533), Jan led the new believers in taking over the city hall on February 23. They made Berndt Knipperdolling mayor, and four days later they passed a law that all adults who refused baptism upon confession of faith had to leave the city.

In line with Melchior Hofman's prophecies, the Anabaptists began to speak of Münster as the New Jerusalem. Hundreds and soon thousands of newly baptised believers began to come on foot, by boat, and on horseback from all over the low countries. They came to live in what they believed was the city of Christ. In the city they surrendered all private property and returned to living in community of goods. Berndt Rothmann published a book on the restoration of the apostolic church. But the Roman Catholic and Protestant authorities of northern Germany did not leave the "New Jerusalem" in peace.

The bishop of Westfalen, Franz von Waldeck, called for arms and early in 1534 laid siege to Münster. The Anabaptists, under Jan van Leyden (who on August 31, 1534, declared himself the king of the New Jerusalem), took up arms. Berndt Rothmann published another tract in which he explained that the children of Jacob needed to help God punish the children of Esau. Then they went out to attack the bishop, and on several occasions drove him and his soldiers back.

Within the besieged city, the twelve apostles who served as King Jan van Leyden's council and the prophets who received visions and interpretations kept informing the people of what was about to take place. A young woman, Hille Feicken, received the revelation that she was to go out into the camp of the enemy and slay the bishop like Judith killed Holofernes. But her brave attempt ended in disaster. They caught her and promptly put her to death. Other prophecies also failed, and the messengers sent out to the Anabaptist brotherhoods of the Netherlands fell one by one into the enemies' hands and were killed.

By the end of 1534 things looked dark, and the hearts of the people began to waver. King Jan van Leyden had turned, like the kings of the Old Testament, to having more than one wife, and others followed him. Berndt Rothmann himself took nine wives. But supplies were running low, and sickness, hunger, and treachery were taking their toll. On January 25, 1535, the bishop's army broke into the city and the

---

[15] This resumé has come down to us as the confession of faith of the South German Anabaptists, edited and enlarged by Pilgram Marpeck and Leupold Scharnschlager in 1531.

last terrible battle began. Blood ran through the streets. Berndt Rothmann escaped, but they caught Berndt Knipperdolling, Jan van Leyden, and others. Put in iron cages for display, they got carried around the country for several months until the bishop's men tortured them to death and let the ravens eat their bodies hung from the tower of the Sankt Lamberti church.[16]

Melchior Hofman learned about the tragedy at Münster while sitting in the tower prison at Strasbourg. An old prophet in Friesland had told him that he would be in jail for six months, after which he would escape to lead the Anabaptist movement into victory over the whole world. But five years had passed, and his imprisonment was getting worse. His legs were swelling and he felt sick. They let his food down to him through the ceiling, and all pleas for paper and ink fell on deaf ears. For some time he wrote his ongoing prophetic revelations onto the flyleaves of the books he had with him. Then he tore his bed sheet into strips and wrote on cloth until he ran out of that too. But his prophecies failed. His singing and shouting in prison got weaker as his health declined. Those who had once shared his vision scattered and fell away.

Melchior Hofman died in his cell at Strasbourg ten years after the fall of Münster, in 1543, a broken man.

But it took more than personal mistakes, mistaken teachings, a mistaken emphasis, and mistaken prophesies to break the Anabaptist movement. It took . . .

16 The "Anabaptist cages" still hang as a warning to rebels, from the church tower today.

A Bull in the China Shop

Clustered around its Benedictine monastery, Mönchen- Gladbach on the plains of the lower Rhein in Germany, was a city of song. Its monks sang. Choral groups of nuns from the convent of Neuwerk sang. The music of the great organ in the bishop's church broke into thousands of crystal echoes among the vaulted arches and gothic stonework high above those who came for morning mass.

But in the 1530s other songs began to stir the hearts of the people of Mönchen-Gladbach. Anabaptist believers, gathered secretly in city homes at night, sang to Christ and loved him. They sang about giving up all they had to follow him, and it wasn't long until the whole city discovered the truth of what they sang.

In the winter of 1537 they caught one of the Anabaptists, Vit Pilgrams, and tortured him on the rack. Failing, after months of barbarous cruelty to make him recant, they burned him at the stake on May 26, with a bag of gunpowder pulled up to his chin. Then they caught Theunisz van Hastenrath, the first Anabaptist messenger in Mönchen-Gladbach, and killed him too. The man who took his place was a bagmaker named Lambert Kramer.

Lambert loved Christ and spoke of him on every opportunity. He held secret meetings in his home,[1] and provided Menno Simons with a place to stay when he came through the area. On one occasion the authorities tore his house down and took his possessions because of his Anabaptist activities.

A close companion of Lambert Kramer was a charcoal maker named Zelis Jacobs. Zelis spoke bravely of Christ. They chose him to be a servant of the Word, and in the 1560s he ordained two young men, Matthias Servaes and Heinrich von Krufft, to help him. Under the direction of Zelis and these young men the believers met at night to sing and pray in a stone quarry between Mönchen-Gladbach and the village of Viersen.

The songs of the Anabaptists lifted their spirits to God. They did not stop singing when Matthias Servaes and 56 others fell into the hands of the authorities in 1565. But their songs took on a sorrowful note when the news of something much worse than that came to their ears.

Disagreement in the Church Community

Little by little the believers of Mönchen-Gladbach became aware of strange things happening among the Anabaptists of the Netherlands. Reports came of sudden excommunications and harsh shunnings—husbands refusing to eat or sleep with their wives, and many put out of fellowship for trivial reasons. The Dutch Anabaptists, it

---

[1] Lambert Kramer, after joining the Anabaptists, lived for some time in the village of Visschersweert.

seemed, no longer used excommunication to deal with clearly evident sins but as a quick fix for any disagreement among the brothers. Anyone who questioned what the church (that is, the most widely respected elders like Menno Simons, Dirk Philips, and Leenaerdt Bouwens) decided was in danger of getting "delivered unto Satan." Then, in 1555, things came to a head in the Dutch town of Franeker.

The tradesmen and merchants of Franeker, on the flat land only ten miles from Leeuwarden in Friesland, were not poor. They lived in cosy rooms above their shops that lined the city's cobble stoned streets. The farmers around Franeker, who tended cows and gathered hay for the winter, were not poor either. But they were hungry—hungry for the truth first preached by Anabaptist messengers in the 1530s.

Within a few years after the first Anabaptists passed through Franeker, a large congregation of believers gathered there behind closed doors, watchmen peering out of candlelit rooms to advise of danger on the street. Two hundred and fifty, three hundred, five hundred, and eventually more than six hundred baptised members took communion there. With the children, the group numbered well over one thousand souls, but Satan was not pleased and did all in his power to make trouble.

After several harsh and sudden excommunications (to which many brothers and sisters objected), the elders at Franeker excommunicated a teacher of the Word, Hendrik Naeldeman, and all those who like him failed to support what they had done.[2] The news of this reached the lower Rhein area. Then, while Matthias Servaes was still in prison, Lambert Kramer, Herman van Tielt, and Hans Sikkens travelled to Wüstenfelde, the little village on the plains of Schleswig-Holstein, 300 miles north, to find out what was going on.

The men stayed in Menno Simons' home. Lambert and Menno had been good friends from years earlier, and they had a pleasant visit. For two days they discussed the matter of the ban (excommunication)—when to use it and when not. Other leaders from the area came, and many shared their views. Then Herman and Hans left and Lambert stayed for two more days, visiting with the Simons family.

On his trip north Lambert was impressed with Menno Simons and the positions the Dutch leaders were taking. But in thinking about it on the way back, and after speaking with the believers in his home congregation, something did not seem right. How could excommunication be used so freely? Was it right to "deliver unto Satan" where there was no clearly committed sin, and in cases when the transgressor was already repentant? Was it right to demand such drastic separations from those within and those who had been put out of the congregation?

Caught between the Dutch Anabaptists and their hardline position on one hand and the more moderate brothers of Switzerland and southern Germany on the other, the believers on the lower Rhein became steadily more

[2] Hendrik Naeldeman and those who believed like him were put out of the Franeker congregation in the first mass excommunication that took place among the Anabaptists.

uncomfortable.

In the spring of 1557 Menno Simons and Leenaerdt Bouwens called a meeting (at Köln am Rhein) to discuss things. They invited Lambert, Zelis, and other Anabaptist leaders of the surrounding towns. Matthias Servaes could not come. But writing from his cell in the Bayen tower prison within easy walking distance of where the meeting took place, he admonished the believers to take a cautious and moderate position in the spirit of Christ. Then, several months later, Lambert and Zelis travelled south—this time to meet with Anabaptist leaders in the city of Strasbourg.

Prosperity and material peace, who should wish for anything less? As the Frisian Mennonites became ever more deeply involved in the fast-growing economy of the Netherlands (many of them buying land and milking cows) they left their "martyr complex" behind and became well-liked respectable citizens, willing to serve God in private and become "the quiet in the land."

The Breakdown

From all over southern Germany, Switzerland, and the German regions of France, the brothers came. In Strasbourg they met in a believer's house and read a letter Menno Simons had written asking the South German believers to accept his position on excommunication. Menno Simons called on the Swiss and South Germans to draw stricter fellowship lines and to separate themselves from all those who did not. But they prayed about the letter and discussed it at length until they decided to kindly but firmly reject it. They wrote up a letter in answer, asking Menno and the Dutch Anabaptists to reconsider, and to handle church discipline in the spirit of Christ, not in a rash authoritarian way. In the letter, the South German and Swiss brothers stated their hope that this issue would not divide them, but that they could keep on following Christ together.

Their hopes met disappointment.

Lambert and Zelis, travelling north to Mönchen-Gladbach, carried the letter to believers in the Netherlands who reacted strongly to it. The Dutch believers called it false doctrine, an accomodation to the world, and other uncomplimentary things. Menno Simons replied with a strong letter, which he called a *Thorough Explanation and Account of Excommunication.*[3] He sent it to Lambert and Zelis. After thinking about it for some time they wrote back.

Neither Lambert the bagmaker nor Zelis the charcoal seller could write like Menno Simons. Neither of them wanted a controversy. But they called Menno to reconsider and to return to the more moderate view on excommunication that he formerly held. They told Menno in this letter that they would rather be excommunicated themselves than go along with his extreme and un-Christlike way of putting people out of the church community.

Menno wrote a reply: *A Thorough Answer, Full of Instruction and Counsel, to Zelis and Lambert's Undeserved and Unjust Accusations, Their Slander and Bitter Name-Calling About Our Position Which Is, As We Believe, the True Teaching of the Holy Apostles in Regards to Excommunication and Shunning.*[4] Soon afterward[5] Dirk Philips and Leenaerdt Bouwens travelled south along the Rhein, through Köln and Viersen and Mönchen- Gladbach, all the way down to southern Germany, on a terrible mission. Everywhere they went they read a letter, written by Menno Simons, excommunicating Lambert Kramer, Zelis Jacobs, and all the South German and Swiss Anabaptists with them.[6]

More Trouble in Franeker

No sooner did Dirk Philips and Leenaerdt Bouwens get back from their trip south than they had serious matters to take care of in Friesland. Menno Simons died shortly after their return and Leenaerdt Bouwens became the leader of the Anabaptists in the region. But not everyone was happy.

Many brothers in Friesland felt that Leenaerdt "lorded it over the flock," and they questioned his taking of money for preaching. They also wondered about his drinking of wine (it seemed like he drank too much). Finally, in 1566, under Dirk

3 *Grondelijk Onderwijs ofte bericht van die excommunicatie,* 1558

4 *Antwoort aan Zylis und Lemmeken . . .* 1559

5 1559 according to the Julian calendar

6 After the great excommunication of 1559, the Anabaptist movement was permanently divided into two camps—those who held the strict authoritarian view of the north, and those who took the more moderate position of the Swiss and South German believers. Seventy years later, in 1632, those of the north set down their views in the *Dordrecht Confession of Faith.* This confession (which teaches the rigid view) was adopted by Jakob Amman and his followers (the Amish) in France and Switzerland in 1660. In 1725 it was also adopted by the Swiss and South German brothers who had settled in Pennsylvania. About that time, the Swiss and South German Anabaptists in America became known as *Mennonites.*

Philips' direction, Leenaerdt lost his responsibility as an elder in the church community.

Then came the question of how to replace him. The ordination (to take place in Franeker) brought to light a longstanding difference between the native Frisian brothers and the Flemish families who had moved in from Belgium to escape persecution.

The Frisians thought the Flemish dressed in fancy clothes. The Flemish, in turn, thought the Frisians lived in houses that were too fancy. When a Flemish brother, Jeroen Tinnegieter, was ordained by the elders at Franeker, the congregation divided at once. Leenaerdt Bouwens sided with the Frisians (and took up his responsibility again). Dirk Philips sided with the Flemish, and the two men who had worked closely together, sharing many dangers, joys, and sorrows in the Lord's work for many years ended up excommunicating each other. With that, they excommunicated en masse all those who supported each other, and the two groups—Flemish and Frisian—shunned one another completely.

In the early 1550s Menno Simons had written a compassionate letter to the congregation at Franeker imploring the brothers there "for God's sake to pursue peace. And if you have with words collided too roughly against each other, then purify your hearts and be reconciled in Christ Jesus. . . . If you are baptized into one Spirit, then fulfill my joy and be of one mind with me in Christ. Build up and destroy not. Let one instruct the other in love, and do not disrupt, so that blessed peace may be with all the children of God and remain with us unbroken and unto eternal life." But as a result of his own teaching on excommunication, Menno's good desires came to nothing, and the bull of authoritarian church leadership began its rampage in the china shop of the Anabaptist movement.

The Exaltation of Brotherhood Authority

Not many years after he left the Roman Catholic church Menno Simons had written:

> We counsel and admonish everyone to take good heed to the Word of God. . . . We have not directed you to men nor to the teachings of men, but to Jesus Christ alone and to his holy Word, preached and taught by the apostles. All teachings that do not agree with the teachings of Jesus Christ and of his apostles, no matter how holy they may appear, are accursed.[7]
>
> Christ commands all true messengers and preachers to preach the gospel. He does not say, "Preach the doctrines and commands of men, preach councils and customs, preach interpretations and scholarly opinions." He says, "Preach the Gospel! Teach them to observe all things that *I* have commanded you" (Matt. 28:20).[8]

---

7 *Van die gheestelicke verrysenisse* . . . ca. 1558

8 *Dat Fundament des Christelycken leers* . . . 1539

> We look not to lords or princes, to doctors and educators. We look not to the councils of the fathers nor to customs of long standing. For no emperor, king, doctor, educator, council or decree can stand against the Word of God. We dare not be bound by men. We are bound by the commands of Christ, by the pure teachings and practice of the apostles. . . . Doing this, we shall neither deceive nor be deceived.[9]

With a clear vision of Christ's authority, Menno Simons rejected the belief that the church stands between God and man and stepped out of Roman Catholicism. But toward the end of his life his vision got blurred and his teaching changed.

In the end, Menno submitted to the authority of a new "mediatorial church"—that of the Anabaptist church he had helped to establish. His earlier love for Christ gave way to an inordinate affection for the church.[10] And, thanks to the writings of his old age and of the Dutch and Alsatian (Amish) Anabaptists who followed him, his later position prevailed.[11]

Four hundred thirty five years after Menno Simons died, I listened to a Mennonite bishop preaching on "The Anabaptist Key to Sound Doctrine." He said:

> The Anabaptists discovered the key to defining and maintaining sound doctrine. They discovered the "filter of the brotherhood." No doctrine can be known to be Biblical unless it passes through this filter of the Biblical brotherhood. Therefore, all personal convictions must be presented to the brotherhood, where sound doctrine is defined, the Scriptures are properly interpreted, and the truth is discovered.
>
> It is in submission to this Biblical brotherhood that we find doctrinal stability. . . . God has charged the Biblical brotherhood to bring the Bible to the people. . . . So may God help us to reconfirm our commitment to the brotherhood—the basis of our faith, our source of stability, and the place from which we may go out to evangelise the world.

The bishop's sermon was well presented, and it expressed what Menno Simons, Dirk Philips, and Leenaerdt Bouwens no doubt believed by about the 1550s. But it was not the teaching that gave birth to the Anabaptist movement. And it certainly was not what many Anabaptists of Switzerland and southern Germany

---

9 *ibid.*

10 In 1558, two years after he excommunicated Hendrik Naeldeman and a large part of the Franeker congregation, and the year before he excommunicated all the south German and Swiss Anabaptists, Menno Simons wrote to his brother-in-law Reyn Edes: "Oh my brother Reyn! If I could only be with you even a half day and tell you something of my sorrow, my grief and heartache, and of the heavy burden that I carry for the future of the church. . . . If the mighty God had not strengthened me in the past year, as he is now doing also, I would have lost my reason. There is nothing on earth that I love so much as the church yet just in this respect to her must I suffer this great sorrow."

11 J.C. Wenger, speaking of Menno Simons in the introduction to his complete works (Scottdale, 1955), exclaims: "It is right that the church he served should be called *Mennonite*!" Considering the disastrous effects of Menno's later position on the Anabaptist movement, that observation may (ironically) be only too correct.

believed.

The Anabaptist movement began with the belief that the church was *not* called by God to "bring the Bible to the people," the truth is *not* found in consensus, and church councils do *not* have the right to define or interpret the teachings of Christ. Menno Simons, in the earlier years of his ministry, wrote, "Our *concilium* (council) is what was written in the Scriptures. . . . Nothing may be preached in Christ's kingdom but the King's commands. Nothing may be taught in Christ's house and church but Christ the husband's own words. The entire household must govern itself according to him."[12]

Once this changed it did not take long until they had. . .

Still More Trouble in Franeker

After the tragic division of 1566, that divided most Dutch Anabaptists into *Frisian* and *Flemish* congregations, the Flemish group in Franeker needed a new meetinghouse. Their elder, Thomas Bintgens, entrusted with the church's money, was happy to find a bargain. A poor man of the city (a drunkard) had been forced by his creditors to sell his house to the highest bidder. The drunkard knew Thomas Bintgens. He offered to sell him the house for 700 florins, but to avoid the possibility of higher bids, he falsely made the receipt to read 800 florins.

Thomas Bintgens did not think much about this insignificant detail. He gave his report to the other ministers, not sparing any information, and expected them to be pleased.

They were not pleased. In fact, Jacob Keest, Joos Jans, and Jacob Berends were horrified. "You mean you bought the house from that drunkard without talking to his creditors!" they exclaimed. "How could you do such a thing as accept a false receipt!"

No sooner was Thomas confronted with his error than he repented heartily. "I would rather pay for the house two times with my own money than offend someone," he declared. But his fellow ministers were not satisfied.

"Thomas needs to be silenced," they decided. "Such a major lack of judgement shows that he is not qualified to serve in the ministry." But many in the congregation did not agree.

"Thomas is a good man," they said. "In fact, he is more consistent in his daily life and deals more forthrightly with sin and worldliness than the other ministers."

It was true. Thomas Bintgens had been the most "conservative" among the

12 *Dat Fundament des Christelycken leers . . .* 1539

Flemish Mennonite ministers at Franeker. Before long the "conservative" members of the congregation rallied around him, while the "liberals" supported his opponents. On three occasions, committees of elders from other congregations—Haarlem, Amsterdam, Groningen, and elsewhere—were called in to settle the dispute. But they could not bring the conflict to a conclusion, and once more they resorted to excommunication to settle their differences.

Both groups excommunicated and began to shun each other. And the division spread throughout the Netherlands and northern Germany. Before many years had passed, practically all the Flemish Mennonite churches had divided into conservative "House-buyer" and more liberal "Contra-House- buyer" groups.[13]

The Trouble Increases

As the Anabaptists of the Netherlands turned their energies to enforcing their authority and the rules they had made upon one another, those who once persecuted them relaxed. By the end of the sixteenth century the Roman Catholics and the Protestants no longer feared the Dutch Anabaptists. Instead of warning people against them, they joined in making fun of their many divisions and small-minded rules.

It was true. As their focus shifted from following Christ to submitting to brotherhood authority, the rules of the Dutch Anabaptists multiplied. Every area of life from the kind of tools and trades one used in making a living to the exact style of clothing, shoes, hats, and haircuts became important. In 1589 the Frisians (Leenaerdt Bouwens' group) divided into *Harde Vriezen* and *Slappe Vriezen* (Hard Frisians and Slack Frisians). The Hard Frisians (who considered themselves the only church of Christ) soon divided into the *Jan Jacobsgezinden,*[14] *Thijs-Gerritszvolk,* the *Pieter-Jeltjesvolk,* and dozens of other tiny groups and subgroups.[15] Some of the Slack Frisians united with Hendrik Naeldeman's group (the Waterlander Mennonites), and some joined the Anabaptist congregations of the lower Rhein. At the same time the Flemish Mennonites (Dirk Philips' group) split into *Oude Vlamingen* and *Zachte Vlamingen* (Old Flemish and Slow Flemish), and both of these groups broke up into many more: the *Vermeulensvolk,* the *Vincent de Hondvolk,* the *Thomas Snepvolk,* and the *Jan-Evertsvolk* to name a few.

Practically every group "delivered unto Satan" the group from which it came and got "delivered unto Satan" in return. Within thirty years of Menno

---

13 The unfortunate names, especially the former, remained in use for a long time. One hundred and fifty years after Thomas Bintgens, a Dutch catechism was still called *Mennonite Book of Questions . . . As Used in the Fellowship of Anabaptist Churches Called House-buyers.*

14 This group, the longest-lasting of all the little conservative groups, existed on the Dutch island of Ameland until 1855.

15 Historian and author Pieter Jansz Twisck was the leader of a "Hard Frisian" group called the *Jan-Pietersz-Twisckvolk.*

Simons' death, most Dutch Anabaptists had gotten excommunicated three or four times by other Anabaptists who claimed to have authority over them. Among the few exceptions were the *Bekommerde Vriezen* (Concerned Frisians), who refused to excommunicate the rest, and the *Stilstaanders* of Zeeland who did not take sides with any group but got "delivered unto Satan" and shunned by them all.

Then, as a final shattering of Dutch Anabaptism the *Lammerenkrijgh* (War of the Lambs) broke out in the 1650s. It started in the large Flemish congregation *bij 't Lam* (by the Lamb) in Amsterdam.

The War of the Lambs

The congregation by the Lamb chose Geleyn Abrahamsz, a 26- year-old medical doctor, to serve them as a teacher of the Word in 1648. Geleyn had grown up in a *Stilstaander* congregation on the island of Schouwen-Duiveland in the Dutch province of Zeeland. As a child he had been taught to speak sparingly and deliberately, to dress simply, and to live a modest life.[16] He did not learn much about the other Anabaptists in the Netherlands until he went to study medicine in the city of Leyden. Then he married a Mennonite girl from Amsterdam and settled there.

Geleyn's first goal as a teacher was to bring the Anabaptists of Amsterdam to unity. But many of them opposed him. They clung to the confessions of faith and their written lists of rules that divided them. This grieved Geleyn and raised questions in his mind. On January 11, 1657, he presented to the congregation by the Lamb a paper for them to consider. In his paper and in his conversations with the leaders, he asked these questions:

1. To what degree may leaders exercise authority over their congregations? May leaders ever decide what the members of their congregations should believe?
2. May a congregation or denomination claim to be the only church of Christ?
3. May the authority of human leaders ever override the authority of the conscience?
4. May statements of belief or interpretations of Scripture be considered

[16] The *Stilstaanders* of Schouwen-Duiveland, who wrote a book against taking part in harsh judgements and divisions, tried to follow Christ in the way they lived. They lived in unadorned houses and shared what they had with the poor. Another young man of their congregation (a friend of Geleyn Abrahamsz and about the same age) was Pieter Cornelisz Plockhoy. While Geleyn studied medicine in Leyden, Pieter travelled to England where he wrote *The Way to Peace* and *The Way to Happiness for the Poor*. In 1663 he and his wife set sail with 25 families to the New Netherlands where they settled at Horekill on the Delaware River. They lived in community of goods and concerned themselves with the spiritual and social needs of the Dutch colonists and their black slaves until the Anglo-Dutch war scattered them. Theirs was the first Anabaptist settlement in the New World.

infallible? Is there anything infallible outside of the Scriptures themselves?

Geleyn's questions struck the congregation by the Lamb to the heart. They all knew how Geleyn lived and what he taught.

None of the other Anabaptist leaders in Amsterdam followed the example of Christ as he did. But a number of the older leaders saw his questions as a threat to the Anabaptist-Mennonite movement itself. They called a great meeting at Leyden, inviting leaders from all over the Netherlands and northern Germany to come and discuss Geleyn's questions. They chose Thieleman Jansz van Braght, the compiler of the *Martyrs Mirror*, to be their moderator.

At this meeting Geleyn explained his belief that the Scriptures are a sure guide and that every man needs to study and follow them in a personal way (not only in a way prescribed by the brotherhood). He believed that all truth can be understood by everyone who comes to know Christ and who learns from his words and example. Finally, he believed that God will judge us not so much by what we believed as by what we did, and that if we seriously follow Christ our common goals and lifestyle will bring us together in harmonious brotherhood.

At this, the Dutch Anabaptist leaders shook their heads. "The man is doing away with sound doctrine," they said. "He is replacing the established positions of the church with a strange emphasis on lifestyle."

When Geleyn challenged the infallibility of the Mennonite confessions of faith, many of those who had come for the meeting rose in their defence. "The confessions of faith have come down to us from the time of the martyrs. They present a Biblical view," they insisted.

"But the martyrs did not all believe the same things," Geleyn reminded them. "Even Menno Simons changed some of his beliefs along the way."

At this, the Dutch leaders decided that Geleyn would either need to give up his views or be silenced. He responded with another question: "May a meeting of elders silence a man who was chosen by a congregation to lead them? Shouldn't that silencing be done by the congregation itself?"

This last question fell on deaf ears.

Most of the members of the congregation by the Lamb could not go along with the silencing of Geleyn Abrahamsz. They knew that he was a godly man, blameless in his private life, and an example to the unbelievers. But some wealthy families who held fast to the old conservative position withdrew under the leadership of Samuel Apostool and founded yet another Mennonite group in Amsterdam—the one that met in a meeting house called *de Zon* (the Sun). Much to the distress of Geleyn Abrahamsz and the congregation by the Lamb, the division spread rapidly, and within a few years the Dutch Anabaptists had regrouped under the new names of *Lamisten* and *Zonisten* (those of the Lamb and those of the Sun).

Among those who sided with the Lamisten were the remnants of the once flourishing Anabaptist congregations of the lower Rhein. But . . .

Their Singing Died Away

After they beheaded Matthias Servaes on Saturday, June 30, 1565, his companion Heinrich von Krufft wrote a song:

> My joy in this life is taken away. Into anxiety and grief have I come. Therefore, I sing with a sorrowful spirit, and if it doesn't sound nice, I ask you not to hold it against me.
>
> Ezra says that there will be a great falling away. Oh God, the pain! . . . The righteous suffer persecution in every place. Wickedness is taking over. They kill those who teach the Word of God. Oh God, where shall I turn?
>
> In the name of the Lord I lift my eyes to the hills from where my help comes.[17]

Persecution caused grief to the Anabaptists of the lower Rhein, but it was a small grief compared with the sadness of seeing the church disintegrate.

After Menno Simons excommunicated Lambert Kramer, Zelis Jacobs, and all the Swiss and south German brothers with them in 1559, the Anabaptist movement entered a time of confusion and distress. What Zwingli, Luther, and the Pope could not accomplish through force, the terrible abuse of brotherhood authority accomplished in the space of a few years.

In the north, the movement broke into dozens of quarrelling fragments. In the south, many got discouraged and fell away. Thousands of Anabaptists, including most of those in the lower Rhein area, gave up and joined the state churches. Among those who remained (mainly in out-of-the-way rural areas in France and Switzerland), Jakob Amman introduced the same disastrous teaching. Then the proud spirit of "we are the ones who own the truth" and "following Christ means submitting to us" was carried by what was left of the Mennonites, the Amish and the Hutterites to America to reproduce itself a hundredfold there.

Four hundred and fifty years later, Mönchen-Gladbach is still a city of song. But its music is *Rock and Roll* and *Reggae* . . . and the songs of those who follow Christ in that city are practically unknown.

The Anabaptist congregation at Mönchen-Gladbach died out in 1654.

[17] *Ausbund*, 24

Zu de Gmehsleid[1]

Zwansig Joa zrick hen mei Schweschda un ich viel gschwetzt von die Sacha. 'S hot vleicht net viel gebatt weil ma woara all zweh jung, neibekäat, un mit wenig Äafoaring. Juscht mia hen vielmols, meiats im Winta wans kald un schneeig woa draus, im Schtall bei de Millichhausdäa gschtanna un gschwetzt. Mia hen wichtige Dinga gfrohgt un gwunnet was in de Zukunft woa fa uns.

Uf ä Seid hemma Bang kat. Mia hen Bang kat von de Welt un von de weltlicha Mennischda um uns rum. Mia hen uns nix von sellem gleichstella wella. Unsen äfacha Lewaswandel, unse Muttasproch un alles was ma glennt hen von unse Fäafedda woa uns unaussprechlich viel wäat. Unsen ehnschichsda Ziel woa mehna davon zu wissa un bessa nochzukomma was sie uns glennt hen.

Uf de anna Seid hemma aa Bang kat. Mia hen net zu a Gmeh käada wella, wo de Leid net bekäat woara un wo ma so viel von de Zeit Unruh kadda hen iwwa Glehnichkeida. Mia hen nix zu du hawwa wella mit schendliche Sacha unnich de Junga un mit a leichtsinnig, unbekimmad Lewa. Mia hen oft gwunned eb eiats a Gmeh is was de alda Gebraucha halt, was geischtlich und evangelisch is, un was a Licht is fa de Welt.

Jetzt is 's zwansig Joa nochhäa. 'S hot schon viel gewwa in de Zwischichzeit. De Häa hot uns darrich viel fremme Bletz gfiad awwa 's is ma jetzt noch deitlicha wie 's ehmol woa es de Fäafedda uns ebbas wichtigs zu sahwa hen. Ich freh mich es mia ihre Stimm widda häara kenna in dem Buch, un ich hoff was sie zu sahwa hen kann eich—mei mennischda, huttrische und amische Gmehsleid—so viel helfa wie 's mich kulfa hot.

This book, many parts of it quoted from people in danger of their lives, in prison, and on death row, was not written for anyone's enjoyment. It was written to trouble and perturb, perhaps even to vex those who read it, because it is in trouble and vexation of spirit that one may stumble onto the narrow, problematical, almost unknown way that leads to eternal life.

The way to eternal life is so different from what we expect that many of us do not recognise it when we first see it. It is unreasonably rough and narrow. The cross is unreasonably heavy and much more unhandy to carry than what we could possibly have imagined. Nearly all the people we know (even "respectable" and "balanced" people) are opposed to it. But in the depths of all the trouble it brings us, we come to "know Christ and the community of his sufferings," and in knowing him we discover eternal life.

---

[1] For a short time I will switch to my native tongue, the archaic dialect (a form of *schwäbisch-pfälzisch*) spoken by the Anabaptists of southern Germany, and still in use among many of their descendants today. The material in these paragraphs is, for those who are unable to read it, not crucial to understanding the chapter.

Nearly five centuries have passed since our Anabaptist forefathers left the state churches. We have survived! We still try to dress, talk, and live like Anabaptists, but what has come down to us from our ancestors' time is not a great amount.

Two scenes from my home area, in the Waterloo Region, Ontario, Canada. An Old Order Mennonite meetinghouse (above) and the sign announcing a Canada Day picnic at an Ontario Conference Mennonite church.

Like our refugee ancestors arriving at the docks of Philadelphia or Buenos Aires, we stand among the treasured baggage of our past while peering anxiously at the new land that lies before us. Some of us rejoice. Others weep. We face an uncertain future. Do we have what we need?

Many of us who carry our Anabaptist names with pride— Brubacher, Troyer, Amstutz, Graber, Kleinsasser, Klaasen, and Schroeder—have returned in thought and practice to the world. Those of us who haven't done that, clinging to the traditions and the language of our forefathers, have split into almost innumerable little groups. Some of us speak to all the world about our glorious heritage. Others are ashamed of our reputation. Some of us glory in what we have accomplished while others despair at how we have failed. But like the newly- arrived immigrants, we have little time to stand and ponder.

Some of us think we should go back to "recover the Anabaptist vision." But we cannot go back. We must go on to perfection.

And even if we could go back, their vision would not be ours. Vision is a personal matter. God must open our eyes!

Some of us glorify the Anabaptist movement. The Anabaptists themselves did not. They saw themselves as nothing before a glorious God.

Some of us treat our historic faith and the traditions that come with it like sacred heirlooms. ("Watch out you don't break them!") They did not. Their faith was original and they tested it in practice. Innovations that brought them closer to Christ were in demand.

We claim to be the custodians of the Anabaptist movement today. But our apostasy and divisions have devastated our credibility. Are we "real" Anabaptists, or do we only pretend to be Anabaptists like actors in a play? From the world's point of view our claim is weak—like the Catholics' claim to be the original Christians or the Jews' claim to be the children of Abraham.

We enjoy thinking of ourselves as a "special" and "peculiar" people. But what if we aren't as special as we think we are? What if the Lord should open our eyes and we would see that we are not so different from the rest and really no better? Could we live with that?

The time has come to stop depending on our "glorious heritage," which threatens to become the brazen serpent before which we fall instead of falling on our faces before God. If our heritage gives us a sense of dignity (*we* are the descendants of the Anabaptist martyrs), we would be better off without it.

The time has come to stop staggering along wall-eyed, with one eye on Christ and one on the church structures we have built, trying to promote one while preserving the other at all costs. God will not accept such a stubborn doublemindedness.

The time has come for a return to the original pattern—that of Christ and the apostles, rather than the patterns handed down by our ancestors. When they put us to cutting rafters at a barn raising, what does the *Schreiner*[2] say? Doesn't he tell us to use the first rafter we cut as a pattern for all the rest? What happens if we don't?

---

[2] head carpenter

The time has come to stop handling our worn-out traditions with German frugality, fixing and patching and mending and insisting on handing them down. But the time has also come to rediscover and put to creative use the good traditions we have lost. Then, while sorting out what we need for today and looking forward to a *frohe Ewigkeit* (glad eternity),[3] we do well to remember that preserving our way of life will not keep us safe. Neither will changing our way of life. More divisions are not the answer. Neither is an ungodly ecumenism.

In 1907 the Mennonites of France began to publish a paper which they called *Christ Seul* (Only Christ).

That is the answer.

If we turn to Christ he will build his kingdom with us again.

[3] From a headstone in the first Mennonite cemetery of the Americas in Germantown, Pennsylvania.

To the "Outsiders"

On hazy summer afternoons, while the grownups worked elsewhere, we children played house on the back yard. Even though we didn't know English yet, we would dress up, pretend to be stylish and ignorant, and call ourselves *die Stoltze* (the proud ones). That is how we Mennonite children in southern Ontario learned to think of those who were not part of us.

Later on we called them by the more grown-up term: "Outsiders." And in years since then, we have also learned the meaning of the gently derogatory terms: "seekers," "converts," and "new Christians."

If you, a person without Anabaptist background, have felt some of that spirit come through in this book, I am sorry. If exclusive Anabaptist terms, names, and ideas have left you feeling like an "outsider" I will now correct that impression. I will go right out into the "world" and show you a man (an American Indian) who lived and died for Christ.

Following Christ and living in community with him is not the exclusive privilege of Swiss, German or Dutch people of Anabaptist background. Anyone may answer his call and people from all over the world, from all walks of life have done and are doing so.

Glikhikan, captain of the Lenni Lenape Wolf Clan, speaker in the council of Kaskaskunk, and principal advisor of the great chief Custaloga, grew up learning how to fight. The Lenni Lenape were not a particularly warlike tribe, but the violence of the American frontier turned even "good men" into fighters during the eighteenth century.

Glikhikan grew to manhood during the French and Indian wars. In raids upon hostile Indian neighbours he learned how to handle a tomahawk with skill—three quick slashes and he could lift a victim's scalp in triumph.

The Lenni Lenape learned to respect Glikhikan and, as a symbol of their bravery, he inspired their imagination. Not only did he become a leader in battle, he became a great orator, speaking around their council fires at night with the wisdom of shamans long gone. It was this gift of speech which brought Glikhikan into contact with the "Black Robes."

For many years, black-robed missionaries from Quebec had braved the hardships of the frontier to bring the Christian (Roman Catholic) faith to the Indians. Glikhikan studied what they said. He concluded that what the Black Robes said was true, but that it must be the Great Spirit's message to people across the sea. Therefore what the shamans of the Lenni Lenape said was not to be rejected for it.

Glikhikan's first opportunity for a public debate with a Black Robe occurred at Fort Venango in what is now northwestern Pennsylvania. The Black Robe was a Jesuit priest, and, in the eyes of all the Indians present, Glikhikan silenced him completely.

Some time later, when new Black Robes (Moravian missionaries) appeared in western Pennsylvania, the Lenni Lenape called on Glikhikan again. With a band of shamans he travelled, eager for debate, to meet the intruders in their camp on the Allegheny River.

Things were not like Glikhikan had expected. Instead of a squalid frontier camp of Frenchmen or English Americans he found only Indian people like himself. Instead of lazy soldiers flirting with the women and traders selling rum to drunken Indians, he found a quiet industrious people living in log shelters. The street between the shelters was swept clean. The Indian women, dressed in long skirts and with their hair done up under white caps which they tied under their chins, took care of children with strange names: Johanna, Maria, Benigna, Gottlob, Israel, Michael, etc.

Everywhere, Glikhikan and his men saw signs of peace and order. Corn and pumpkins grew in neat clearings behind the log cabins. Farm tools hung from the porch roofs. And when a group of men, led by a Monsee whom they called Anthony, came to greet him and to invite him to a community fellowship meal, Glikhikan was speechless. This religion was not at all like that of the Black Robes from Quebec. All his cleverly prepared arguments against it no longer seemed to fit and he told Anthony to go ahead and speak first.

Anthony spoke of the Maker of all things and sat down.

After a long silence, Glikhikan still did not know what to say. He motioned for Anthony to speak again.

Anthony now proceeded with the story of the Son of the Maker of all things, and how he let men kill him so he could give new life to all.

"I believe your words," was Glikhikan's reply. Then he rose, and with his companions following in silence, they returned to the camp of the Lenni Lenape several days journey south.

On his return, Glikhikan asked chief Custaloga to invite the Christian Indians, with their black-robed teachers, to come and show the Lenni Lenape how to live. Only too well did he know the evil superstitions, the vices and violence which kept his people bound. Custaloga, somewhat hesitantly, agreed, and before long, a new village called Langunto Utenuenk which means city of peace (*Friedensstadt*, in the language of the Black Robes) stood on the shores of the Beaver River, northwest of Fort Pitt.

Many of the Lenni Lenape resisted the teachings of the Christian Indians. They bought rum and staged wild feasts and dances next to Langunto Utenuenk to entice the Christians back into their old way of life. But the Christians (whom the Lenni Lenape suspected of being under a powerful spell) could not be distracted. They kept on farming during the day, paying their debts, sharing their belongings with others and meeting to sing and pray in the evenings.

Glikhikan, after some months of observation, packed up his wife and family and went to live at Langunto Utenuenk. There he heard one of the Black Robes (David Zeisberger, a native of Zauchenthal in Moravia) speak in the meetinghouse and his heart broke. He began to weep and walked back to his shelter, his eyes blinded with tears. There he promised his life to the Son of God and great peace came with his baptism not long before Christmas in 1770.

Within a few months of his baptism, Glikhikhan, (or Isaak, as they now called him) left on his first missionary journey into the Ohio River Valley. Anthony the Monsee, Jeremiah a converted Mingo chief, David Zeisberger and another Lenni Lenape man accompanied him. Everywhere he went, Isaak Glikhikan, due to the respect the Indians felt for him, found a ready audience.

Chief Custaloga, nevertheless, found Glikhikan's conversion a let-down and told him so. "What do you expect?" the chief asked him. "Do you think that you will get a white skin for accepting the white man's religion?"

Isaak told him, no. He did not want a white skin. He wanted to know the Son of God and live with him forever.

Another Lenni Lenape tribal leader whom they called Koquethagakhton (White Eyes) had been Isaak Glikhikan's boyhood friend. When Koquethagakhton asked him about his conversion, Isaak reminded him of a promise they had made long ago. "Do you remember," he asked, "when I set my tobacco pouch between us and gave you permission to take from it for the rest of your life? Do you remember how we promised to share everything between us, and that if one of us finds a good thing to be sure to inform the other? Now I have found that good thing, and I want to share it with you. I have found new life with the Son of God."

On several occasions Isaak Glikhikan met danger as a Christian. But he met it without arms. When new Christian villages sprang up in Ohio's Tuscarawas valley the Wyandots, a warlike tribe from the North fell upon them. Isaak Glikhikan went out to meet them, loaded with gifts and speaking peace. Pomoacan, the Wyandot chief, listened to him and did the Christian Indians no harm.

Not long after this, during the Revolutionary War, when a young girl from the Christian villages escaped the Wyandots on horseback, Isaak Glikhikan was in trouble again. The girl, a converted Indian prostitute, was his relative. The Wyandots surrounded his house, war whoops and cries to scalp him shattering the night. Isaak opened the door, stood in the light of his lamp and silence fell upon all.

"I would fight you," Isaak said. "I know how to fight and I scalped many a warrior before you knew your right feet from your left. But I fight with my bow and tomahawk no longer. I fight with the power of the Great Spirit. I no longer fight those who do evil, I fight evil itself. Here I am. You may capture me and take me to your chief!"

The Wyandot chief released Isaak Glikhikan, but more trouble was not long in coming.

Caught between the British and the Americans in the Revolutionary War, the Christian Indians of the Tuscarawas Valley aroused the suspicion of both. Trying to treat all men alike they gave lodging to armed bands of both sides of the conflict. Finally the British General in Fort Detroit ordered the Wyandots to remove the believers to far northern Ohio.

The order from Fort Detroit came in late August. The corn was not yet ripe and the pumpkins still too small to harvest. With great sadness the Indians left their prosperous villages *Gnadenhütten* (Shelters of Grace), *Schönbrunn* (Beautiful Fountain) and Salem, behind. The overland march was long and rough. Some little children died. Food was scarce, and before winter set in, starvation faced them at the Wyandot camp.

For several months the Christian Indians could buy and ration corn. (Even in their captivity, white traders reported, they paid their debts and bought nothing but necessary staples.) But by February there was no more. The supply of edible roots and wild game had been depleted. Then Isaak Glikhikan and almost a hundred people turned back to the Tuscarawas valley.

Both white and Indian friends warned the Christians about the danger of returning to that war-torn region. But their need was so great they felt they had to go ahead. And there, digging corn from beneath the snow in the abandoned village of Gnadenhütten, a band of American militia found them in early March.

The Christian Indians received the Americans with accustomed hospitality. Colonel David Williamson and his men even appeared to be interested in their faith. Isaak Glikhikan and an older minister named Tobias, spoke earnestly to the young white soldiers. The soldiers told them, "You are good Christians!" and called the remainder of the believers together during the following day.

After two nights among the Christian Indians, the Americans revealed to them their true intentions. Up to this point they had deceived them by telling them of a new and peaceful location to which they would lead them. Now, with around ninety men, women and children gathered before them, the Americans changed their story. They began to accuse the Christian Indians.

"You are warriors," they said. "And we know that you are thieves. Look at all the metal pots, the tools and the white men's clothing among you. You stole that from our frontier settlements."

The Christian Indians were almost too surprised to speak. "We do not go to war anymore," Isaak Glikhikan explained. "We are followers of the Son of God and do no men harm." But the Americans would not listen to them. They took a vote. Colonel Williamson ordered all his soldiers in favour of sparing the Indians to step forward. Only sixteen did so, leaving the great majority in favour of killing them on the spot.

Isaak Glikhikan, captain of the Lenni Lenape Wolf Clan, seasoned warrior of many battles in the wilderness and expert with the tomahawk, looked the Americans in the eye. "We belong to Christ," he said. "We are ready to die. But, will you allow us to spend one more night together at this place?"

The Americans allowed it. They put all the men in one of the log houses of Gnadenhütten and the women in another. There the Christian Indians confessed their faults, prayed together and sang. All night long they encouraged one another and called out to Christ before whom they knew they would stand on the following day.

The massacre began in the morning. The first one the Americans clubbed to death and scalped was Abraham, an old Mohican brother who had believed in Christ for many years. Then followed the five ministers, Jonas, Christian, Johann Martin, Samuel and Tobias; seven married men: Adam, Heinrich, Lukas, Philipp, Ludwig, Nikolas and Israel; the young men: Joseph, Markus, Johannes, Abel, Paul, Heinrich, Hans, Michael, Peter, Gottlob and David; and the little boys: Christian, Josef, Markus, Jonathan, Christian Gottlieb, Timotheus, Anton, Jonas, Gottlieb, Benjamin and Hans Thomas.

Dying with Christian names, dying like Christ rather than take sides in the American Revolutionary War, the Indian believers of Gnadenhütten did not resist their murderers.

One young man, Jakob, managed to escape and crawl beneath the floor of one of the "slaughterhouses" where the soldiers took the believers in groups of three or four, to smash their skulls with a cooper's mallet. But so much blood ran down between the floor boards that he had to leave. He made a break for the woods and was one of two survivors who returned to the rest of the Christian Indians in northern Ohio. The other survivor was a young boy named Thomas. The Americans left him for dead among a pile of corpses. But in the night, when everyone had gone, he came to and crawled, stunned and bleeding through the woods to Neuschönbrunn where he found help.

The Christian Indian women died, like the men, without resisting the Americans. One after another: Amelie, Jonas' wife, Augustina, Christian's wife, and seven other married women, Cornelia, Anna, Johanna Salome, Lucia, Lorel, Ruth and Johanna Sabina met their death. The unmarried sisters from whose heads the American soldiers jerked white prayer veilings to scalp them, were Katherina, Judith, Christiana, Maria, Rebekah, Rachel, Maria Susanne, Anna and Bathsheba (daughters of the Indian minister, Joshua), Julianna, Elisabeth, Martha, Anna Rosina and Salome. Then there were eleven little girls: Christina, Leah, Benigna, Gertrud, Anna Christine, Anna Salome, Maria Elisabeth, Sarah, Hannah (the child of Maria the widow) and Anna Elisabeth. Besides these, and five unbaptised seekers, the Americans clubbed twelve babies (too young to scalp) to death.

Isaak Glikhikan, leader of the Christian Indians at Gnadenhütten, was not the first to be killed. Perhaps he stayed back to comfort the new in the faith and the children among them. Perhaps he hoped to encourage the sisters in the other house. But when they laid hands on his wife, Anna Benigna, and on him, he died as he had lived—for Christ in whom he believed.

It was March 10, 1782, the day of his last battle . . . and greatest triumph.

You, North Americans, Latins, Blacks, Orientals, Catholics, Protestants . . . whoever you are, have you considered doing like Isaak Glikhikan?

Have you considered living like Jesus, no matter what happens—no matter how great a cultural adjustment it may involve, and regardless of what it might do to your career and reputation? Nothing stands between you and glorious triumph in Christ except the cross.

A deep discouragement and pessimism threatens to take a hold of many who seek for the truth. Listening to what they say one could think "the old ship of Zion" was going under. But it is not! One could think the church community was in trouble. But it is not!

Christ said, "Look up! Your redemption draws near!"

Paul said, "God wants men to seek him, to reach out and find him, though he is not far from each one of us." The Lord Christ walks on ahead. Shall we run and catch up? Waiting on our friends is not necessary. Neither waiting on our churches, our wives, husbands or children. It is time to get up and go like the fishermen of Galilee, the Anabaptists, and the Indians of the Tuscarawas valley.

If we have not prayed to Christ, now is the time. No one can follow him while being afraid of talking directly to him. "Whoever comes to me I will never drive away. . . . I am the way. . . . Everyone who looks to the Son and believes on him will have eternal life, and I will raise him up at the last day."

The Spirit of Christ fills those who spend time with his life and teachings in the Gospels, especially the Sermon on the Mount. It is not much material. But it is enough, and the more time one spends with it the more extensive it becomes.

Above all, when the voice of Christ is understood it must be followed. I believe that as you "outsiders," "Greeks," and "Syro-Phoenicians," do that, marvellous works shall be accomplished. Not the least of them may be to reorient and mobilise what is left of the Anabaptist movement.

We, the Anabaptists' descendants, have shown ourselves to be a difficult group to work with. We learn slowly (since we tend to think we already know all we need to know). We hate to change, even for the better. It is next to impossible for us to admit that we are wrong, or that someone else has a better way of doing things. Our steadfastness, in many cases, has degenerated into sheer blockheadedness. We are by nature withdrawn, proud, and self-righteous. But many of us, little by little, are coming to realise that without you and your convictions, our movement will surely disintegrate further and die. You have great things to teach us—about reaching out to the poor, about forgiveness and equality, about keeping the Gospel a simple one. Don't let us down!

The Anabaptist movement was never stronger than when it consisted of more than a hundred thousand "new Christians" without a single experienced person among them to say how things should be done.

You can be part of something like that.

The Last Chapter

In the beginning of this book we compared the Anabaptists with Samson. In following chapters we saw the great strength whereby they overcame their trials. But we also saw the mistakes they made and how, in less than a hundred years, the great strength left them and their movement began to fade away.

By the mid-1500s the European Reformation age was definitely over.

Huldrych Zwingli, at odds with Luther and not able to get help from Strasbourg, turned to the king of France and to the Doge of Venice for help. But no one responded and Catholic troops from the "forest cantons" of Switzerland attacked Zürich. In the battle of Kappel, just south of the city, Zwingli died clutching his sword in death on October 11, 1531.

In 1543 Sebastian Franck died alone at Basel.

On February 18, 1546, Martin Luther died. For several years he had been threatening to leave the city of Wittenberg, which he called a "den of robbers, harlots, and shameless rogues." Plagued with rheumatism, he had become a crabby old man— angry at the Protestant church for failing to live right and angry at all the rest (Catholics and Anabaptists) for opposing him. He spent his last months writing the books: *Against the Anabaptists*, *Against the Jews*, and *Against the Papacy at Rome, Founded by the Devil*. After a snowy trip to Eisleben in Sachsen-Anhalt to settle a quarrel between the counts of Mansfeld, Luther took sick and died during the night.

King Henry VIII, Reformer of the Church of England, died in London on January 28, 1547. Not long before this he had beheaded Catherine Howard, his 20-year-old queen and next to last wife (of six).

Four years later, Martin Bucer, the Reformer of Strasbourg, also died in England. His later years were filled with scandal and strife. Philip of Hesse, the German prince and protector of the Protestant church (for whom Peter Rideman wrote his confession of faith) had marriage problems. Martin Bucer, using the Old Testament, finally convinced Luther and Melanchthon that it was alright for Philip to have two wives. But all three Reformers lied about it in public and brought reproach upon themselves. Then, under orders from the Emperor Charles V of the Holy Roman Empire, Martin Bucer came up with a plan to reunite the Protestants with the Roman Catholic church. His efforts failed. He lost friends on both sides and finally got expelled from Strasbourg.

In 1556, Peter Rideman[1] died on the far side of the Carpathian mountains

[1] Before his death, Peter wrote the hymn: "Altogether free, Jesus has loosed us from death and Satan's power."

in Slovakia. And shortly before Christmas, Pilgram Marpeck died at Augsburg in Bavaria. Before his death he made one last trip through Württemberg, Strasbourg, Sankt Gallen, the Rhaetian Alps, and Austria. Everywhere he found Anabaptist groups quarrelling, excommunicating, and shunning one another. He pled with the brothers to not excommunicate so quickly and to not make rules about how to live in community of goods. But only a few paid any attention.

Then on January 31, 1561, Menno Simons died at Wüstenfelde in Holstein—crippled, a widower, and deeply disappointed in his divided church. Three years later John Calvin died in Geneva.

The thatched cottage where Menno Simons lived, and where he ran a small printing press in his last days, still stands in good repair near Bad Oldesloe in Schleswig-Holstein. But his grave-marker, moved by the dairy farmer that now runs the Wüstenfelde estate, stands overgrown with brambles in a fence row, several km away. Menno would have wanted it like this—no earthly monument, no foundation other than Christ alone.

Calvin's last years had grown steadily more difficult. Jerome Bolsec, an influential member of his church opposed him in public, saying that with his doctrine of predestination he had turned God into the author of evil. Calvin banished him and had another opponent, Michael Servetus, burned at the stake. Calvin's reformed Christianity had spread throughout France, but his followers embarrassed him in 1560 by trying to kidnap the sixteen-year-old king (King Francis II, son of Catherine de Médici and husband of Mary Stuart, Queen of Scots). This incident, among others, led to a 36-year war between Calvin's church and the Roman Catholics. John Calvin, sick, and distressed by the war (which he supported), died before the Protestants suffered overwhelming defeat in the massacre of Saint Bartholomew's day.

Dirk Philips died at Het Falder in East Friesland in March 1568. Excommunicated by Leenaerdt Bouwens and the Frisian Mennonite church, he said he did not worry about that because he no longer considered them the church nor the children of God.

Kasper Braitmichel, Peter Walbot, Leupold Scharnschlager, Ulrich Stadler and the remaining Anabaptists quoted in this book all died before the end of the sixteenth century.

Spain and her Habsburg allies were filling their coffers with New World gold. Questions of religion took second place as much greater and exciting issues of conquest and commerce arose. England and the Netherlands became great powers. The Ottoman Turks continued to advance from the south.

The End of Persecution

As the focus of European attention shifted, the Anabaptists broke up into many little groups, and their numbers declined rapidly. The world no longer feared them, and public executions gave way to fines or lesser punishments.

In southern Germany and Austria the Jesuits calmly went ahead with their "counter-reformation" until not only the Protestants, but practically all the Anabaptist residents of those areas had returned to Roman Catholicism.

From Switzerland's valleys the Anabaptists retreated into pockets of safety: the Horgen mountains west of Lake Zürich, the Jura region and the Kurpfalz (Palatinate).

In the Netherlands the Anabaptists gained toleration under the Dutch government, but they had to build their meetinghouses out of sight behind other buildings and pay special taxes. In this seclusion they prospered, becoming bankers, whalers, and merchants. By the mid-1600s they owned an important share of the Dutch East India Company.

The Flight from Switzerland

What happened to the Anabaptists is a long and involving story. I will illustrate it only by telling about my own family (the Hubers/Hoovers) who fled from Switzerland. Anyone else with Anabaptist roots could do the same, because more or less the same thing happened to all Anabaptist families.

My Huber ancestors got converted in the first wave of Anabaptist revival in central Europe. The Protestants executed Ulrich Huber of Signau at Bern in 1538. Johannes Huber, a shoemaker of Braunöken was arrested in 1542 at Wasserburg in Bavaria. Tied to the stake, he was still conscious after the fire had singed off his hair and beard. The presiding magistrate gave him an offer to recant and go home to his family. But he refused, and promptly died.

The Hubers remained Anabaptist. Toward the close of the sixteenth century when thousands apostatised, they kept the faith, but they feared the *Täuferjäger* and withdrew farther and farther up the Alps. Some of them chose the Horgerberg and the Albis, sunny meadows high above the shimmering lakes of Zürich. They avoided going down into the heavily populated valleys. Friends of the hidden Horgerberg Anabaptists did their business for them. But their two preachers, Hans and Heini Landis, were discovered and arrested in 1589. Nineteen years later Hans Landis and deacon Jakob Isler were arrested again and escaped. At that time about 40 Anabaptists remained to gather in secret meetings in barns or forests of the Horgen area.

In 1613 Hans and Jakob with four other men were arrested and faced with banishment or galley slavery. Some of them escaped and found their way home from the Solothurn castle prison. Then Zwingli's churchmen caught Hans Landis again and beheaded him on Sept. 29, 1614.[2]

In 1637 the Zürich government in a concentrated "Anabaptist chase" arrested everyone they could of the Horgen congregation. They confiscated their property and held the people in Zürich until 1640. Hans Huber was arrested again in 1654, then they all left and the church at Horgen ended.

Untere Siten, the house and farm just outside the village of Hirzl, on the Horgerberg, where Hans and Margarethe Landis lived until his final arrest and execution in 1613. Asked if he had anything more to say before they beheaded him, he replied: "*Ich weiss nüt fil me zuo sägen, dan ich möchte allen mänschen gunen, das sy zuo erkantnus iren sünden kemind und büsstendind, das sy möchtid sälig werden, das möchte allen mänschen guonen* (I don't have anything more to say than I would wish for all people to acknowledge their sins and repent so that they might be saved. That is what I would wish for all people)." Margarethe, sixty years old, suffered arrest and banishment and their property was confiscated.

Other harassed Swiss congregations held out longer in mountain regions further from Zürich and Bern. But eventually all the Anabaptists who refused to conform to the state church moved to Alsace and the Kurpfalz or escaped to the Netherlands and America. The last nonconformed Anabaptists to leave Switzerland were the Sonnenberg people.

The Sonnenberg congregation, hidden in the Jura mountains, existed for centuries in seclusion, cultivating stony land with little water. They wove their own clothing and built their barns in secret places, suitable for their meetings. In the wintertime the congregation met in large upstairs rooms of the members'

[2] Hans Landis, elder of the Horgerberg Anabaptist congregation, and the last martyr in Switzerland, was the ancestor of a great number of Mennonites living in Pennsylvania, Ontario and Virginia, today.

homes. There they sang from the *Ausbund* and ate pea soup with milk coffee. In the 1800s all their conservative members moved to Kidron, Ohio.

The Anabaptists remaining in Switzerland stopped making proselytes. They accepted noncombatant military service, and the last active congregation in the Emmental, at Langnau, entered a peaceful partnership with Zwingli's Reformed Church in 1947.

The Schweikhof, above Ebertswil in the Canton of Zürich, where my Huber ancestors lived.

The Flight from Germany

Jakob Huber fled Switzerland for southern Germany in the late 1600s. There he settled with his family in the Kurpfalz. The Anabaptist movement had swept through the Kurpfalz almost two hundred years earlier. But persecution and the Thirty Years' War had nearly extinguished it. Fighting had devastated the land. Its rulers, anxious to rebuild their estates, now invited Swiss Anabaptists to settle on them. They decided to tolerate them for their industry, even though they had earlier killed them. The Anabaptists showed their gratitude for this toleration by not making their faith a public spectacle.

Immigrants from Switzerland poured into the Kurpfalz. Hundreds and hundreds came down the Rhein—large families with babies and bundles on their backs, austere mountain folk who scorned beds to sleep on piles of straw on the floor. The men came in dark "Anabaptist" clothes and beards. Their wives, wearing black head coverings, spoke nothing but the dialect of their Swiss mountain homes. But things did not go well in the Kurpfalz. The Kurfürst, Philipp Wilhelm, who had invited the Anabaptists, fled from a French invasion and died in Vienna. His son was a strict Catholic and demanded high "protection fees" from the Swiss. Then word came from America—William Penn's America where people could live way out in the woods all by themselves. To the Anabaptists of the Kurpfalz, such a place seemed too good to be true, a place almost as desirable as heaven. By the spring of 1717, three hundred of them embarked at Rotterdam for the Atlantic voyage to Philadelphia. Among them travelled Jakob Huber, my Swiss ancestor, with his son Ulrich and family.

The Hubers settled in Lancaster County, Pennsylvania. They worked hard to wrest a living from the frontier. No one bothered them anymore. Gathering in log homes to sing from the textit{Ausbund}, their troubles in Europe became a legend in the minds of their children while they relaxed in their newfound peace and prosperity.

In America the Anabaptists stopped calling themselves *Schweizer Brüder* (Swiss Brothers) and adopted the name Mennonite. With persecution out of the picture, money in their pockets, and vast landholdings to their names, they kept some Anabaptist forms. But their zeal to bring others to Christ died away and they were content to be the quiet in the land.

Even so, they fared better than those who stayed behind. There, in Germany, they lost not only their zeal to evangelise. They lost their separation from the world and their nonresistance as well.

In World War I a few German Mennonite youths still opted for noncombatant service. But in World War II they supported Hitler almost to a man.

The Flight from Democracy

The American revolution came upon my Huber ancestors snugly settled in West Manchester Township, York county, Pennsylvania. Ulrich Huber's son Jakob had married Barbara Schenk and bought land there. But the Hubers did not trust the new "United States" government. They feared they would lose the privileges and the religious freedom they had gained at long last under the British crown. Therefore Jakob Huber with his son David started north on horseback to Upper Canada. They crossed the Niagara River and followed the Lake Erie shore west through Iroquois lands into virgin territory until they came to an area of maple trees and plentiful springs of water. They claimed and deeded 2,500 acres of lakeshore property on both sides of the mouth of the Stony Creek between present day Selkirk and Rainham, Ontario. Two years later Jakob Huber with six married sons and three married daughters arrived to make this place his home.

Far from Switzerland, far from the ideals and vision of Johannes Huber who wouldn't give up at the stake, the Hubers were the first white settlers in this part of British North America. Local records say they were "among the most respected and substantial yeomen of Haldimand County."

Jakob Huber died in 1810 at the age of eighty-one years. They buried him behind the little Mennonite meetinghouse on Hoover's Point. (The name Huber became anglicised to Hoover upon the move to Canada.)

The Flight of the Old Order

Anabaptists respected instead of persecuted, Anabaptists improving the world's economy instead of turning the world upside down—in Canada the Mennonite settlers learned how to be "nice people" among their Anglican and

Iroquois neighbours. The world liked them, and before long they came to like the world too.

David Hoover's son Jacob fell in love with Elizabeth Brech, a Catholic immigrant from Düsseldorf on the Rhein. She joined the Mennonites to marry him and became the mother of eleven children. Jacob became deacon in 1838, and he lived with his family in the original Huber house built of rough logs and hand-hewn boards within a stone's throw of the lake. Their fourth child, Peter Hoover (my great-grandfather), was one of their few descendants who stayed Mennonite.

Peter Hoover did not just stay Mennonite. He became an Old Order Mennonite, a guardian of what little there was to rescue of Anabaptist tradition: the German language, simple meetings, and plain clothes.

Peter had a sailboat. It was given to him by two boys who fled across Lake Erie from Ohio to escape military service during the Civil War. Peter loved to sail. He loved to sing and played a violin on the sly until his father burned it. He loved to dance until one night he came to the neighbours' house. Peeking in the window before entering, he saw what looked to him like devils leaping and swirling. He turned around, went home, and decided to "stay plain."

Several years later he married Maria Wideman of the Mennonite settlement north of York (Toronto), Ontario.

Peter and Maria were not married long until D.L. Moody's "Great Awakening" hit the Mennonite Church. Suddenly prayer meetings, revival meetings, church picnics, fancy clothes, politics, the temperance movement, foreign missionary societies, and a host of other innovations threatened to take over their quiet little church on the shore of the lake. Peter and Maria withdrew their membership. They began to meet with a few other families to become an Old Order congregation. Freeman Rittenhouse was their bishop.

It wasn't that Peter opposed a greater spirituality. He opposed the sudden loss of what he thought was the tradition of the forefathers: the faith of the *Ausbund* and the *Martyrs Mirror*. "*Je mehr gelehrt, je mehr verkehrt,*" was a favourite expression of his (the more educated, the more perverted). So instead of going to Sunday School and revival meetings, he built a spacious new red brick house, a new barn, and a new plain meetinghouse in the sugar bush on the back end of his farm. They called it the Rainham Mennonite Church.

The Flight from Urbanization

The Old Order Mennonites on the Lake Erie shore did not last long. Big cities were too close. Theatres and saloons were too inviting. And with the coming of the automobile, all the old homesteads along the lake became a beach playground.

Peter Hoover's farm, with the house he built in the 1890s, near Selkirk, Ontario—later occupied by my grandparents, Menno and Leah Hoover.

Peter's oldest daughter, Amelia Hoover, remained a spinster for many years.[3] Margaret and Elizabeth died. Charity Hoover married a "man of the world." Only Mary Anne and Peter's youngest child, Menno, found companions and had children who stayed within the Anabaptist tradition. (Mary Anne Hoover Helka and one of her sons, a single man, were the last Old Order Mennonites on the north shore of Lake Erie.)

Peter and Maria, Menno and his family, and a handful of the remaining plain people moved north to Waterloo County Ontario, in the 1920s to "flee from the world." The relatives they left behind gradually adjusted themselves to Canadian society around them.

In 1979 we attended a Hoover reunion at the Mennonite meetinghouse on the back end of my grandparents' farm. A Protestant minister of Tonawanda, New York (a Hoover descendant) had the main speech. Using an acrostic diagram he spoke about our family:

H ospitable neighbours
O pportunistic businessmen
O riginal settlers
V enturesome pioneers
E nergetic farmers
R eligious plainsfolk

Listening to Jakob Huber's descendant speak, dressed in blue jeans and a tee shirt behind the pulpit, I marvelled at how well he summed up the fate of the Anabaptists in America: religion in last place, and that consisting at best of "staying plain." Then another relative sang "Under his Wings" and they brought the big

---

[3] When Amelia finally married she became the wife of Menno Sauder, the independant publisher of the "Elmira Prophetic Mission." They had one adopted son from Russia.

wooden-covered Huber family Bible up from the basement. They wanted me to read from it. Not one of my relatives at the reunion (outside of my own family) understood the German text I read, but when I finished there was a great roar of applause.

Besides my mother, one relative, Mrs. Lanson Jones (of the Brethren in Christ), was the only woman with a veiling on her head at the reunion in 1979.

Mary Jones, faithful soul, wore not only a veiling but a black bonnet over it, with strings tied under her chin. After talking with her I met a younger cousin's new man. She had just divorced her previous one. She grew up on the old Jakob Huber homestead beside the lake. Now she wore a two-piece suit: a cut-off blouse that left several inches of tummy showing between it and her shorts.

The last time I visited Rainham before I moved to Latin America was early in 1981. Slushy snow lay soft on the cemetery. Listening to the music of the surf (the lake has already carried away part of the grounds), I stood for some time looking at Jakob Huber's plain white tombstone. His grandfather, also called Jakob, fled from Switzerland in the 1690s. That Jakob Huber's great grandparents were Anabaptists--burning at the stake but not ready to recant. Then I drove away, past the old homestead, the A.E. Hoover farm, and long lines of summer cottages along the lake, standing with their windows boarded up and silent in the falling snow.

Flight of the Plain People

After reaching Waterloo county, my Hoover grandparents joined the most traditional branch of the Old Order Mennonites: the David Martin group. Taking a stand against screen doors, indoor bathrooms, and painted barns, the bishop of this group refused to buy seed grain from western Canada after he learned it had been harvested with combines.

In the 1950s the David Martin group split. Menno Hoover and numerous ones of his married children (including my parents Anson and Sarah Hoover) left that group to establish a new one. Menno suggested calling it the "Orthodox Mennonite Church."

The Orthodox Mennonites built a new meetinghouse and were yet more conservative than the group from which they came. Menno Hoover planted maple trees around the meetinghouse, but concerned brothers advised him against it, saying that only worldly churches did such. So he dug them up and planted the customary spruce trees. Eventually we buried him among them.

Some of Menno Hoover's descendants, that quickly grew to more than a thousand people after he died (large families blessed with many children and grandchildren).

Among the Orthodox Mennonites I learned the language and became familiar with the history and writings of the Anabaptists. I came to faith and repentance among them. But when I sought baptism as a young teenager I turned to a more progressive Mennonite group.

The End of the Flight?

Several years after I left them, I came back with two friends to visit the Orthodox Mennonites. Their young people had gathered at a farm near Linwood, Ontario. Tracks of many steel- tired buggies had cut through deep packed snow in the lane. Bonnets and shawls lay stacked on a table in the wash house. Wire-rimmed glasses, fire in the woodstove, curtainless windows and a calendar with its picture cut off—everthing in the low-ceiling kitchen surrounded by solemn faces looked like home. *"Wie geht's?"* They timidly shook our hands, not expecting an answer. For a while we sang old, slow songs. A few of my relatives greeted me warily, but most of them had nothing to say. Then we left the narrow, snow-packed lane, the drifted side roads, the rolling farmland, and the black, wintry forests of upper Waterloo County to join heavy traffic on the McDonald-Cartier Freeway to Toronto.

Minutes off the freeway's loops and whining tires on corrugated Canadian concrete, we stepped into the Wideman Mennonite Church. Founded by my Wideman ancestors (Anabaptists from Baden-Württemberg in southern Germany), this is one of many congregations in southern Ontario that big cities threaten to engulf. Less than half of the benches were filled. Wrinkly faces and tottering steps..everyone was old. Tiny net coverings graced some women's silver hair. Here and there I spotted a "cape dress" and one "plain coat." My ancestors' farm nearby had become a golf course. The Almira meetinghouse on that farm was a city storage-rental facility. Another meetinghouse, Altona, stood with broken windows, abandoned on the site of Pickering field, then scheduled to become Canada's largest airport.

I talked that night at Wideman Church with a young boy from Toronto. He was excited about his recent "conversion" to the Anabaptist movement and pressed me for details about them. He told me how he had found the Wideman church through his girlfriend at the university. His "Anabaptist" girlfriend wore slacks and jewellery. She had her hair cut, and he kept his arm around her during the short service. A sister of the Wideman congregation made headlines as the first ordained Mennonite lady pastor in Ontario.

Anabaptists. Anabaptists? I sat deep in thought on the back seat of the car as we headed east out of Toronto that night. Anabaptists in form or in name perhaps, but what about in spirit? Fleeing from the world, fleeing from the cities, fleeing from real or imaginary dangers, some fleeing from fads, some fleeing from dead legalism, fleeing for hundreds of miles and years—but sadly overtaken in the end by them all.

On the wall of my office I have a chart of my ancestors tracing my roots back thirty-two ways to Anabaptists in Switzerland, once to the Netherlands and several times to southern Germany. Beneath that chart hang two photos: one of an Old Order Mennonite meetinghouse, and one of a family reunion near Rainham by the lake in southern Ontario.

Those pictures hurt. They hurt like the news that every so often comes trickling down to Costa Rica: "Did you hear that Paul and Betty left the Mennonites? . . . Nathan has left home and is going to college. . . . All of Jake's children now belong to this cult." Relatives, close friends, "converts" who were once so happy among us, boys I went to Bible School with—one by one they go. The Anabaptist movement can no longer keep them. They go and it hurts, because hardly anyone that leaves comes back.

I do not think the hurt I feel is a personal hurt. I am no longer part of a traditional Mennonite group myself. Rather, I feel for those that lose their Anabaptist distinctives and go back to the world. I have seen the vast majority of my friends and relatives who leave the Anabaptist traditions take on inferior traditions of a society with twisted values.

No, let us not go back. Let us go on with Christ! Let us leave the world and press on toward the goal to win the prize for which God has called us heavenward in Christ Jesus: a new heaven and a new earth where righteousness dwells.

Before they beheaded him at Köln am Rhein in 1557, Thomas von Imbroich left this testimony:

> I am willing and ready, both to live or to die. I do not care what happens to me. God will not let me down. I am comforted and in good spirits while yet on the earth. God gives me friendly assurance, and my heart is encouraged through my brothers.
>
> Sword, water, fire, whatever creature may come cannot frighten me. No man nor foreign being shall be able to pull me away from God. I hope to stay with what I have chosen for myself in the beginning. All the persecution in this world shall not be able to separate me from God.[4]

---

4 *Ausbund*, 23:20-21

Thomas von Imbroich was an Anabaptist messenger and servant of the Word. He preached and baptised and established new congregations along the lower Rhein. He wrote seven epistles and one of the most widely used Anabaptist confessions of faith. When they beheaded him, he was 25 years old. Dare we commit ourselves to Christ like he did?

If so, Christianity will break out from among us again.

How to Find the Anabaptists' Writings

German-language Anabaptist writings still in use among their descendants, such as the *Ausbund*, Menno Simons' *Vollständige Werke*, the *Märtyerspiegel*, Dirk Philips' *Enchiridion*, the *Artikel und Ordnung* of the brothers at Strasbourg and *Güldene Äpfel in Silbernen Schalen* (which includes the writings of Thomas von Imbroich, Michael Sattler, Matthias Servaes, etc.) may be purchased from the publishing house of the Old Order Amish: Pathway Publishers, 2580N 250W LaGrange, IN, U.S.A. 46761.

The *Lieder der Hutterischen Brüder* and four volumes of letters written by Anabaptist leaders in southern Germany and Austria, *Die Hutterische Epistel*, are available from the Schmiedeleut Hutterian Brethren at the James Valley Bruderhof, Elie, MB, Canada, R0H 0H0 (204-353-2148).

An English translation of the *Martyrs Mirror* and the writings of Menno Simons, Balthasar Hubmaier, Conrad Grebel, Dirk Philips, Michael Sattler, Pilgram Marpeck, and others are available from Herald Press, 616 Walnut Ave. Scottdale PA 15683 (412-887-8500). Select writings of Peter Rideman, Peter Walbot, Andreas Ehrenpreis, Claus Felbinger, and the voluminous chronicle of the Hutterian Brethren are available in English from Plough Publishers, Spring Valley Bruderhof, Rte. 381 N., Farmington PA 15437 (800-521-8011).

All of the preceeding, and the remaining known Anabaptist materials in their original languages or translations are available at the Mennonite Historical Library 1700 S. Main Street, Goshen IN 46526-9989 (219-535-7418); the Menno Simons Historical Library, Eastern Mennonite University, Harrisonburg VA 22801-2462 (540-432-4177); and the Mennonite Archives of Ontario, Conrad Grebel College, Waterloo ON N2L 3G6 (519-885-0220). Competent personnel at all of these locations are pleased to assist those who visit, write, or call. The Mennonite Historical Library at Goshen holds 45,000 volumes, the oldest dating from 1516. The collection is especially rich in South German and Swiss materials. The Menno Simons Library at Harrisonburg, holding a large number of Dutch and North German works, has 25,000 volumes. The Mennonite Archives of Ontario has access to a vast collection of Anabaptist source materials on microfilm.

For preliminary English-language research on the Anabaptists we suggest the following informative books (even though some conclusions drawn in them are not our conclusions):

1. C. Arnold Snyder, *Anabaptist History and Theology*, Pandora Press, 1995.
2. Walter Klaassen, editor, *Anabaptism in Outline,* Herald Press, 1981. Translations of Anabaptist writings on a wide variety of subjects.
3. Cornelius J. Dyck, *Spiritual Life in Anabaptism,* Herald Press, 1995. Includes many valuable translations.

4. George Williams and Angel Mergal, editors, *Spiritual and Anabaptist Writers,* Westminster Press, 1992. Includes important writings by George Blaurock, Conrad Grebel, Michael Sattler, Obbe and Dirk Philips, Ulrich Stadler and others.

5. James M. Stayer, *The German Peasants' War and Anabaptist Community of Goods,* McGill-Queens University Press, 1991. Invaluable for the under standing of the Anabaptist movement in southern Germany and Austria.

6. Werner O. Packull, *Hutterite Beginnings,* Johns Hopkins University Press, 1995. Without a doubt the best book available on the subject. Includes the story of the Gabrielites and Philippites.

7. John Horsch, *The Hutterian Brethren,* Macmillan Bruderhof, *1985.* An inexpensive and truly inspirational history.

8. C. Arnold Snyder, *The Life and Thought of Michael Sattler,* Herald Press, 1984.

9. John L. Ruth, *Conrad Grebel, Son of Zurich,* Herald Press, 1975.

10. Cornelius Krahn, *Dutch Anabaptism,* Herald Press, 1981.

11. Cornelius J. Dyck, *An Introduction to Mennonite History,* Herald Press, 1981. Includes a valuable overview of the Anabaptist movement.

The *Mennonite Encyclopedia* and the issues of the *Mennonite Quarterly Review,* published at Goshen College, offer information about a wide variety of subjects pertaining to Anabaptist life and thought.

Historical research may help you, but Hans Langenmantel, beheaded with his foster son and housekeeper on May 11, 1528, wrote: “Neither spirit nor soul can ever be fed except in following the living Word of God.” That is still true.

Made in the USA
Middletown, DE
07 March 2020

85981440R00130